SEA OF READINGS

SEMEIA STUDIES

Steed V. Davidson, General Editor

Editorial Board:
Pablo R. Andiñach
Eric D. Barreto
Denise K. Buell
Jin Young Choi
Masiiwa Ragies Gunda
Jacqueline Hidalgo
Monica Jyotsna Melanchthon

Number 90

SEA OF READINGS

The Bible in the South Pacific

Edited by
Jione Havea

SBL PRESS

Atlanta

Copyright © 2018 by Society of Biblical Literature

All rights reserved. No part of this work may be reproduced or transmitted in any form or by any means, electronic or mechanical, including photocopying and recording, or by means of any information storage or retrieval system, except as may be expressly permitted by the 1976 Copyright Act or in writing from the publisher. Requests for permission should be addressed in writing to the Rights and Permissions Office, SBL Press, 825 Houston Mill Road, Atlanta, GA 30329 USA.

Library of Congress Cataloging-in-Publication Data

Title: Sea of readings : the Bible in the South Pacific / edited by Jione Havea.
Description: Atlanta : SBL Press, 2018. | Series: Semeia studies ; Number 90 | Includes bibliographical references and index.
Identifiers: LCCN 2018005067 (print) | LCCN 2018011745 (ebook) | ISBN 9780884142775 (ebk.) | ISBN 9781628372021 (pbk. : alk. paper) | ISBN 9780884142782 (hbk. : alk. paper)
Subjects: Bible—Criticism, interpretation, etc.—Oceania.
Classification: LCC BS511.3 (ebook) | LCC BS511.3 .S377 2018 (print) | DDC 220.60996—dc23
LC record available at https://lccn.loc.gov/2018005067

Printed on acid-free paper.

Contents

Preface vii

Abbreviations xi

Islander Criticism: Waters, Ways, Worries
    Jione Havea... 1

Island Twists

Island Prodigals: Encircling the Void in Luke 15:11–32
with Albert Wendt
    Mosese Ma'ilo 23

Wet Bible: Stor(y)ing Jonah with Sia Figiel
    Jione Havea... 37

Native Texts: Samoan Proverbial and Wisdom Sayings
    Levesi Laumau Afutiti 53

Ko e Punake mo 'e ne Ta'anga, pea mo e Folofola (Composer,
Composition, and the Canon)
    Tangikefataua Koloamatangi 69

Island Turns

Lifting the Tapu of Sex: A *Tulou* Reading of the Song of Songs
    Brian Fiu Kolia.. 85

Moses, Both Hebrew and Egyptian: A Samoan *Palagi* Reading
of Exodus 2–3
    Martin Wilson Mariota 103

Sipora (Zipporah), Both Native and Foreigner: A *Marama iTaukei* Reading of Exodus 4:24–26
Inise Vakabua Foi'akau 117

Not Just a Bimbo: A Reading of Esther by a Singaporean Immigrant in Aotearoa New Zealand
Angeline M. G. Song...131

The Priestly *Ger* (Alien) Meets the Samoan *Tagata Ese* (Outsider)
Makesi Neemia 147

Jesus the *Fiaola* (Opportunity Seeker): A Postcolonial Samoan Reading of Matthew 7:24–8:22
Vaitusi Nofoaiga 163

Across the Sea

Is My Island Your Island? A Response in Three Keys
Fiona C. Black..181

Not @ Sea: Finding and Foraging among Family Resemblances across the Oceans
Gerald O. West...191

Going with the Flow
Daniel Patte..203

Ancient Roots of the Islander Narrative of Inferiority
Camilla Raymond 213

Contributors..221

Ancient Sources Index..225
Modern Authors Index...229
Subject Index..233

PREFACE

Kissing point, the place where saltwater (from the sea) meets freshwater (coming down a stream or river), is appropriate for describing the interweaving of islander backgrounds, wisdoms and readings, and responses and engagements in this collection of essays. To be more precise, bearing in mind that precision is not rigid with respect to waters, this work is the confluence of two kissing points.

First, this collection of essays developed as fruits of several *meetings* (read: conferences, intersections, discussions, revisions, edits). Over the past twenty-five years or so, islander criticism has been ebbing and flowing, seeking attention at gatherings of the Society of Biblical Literature. Then in 2009, at the New Orleans gathering, a Society of Biblical Literature group began to form. The Islands, Islanders, and Bible unit had its first session at the 2010 Atlanta meeting, then took on the new name Islands, Islanders, and Scriptures in 2013. Out of these meetings came *Islands, Islanders, and the Bible: RumInations* (SBL Press, 2015), to which this *Sea of Readings* is a companion from a specific island location, Pasifika (Oceania, South Pacific).

Presented at conferences and then later redrafted, reviewed, and revised for publication, most of the essays in this collection had an early germination at meetings (read: intersections) of OBSA (Oceania Biblical Studies Association) with islander criticism. OBSA was conceived during the 2008 International Meeting of the Society of Biblical Literature at Auckland (Aotearoa New Zealand) and has met since 2010 at different islands with the support of Trinity Methodist Theological College (New Zealand), School of Theology at the University of Auckland (New Zealand), Malua Theological College (Samoa), Piula Theological College (Samoa), University of the South Pacific (Tonga campus), Siaʻatoutai Theological College (Tonga), Siasi Uēsiliana Tauʻatāina ʻo Tonga (Tonga), Pacific Theological College (Fiji), and many generous friends (with gifts of time, insights, and resources). The publication of *Sea of Readings* is supported by a grant from the Rev'd Veitinia Waqabaca's Literary and Theological Studies Foundation, administered by Parramatta Mission (of the Uniting Church in Australia). To one and to all, *Vinaka vakalevu* (Fijian, lit. "many [boat-load-of] thanks").

Not all OBSA presentations are included in this collection. Pasifika Islanders are not keen to submit their thoughts into writing, which is expected of thinkers from oral preferring cultures. Two of the essays (Afutiti and Song) in this collection were not presented at an OBSA gathering,[1] and sadly, two of the contributors, Afutiti and Koloamatangi, passed away before this publication came into life.

Second, this monograph is the meeting of Pasifika *twists and turns* with the ebbs and flows from *across the sea*. Hence the three sections of the book: Island Twists contains contributions that twist, like a whirlpool, biblical texts around insights of native Pasifika novelists, composers, poets, and sages. Island Turns contains contextual readings that turn a selection of biblical texts toward, and under, some aspect of Pasifika waters, ways, and worries. The chapters in both sections demonstrate, but in different degrees, how (traditional) historical and literary studies can sit alongside and under cultural studies, with islander and Pasifika manifestations. The third part, Across the Sea, contains engagements by biblical critics who were all asked to launch from the same spot, an essay (by Koloamatangi) that they cannot read. They had to depend on the editor's short introduction, then to reflect on the impact of that experience on reading three other chapters, and thereupon to reflect on the challenges and opportunities that *Sea of Readings* pose for islander criticism in particular and biblical criticism overall. Thankfully, the respondents did not all follow the editor's direction! Raymond wisely ended, rather than opened, with Koloamatangi (a name that means "treasure of/in wind," which acknowledges that the wind continues to gift islanders even when it twists, turns, and changes direction; but the wind, which gains energy from the sea, also causes damage to systems of life in the sea and on the shore). Graciously, nonetheless, all respondents identified more tasks and directions for islander criticism, so there are more kissing points to be reached.

---

1. Angeline M. G. Song's essay draws on her previously published "Heartless Bimbo or Subversive Role Model? A Narrative (Self) Critical Reading of the Character of Esther," *Dialog: A Journal of Theology* 49 (2010): 56–69.

Of course, kissing points are not places to linger. Waters push. Currents are strong. Tides are coming and going. Waters are pushed. Movements.

Language

Language is a barrier in biblical criticism, with the politics and limits of translation as daily food for biblical critics. Language is thus also a house for misunderstanding, for missing the point, and for romanticizing. But the barrier of language is an opportunity. To slow down. To read again. To ponder. To play. To reconsider. To re*con*struct. For language is more than words. Language is also a kissing point for traditions, peoples, ways, cultures, (is)lands, and more.

In Pasifika, English is a colonial language. It comes with *pālangi* (alt. spelling *palagi:* "European," "White," "foreign") sentiments, formalities, and rigidities. People of Pasifika, with hundreds of languages (there are, for instance, over eight hundred living languages in the island of Papua alone), learn English in order to communicate across tribal and national borders. But we do not always follow the English rules. We also creolize in both our speech and writing. For example, the northwestern islands use *Tok Pisin* (Papua), *Pijin blong Solomon* (Solomon Islands), and *Bislama* (Vanuatu), three different forms of creolizing English. Natives of these three island groups may speak, each in her or his creole tongue, and could easily understand one another. They do not need to speak the same tongue in order to communicate, and they do not creolize in the same way. Their different forms of creole are necessary for trade and business and for defying proper English. Thrice.

The written form is not fixed for all Pasifika languages. There are different spellings of the same native words—as an example, Kolia prefers "Sāmoa" (the first "a" is a long vowel when the word is pronounced) because "sā" (sacred) is significant in his reading. There are variants across Pasifika—the references to white Europeans are palagi (Samoan), pālangi (Tongan), and *pākeha* (Māori). Out of respect to the privileging of orality in island circles, consistency in spelling is not sought in this collection.

It is reasonable to expect a book from our region to resist the rules of English. For ideological reasons and for the sake of reducing the number of italicized words in this book, only the first occurrence of a native word in each chapter—out of respect for the authors who write from different native languages—is italicized. In this unconventional approach, bearing in mind that English is a foreign language to our sea of islands, this book problematizes the uncritical assumption that English is the only proper, standard, and academic language. Whose English? Whose English rules? Who decides in the aftermath of European colonization which languages are foreign?

As indicated above, the essay by Koloamatangi is presented in the Tongan language with a short introduction by the editor. Text fields are inserted into the essay, with English translations of key (in the eyes of the editor) phrases and lines, so that non-Tongan readers may get a tweet, a dribble, of Koloamatangi's thinking. Koloamatangi has passed on, but his Tongan words trickle into English in the introduction and text fields. His thoughts are not off limits. This is one way of saying that language is a conduit, a passageway, but not a trap or barrier, in this and in other seas of readings.

Overall, language is like the image on the front cover of this book: a spot, a moment, a flick, on one of the coasts of Papua New Guinea, but common in the *mata-ni-vanua* (Fijian for "eyes-of-the-land"). Language *brings into life*, together, the edge, grass, sand, rocks, branches, leaves, trunks, sea, water, voyage, migration, ancestors, kissing points, another island, another eye-land (*mata-vanua*), another ripple, another wave, another motion, another fare-well, another well-come, another *talanoa*, another.

Abbreviations

AA	*American Anthropologist*
AB	The Anchor Bible
AOTC	Apollos Old Testament Commentary
ARIEL	*ARIEL: A Review of International English Literature*
AS	Advances in Semiotics
ASMS	American Society of Missiology Series
BCT	*Bible and Critical Theory*
BDAG	Danker, Frederick W., Walter Bauer, William F. Arndt, and F. Wilbur Gingrich, eds. 2000. *A Greek-English Lexicon of the New Testament and Other Early Christian Literature*. 3rd ed. Chicago: University of Chicago Press.
BibInt	*Biblical Interpretation*
BIS	Biblical Interpretation Series
BL	Biblical Limits
BP	Bibliothèque de la Pléiade
BTA	Bible and Theology in Africa
BTBull	*Biblical Theology Bulletin*
BZABR	Beihefte zur Zeitschrift für altorientalische und biblische Rechtsgeschichte
CanCul	*Canon and Culture*
CBC	The Cambridge Bible Commentary on the New English Bible
CBR	*Currents in Biblical Research*
CC	*Constitutional Commentary*
ClimC	*Climate Change*

ConC	Continental Commentaries
CP	*The Contemporary Pacific*
Dem.	Demetrius the Chronographer
Dia	*Diacritics*
DiJT	*Dialog: A Journal of Theology*
EBS	Encountering Biblical Studies
ERS	*Ethnic and Racial Studies*
Exod. Rab.	Exodus Rabbah
FAT	Forschungen zum Alten Testament
FCB	Feminist Companion to the Bible
GPBS	Global Perspectives on Biblical Scholarship
HBM	Hebrew Bible Monographs
IBC	Interpretation: A Bible Commentary for Teaching and Preaching
IJPT	*International Journal of Public Theology*
IRM	*International Review of Mission*
IVBS	International Voices in Biblical Studies
JBQ	*The Jewish Bible Quarterly*
JPolyS	*The Journal of the Polynesian Society*
JPS	Jewish Publication Society
JSOTSup	Journal for the Study of the Old Testament Supplement Series
JTSA	*Journal of Theology for Southern Africa*
Jub.	Jubilees
KJV	King James Version
LHBOTS	Library of Hebrew Bible/Old Testament Studies
LNTS	Library of New Testament Studies
LXX	Septuagint
Mo'ed Qat.	Mo'ed Qatan
MR	*Mana Review*
MQ	*Mankind Quarterly*
NICNT	The New International Commentary on the New Testament
NICOT	The New International Commentary on the Old Testament
NIGTC	The New International Greek Testament Commentary
NIV	New International Version
NJB	New Jerusalem Bible
NLR	*New Literature Review*

NRSV	New Revised Standard Version
NTTS	New Testament Tools and Studies
OTE	*Old Testament Essays*
OTP	Charlesworth, James H., ed. *Old Testament Pseudepigrapha*. 2 vols. New York: Doubleday, 1983–1985.
PJT	*The Pacific Journal of Theology*
PostRel	Postcolonialism and Religions
PS	*Pacific Studies*
Pseu	Pseudepigrapha
RECS	Regnum Edinburgh Centenary Series
RT	*Religion and Theology*
RS	Religion and Society
TDOT	Botterweck, G. Johannes, and Helmer Ringgren, eds. *Theological Dictionary of the Old Testament*. Translated by David E. Green. 15 vols. Grand Rapids: Eerdmans, 1975–2015.
TNTC	Tyndale New Testament Commentaries
Trns	Transitions
TT	Texts and Translations
TTCABS	T&T Clark Approaches to Biblical Studies
SBEC	Studies in the Bible and Early Christianity
SemeiaSt	Semeia Studies
SIHC	Studies in the Intercultural History of Christianity
SRA	Studies of Religion in Africa
STCPRIB	Scriptural Traces: Critical Perspectives on the Reception and Influence of the Bible
StudBL	Studies in Biblical Literature
SVT	Supplements to Vetus Testamentum
VE	*Verbum et Ecclesia*
VT	*Vetus Testamentum*
WBC	World Biblical Commentary
WW	*Word and World*
ZAW	*Zeitschrift für die alttestamentliche Wissenschaft*

Islander Criticism: Waters, Ways, Worries

Jione Havea

Islander criticism has slipped into the sea of biblical criticism (see Havea, Aymer, and Davidson 2015) alongside the fleet of minoritized criticisms (see Bailey, Liew, and Segovia 2009). Despite the inconsistent acknowledgment of like-minded and similar-toned biblical critics (see Bailey 2015), islander criticism has gained some recognition through its listing as one of the choices in the catalogue of reading approaches of the Society of Biblical Literature (e.g., in its postmeeting survey). Islander criticism, however, has not held the attention of other context-sensitive colleagues. At the opening event of the 2016 International Meeting of the Society of Biblical Literature at Seoul, South Korea, for instance, islander criticism did not register in the presentations by the five panelists who reflected on the state of contextual biblical interpretation. Since this panel was given the catchy title "Crossing Borders: Biblical Studies from the Four Corners of the World," there is a critical task for islander critics in the academy: to show that the world has more than four corners. As all islands have many corners, so have the physical and ideological worlds. Many corners. Many edges. Many horns. Many extensions. Many ledges. And so is the world of biblical criticisms. Many curves. Many twists. Many turns.

I take on two concerns in this essay, two concerns that pull from each other, for the first one problematizes what i[1] engender with the second. My first concern relates to responses in and to *Islands, Islanders, and the Bible: RumInations*, which noted the ambivalences and broadness of islander criticism (Havea, Aymer, and Davidson 2015). Because what constitutes and passes as islander criticism has not been tightly identified and defined,

---

1. I prefer to use the lowercase with the first person because i also use the lowercase with "you," "she," "he," "it," "they," and "others." My "i" is with respect to, and indebted to, other subjects. See further 37 n. 1.

i drift this essay, first, around and into the hidden twists and risky turns of the politics of identity and the limits of definition. Why identify and define islander criticism? For whom? By whom? From which island? When is a landmass too large to be considered an island? According to whose questions? Whose desires will be appeased with a tightly defined identity? How tight is "tight" (hear: tide) in islanders' mindsets? What might islander definitions feel and sound like? This last question points to the second concern that i tackle in this essay—to identify and characterize islander criticism in an islander fashion. I deal with this concern around three keywords: waters (contexts), ways (customs, orientations), and worries (cautions, anxieties). The three interflow: our watery contexts shape our minds and ways, and our worries have to do with the impacts of the world community, migration, foreign agenda, and cultural appropriation upon our contexts and ways. Consequently, there is swirling and spiraling, ebbing and flowing—the stuff of tides and of orality, one of the native Pasifika (Pacific, Oceania) words for which is *talanoa*[2]—in the following reflection. At the end, therefore, my attempt at defining islander criticism cannot be rigid. But fluid. Watery. Oceanic. Sea-nic. Islandic.

In the course (route) of problematizing and engendering islander criticism, i also locate the essays in this collection. I suggest ways in which these islander voices could be heard together in order that they may be related, for it is an islander thing to relate (see the essays by Neemia and Nofoaiga). We relate, even though we live in separate and distant (is)lands. We relate because we are separate, and by reciprocating we prevent being isolated. To that i quickly add that relations also break up and cause discord between islanders, and Pasifika islanders have a way of tolerating the disruption of relations. In the process of disrupting and interrupting, we assume permission by simply saying, "tulou" (see essay by Kolia). *Tulou* is not the admission of wrong but the announcement that one is about to disrupt. In this connection, the problem is not in the breaking of relations or the breaking of traditions and rules. Rather, the problem is not realizing that breaking relations, traditions, and rules is an acceptable option. I

---

2. The word *talanoa* (used in Fiji, Tokelau, Tonga, Tuvalu, and Samoa) refers to three interrelated entities: story, telling (of stories), and conversation (around stories and tellings). Story (talanoa) needs telling (talanoa) in order for it to come alive, telling (talanoa) needs conversation (talanoa) in order for the story (talanoa) to stay current, and conversation (talanoa) is empty without story (talanoa) and dead without telling (talanoa).

therefore say tulou in advance for the traditions, rules, and relations that i will break. And for those that i fail to break, but should. Tulou!

Islander Under-standings

There are three ways to understand the *islander* in islander criticism. First, an islander is someone who was born and raised on an island *and* whose worldviews and mannerisms would be oriented to the rhythms of island living. Her or his islandedness is due to her or his place (of birth) *and* her or his ways; in other words, she or he is an islander because of her or his context *and* culture.[3] Second, an islander is someone who was born to parents who are/were islanders (in the first definition). She or he does not have to be born and raised on an island, so she or he would not have had the fortune of swaying in the island breeze or feeding upon island grubs.[4] Her or his islandedness is (primarily) by ancestry (*whakapapa* in Māori). Both the island-born-and-raised as well as the island-rooted are islanders but in different ways. They will no doubt have different understandings of what islandedness involves, and that is just fine. Islandedness is not reserved for only one type of islander, and the ones who pass both the place of birth and ancestry tests are not more-islander (or more-native) than the ones who pass one or the other. Islander identity, in my humble opinion, is not about containing something whole and pure (utopia, fantasy), but about having a pinch of something islandic (so islandedness involves being in-between; see essay by Nofoaiga). And no matter whether this is a pinch of context, of culture, and/or of ancestry, it helps to take it with a pinch of salt.

There is more than one type of islander. Similarly, there are many types of islands. Some islands have more land-space (see Boer 2015), wealth (see the essay by Song), colonial power (see Kinukawa 2015), and/or influence (see Mein 2015) than others. Some islands are divided between sovereign powers, like Hispaniola (between the Dominican Republic and Haiti) and

---

3. I imagine context and culture as a combo, and i acknowledge that a culture is always a tapestry of other cultures. When it comes to how one has been cultured in and by a particular context, it is a matter of degree. Some people are more cultured than others, and some people are better placed than others.

4. Overseas-born islanders are caught between island and nonisland cultures (see essays by Mariota, Foi'akau, and Song), and there are also people who have roots on an island but do not see themselves as islanders.

Papua (between Papua New Guinea and Indonesia). Many island groups are occupied by foreign powers, like (in Pasifika) Chamorro/Guam and North Marianas, Tutuila/American Samoa, Kanaka/Hawai'i, Kanaky/New Caledonia, West Papua, Maohi Nui/French Polynesia, and Rapa Nui/Easter Island. Colonizers (e.g., the United States, France, Indonesia, Chile) and colonization have not been "posted" (away) from the Pasifika sea of islands. In terms of size, two southern islands, Australia and Antarctica, are also (confused about being) continents. And there are islands in boroughs (a word that evokes thinking of burrows, holes in the ground), like those that make up New York city, and in lakes and rivers, like those in Canada, Africa, and India.[5] As Andrew P. Wilson (2016) explained in his response to *Islands, Islanders, and the Bible*, there are also tied islands—those connected to a mainland with a land bridge, like Tyre (Kinukawa 2015)—and artificial islands, like those in the Solomon Islands and Dubai and those proposed for tourism development in Barbados by real estate magnate Paul Altman. There are islands, and there are islands! Should there be a correct or wrong kind of island when it comes to islander criticism (Mein 2015; Black's essay in this collection)?

The third sense of islander applies to those who live and think in island-way(s), *as if* they are islanders. They may not have island roots, but they could be more island'er than some people with island-roots. The ones who fit this third sense are opposite of the *fie palagi*—natives who wannabe white Europeans (see essay by Mariota). The island'ers would include foreigners who wannabe native in the way they dress, eat, sit, speak, dance, cultivate, discipline, and tradition. Their islandedness is in their preference and orientation. I coin the Tongan phrase *fie kau* for these island'ers. Fie kau refers to two kinds of people: those who wish to belong (to be included, or to be counted), and those who wish to join (or interfere) in order to correct and to set straight. Fie kau can apply to interfering foreigners as well as to traditionalist islanders in diaspora or at home who act as gatekeepers of islandedness. They think that they are more island'er than other islanders.

Again, there are islanders, and there are islanders. Should there be a correct kind and wrong kind of islander when it comes to islander criticism? Who decides? Defining cultural identities is messy business. While

---

5. Moreover, some nations are scattered like islands, as in the case of modern Palestine being invaded and separated by Israeli settlements and their security (or separation) walls.

definitions are helpful, they do not always account for all the realities of the people involved. Definitions inherently fail. Definitions do not always seize nor benefit the subjects being identified, but they are drawn for the sake of inquiring minds who want to know and/or control. In general, identities are defined in order to see if the defined subjects are acceptable and admissible. For Pasifika islanders in days of old, it was not necessary to define native identities because identities were borne on the faces and tongues of people. Natives used to be able to tell which island a person came from through simple visual recognition of a person's look, shade, and tone. Stereotypes. Migration, cultural appropriation, and intermarriage have made it more difficult nowadays, so modern Pasifika islanders misidentify as well as become casualties of misidentification. And like all other people, islanders discriminate on the basis of stereotypes and (mis)perceptions. Not only do we misidentify our own people, but we also misidentify outsiders and lump them into groups—Europeans, Americans, Asians, Africans—that fail to recognize their differences (according to location, roots, customs, languages, or other cultural distinctions). Islanders too are not free of the traps of producing identities and places as has happened with orientalism.

Not all islanders will endorse my attempt to identify islanders and to characterize islander criticism. I return to this issue again below in this essay. Many islanders will not see themselves in my definition, as Ronald Charles (2016) of Haiti indicated in his response to *Islands, Islanders, and the Bible*, and that is fair enough. Assuming that i, from particular island settings, could capture what islandedness means for all islanders—the illusion of universalism—is both unfair and unreal. The illusion of universalism is better left for critics who favor global optics. Islanders too have illusions,[6] but it is appropriate to bear in mind that the illusion of universalism also brought colonialists and missionaries to the islands in the global south. We are still struggling with the costs of invasion and

---

6. One example of islanders' illusions is in the Tongan proverb, *lau pē ʻe he lokua ʻ ko e moana ʻ hono tāputa ʻ*. The illusion of the lokua (a small fish that lives on the reef) is in assuming that its pool (tāputa) on the reef is the moana (deep ocean) beyond the reef. The proverb, however, has another meaning. It also declares that the tāputa provides all which the lokua needs, so the shallow tāputa is satisfying for the lokua in the same way that the moana is for a larger fish. For the lokua, therefore, the tāputa is its moana. And there is no illusion there. On proverbial and wisdom sayings, see the essay by Afutiti.

occupation, which in some cases were by people from other islands (like Britannia and Japan). Whether and how those invaders and occupiers understood their islandedness is outside of my concerns for this essay.

The illusion of pacificness (that islanders are friendly, laidback, and carefree) has inspired romanticized views with respect to Pasifika's sea of islands. While we dance the *hula,* we also perform the *haka* (Māori) and the *meke* (Fiji), which are reminders of our histories of local and inter-island conflict and violence—similar to what happened in the islands of Sri Lanka and Britannia (Rees 2016)—before European explorers and convicts, colonialists and missionaries, whalers and slavers arrived (Maude 1981; Hamilton 2016). Our ancestors were warrior navigators, and the battles between tribes and across the waters of Samoa, Tonga, and Fiji, for instance, were fierce and bloody. Tension with and violence against people from other ethnic groups continue today, for example, with the Indian and Chinese populations in Tonga and Fiji.[7] Put another way, there are right and wrong, good and bad, kinds of islanders on all islands (Mein 2015). Who decides who is which? And the more critical question is how might the badness of some islands not conceal the badness of other islands?

With other illusions behind my eyes, i answer the questions that have been raised in a way that will not satisfy critics who prefer a tight answer. To be clear, *i decide* above what it means to be islander, and at this occasion, i am aware of the temptations to universalize and to pacify. My aim herein is not to restrict who pass as true islanders, which is the kind of drive that birthed apartheidisms and led to genocides past and present. Rather, i seek to present islandedness as a *site of welcome* where the normal indigenous person (see essays by Afutiti and Koloamatangi) and the outsider (see essay by Neemia), the native prodigal (see essay by Ma'ilo) and the opportunity-seeking Jesus (see essay by Nofoaiga), the Jewish Esther (see essay by Song) and the Midianite Sipora/Zipporah (see essay by Foi'akau), could get comfortable under the same cover (of this book) with subjects like sexuality (see essay by Kolia) and wetness (see Havea in this collection). Welcome is an island thing also, even though some islanders take more welcome than they give. In spite of everything else, welcome

---

7. Together with the ignored genocide in West Papua, under occupation by Indonesia, the "Asia-Pacific" designation of our region is problematic.

and hospitality are two of the assets that visitors nowadays associate with islands and islanders.

In the case of Pasifika islanders, we have come a long way from being pagans and savages in the eyes of missionaries and anthropologists to becoming welcoming and hospitable hosts (and we have not come to terms with how foreign visitors these days still take advantage of us, with flattery). Welcome enables relations and reciprocity. Welcome is thus for those who can flow with our rhythms (see essay by Patte) and for those who are "@ home" with our ways (see essay by West). Welcome is in the pulse of talanoa. Welcome is fluid; it soothes longing souls. Welcome is the spring in the pool of metaphors. Welcome also clears room for diversion.

Diversion: Inferiority

In talanoa fashion, i divert in pursuit of an impulse: Feeling inferior is daily food of minoritized peoples. Sometimes imagined and sometimes imposed, the so-called inferiority complex rouses anxiety and makes people think, behave, and perform in ways that contradict their orientations and preferences. Feeling inferior has many triggers: Body shape and size. Caste. Class. Color. Gender. Heritage. Mobility. Orientation. Qualification. Race. And more. The inferiority complex works within to tame the mind and break the soul, and thus it contributes to the minoritization of people.[8] Feeding the inferiority complex are myths of superiority, from which learned and civil societies are not immune (Rubenstein 1999).

Fear of rejection pushes people to submit to "majoritarian pressures," one of the catalysts in democratic societies (Rubenstein 1999, 619–21). The upshot of their submission ranges from some people feeling recognized, acknowledged, and accepted to some people feeling torn between two or more realities. Among the latter are the hybrids (see essay by Nofoaiga) and the wannabes (or fie palagi; see essay by Mariota) who do not fully buy into the minds and ways of the domineering majority. The hybrids and wannabes do not fully belong to one or the other of the worlds and worldviews across the border. They are in-between, which means that they

---

8. Like other "poisons" (appealing to the Greek *pharmakon*, which also means "remedy"), the inferiority complex can also make people better in who they are and excel in what they do. Notwithstanding, my focus in this section is on the de-meaning impacts of the inferiority complex.

belong to both sides of the border (see essays by Foi'akau and Song). They cross borders with their bodies and in their thinking (Premnath 2007). Since they are at the in-between space, one could also argue that they do not belong to either side. In-between, they do not belong. They are prodigals (see essay by Ma'ilo). As border dwellers, either side of the border does not own them. They are not possessed; they do not belong. In-between, they both belong and do not belong.

Borders, both the physical and ideological types, are potential places for minoritization. And there are minoritized people at all corners of public and academic squares, including religious, theological, and biblical societies; minoritized biblical scholars are too many (see Bailey, Liew, and Segovia 2009). Minoritized biblical critics follow the ways of traditional biblical criticism and push the mainline agendas in part because those were the only tracks offered during our training and because we want to be accepted in the Western academy. What might minoritized biblical critics gain and risk by using the master's tool (especially writing and publishing) to resist the master's interests? Is resistance (as liberation critics have advocated for many years) enough? Should we not also protest (as Steed Vernyl Davidson, in private talanoa)? Protest is an opportunity for minoritized people to shout their voices into the silences of the inferiority complex and into the halls of power.

On the one hand, protest would show that minoritized people have courage and wisdom; we do not approve of the way things are, we want changes to take place, and we can direct how those changes could be effected. Protest is the chief reason behind the various occupy—from the Aboriginal Embassy at Canberra to Standing Rock, at the meeting of South and North Dakota—and #BlackLivesMatter movements, as well as the multiple editions of *Voices from the Margin* that R. S. Sugirtharajah has collected over the past twenty-five years. These efforts affirm, appealing to Gayatri C. Spivak's question, that subalterns can indeed speak. Subalterns have their languages, and they can speak the languages of the masters as well as write in the ways of the masters (see essays by Ma'ilo and Havea). The challenge, however, is getting the masters to hear, to be engaged, and to be accountable.

On the other hand, protest is evidence that minoritized people would, appealing to the popular proverb, still use the same tub after throwing out the dirty bathwater. Without changing the tub (frame, system), the sins of the past could resurface to irritate the infant. In this connection, one might ask if protest on its own is enough?

In the following section, i edge islander criticism by metaphorically putting the tub aside and jumping straight into the sea. To step into islander criticism requires one to step away from "firm terrestrial foundations" (Wilson 2016) onto the sandy and rocky shores of island space and then push off from the shores of certainty into the welcoming, rich, fluid, and treacherous deep (Davidson 2015; Havea 2008).

Islander Criticisms

Pasifika cosmologies divide the world into three domains—the sky (*rangi, langi*) above, the world (*papa, māama*) below, and the underworld (*Bulu, Burotu, Pulotu*) beneath—each with governing deities and multiple versions of talanoa. The deities are legends in crossing between the domains, in tricking and pushing away from each other (e.g., Māori legend of Tāne, Ranginui, and Papatūānuku), and in sneaking treasures (e.g., fire, land, coconut) across the domains. The three domains emerge and overlay in the currents of talanoa.

Waters

One of the elements that link the three domains is water: there are waters in the sky (which also contains guiding stars and air), in the world (consisting of land and sea), and in the underworld (in pools and lakes). Waters fall from the sky unto the world of the living, and waters (as well as fire) rise from the underworld of the spirits. Waters are everywhere, making the world of islanders a water world (parts of which have been tapped, dammed, bottled, and marketed).

In Pasifika, we distinguish between two kinds of water (bodies): saltwater and freshwater, both of which spring from the underworld. Those of us from smaller islands are oriented toward the deep sea (*moana*), and we are naturally saltwater people. The sea is our border, our link, our warehouse (as expressed in the Tuvaluan *fale-o-ika*, "houseful of fish"), our livelihood, our home, our destiny (*mateʻanga*, "to-die-for"), and our burial ground. In other words, for saltwater islanders, the sea is our past, present, and future.

On larger islands, which are also "girt by sea" (Australia's national anthem), the coastal people are saltwater people, while many of the people at the interior (center, outback, hinterland) and the highlands would not have experienced, or even seen, the sea. They would not have sea-orientation like saltwater and coastal islanders. Rather, their orientation would be toward rivers, lakes, and underground water. They are freshwater people (who could find ground water in arid places, as saltwater people could find freshwater at the depth of the sea). This collection of essays (like the *Islands, Islanders, and the Bible* collection), unfortunately lacks a contribution by, though there are concerns for and solidarity with, freshwater Pasifika islanders.

Islanders are oriented toward waters,[9] waters that ebb and wash up but also sweep away and drown. Waters are everywhere, and they leave a significant mark in islander criticism. Three qualities of waters and bodies of waters are characteristics of islander criticism: fluid, limiting, and sustaining. Each quality is complex, having effects that are contrary to one another. Despite their different densities, freshwater and saltwater are fluid, and they function as both border (barrier, access) and fount (of resources, of trouble). In similar fashions, biblical texts and interpretations are fluid, limiting, and sustaining.

Fluid

Waters are fluid, but waters do not necessarily understand what fluidity entails. An islander reader comes to biblical texts and interpretations expecting them to be fluid. Wet. Flexible. Unstable. Shifting. But also powerful. Substantial. Crushing. And so forth.[10]

There are waters in the text that many critics read over. An islander reading of the Priestly creation story in Gen 1–2, for instance, would foreground the ways in which the events of creation are located around waters, above and on earth below, as well as at the "face of the deep" beneath (Gen 1:2). The waters had the capacity to "bring forth living creatures" (Gen 1:20), so the waters cocreated with God and with the land (Gen 1:11). In this islander reading, the waters and the land are the cocreators that God

---

9. Our orientation towards waters is with respect to our island setting, with two trajectories in mind: the postmodern affirmation of liquidity (led by Zygmunt Bauman) and the alternative (post)truth politics according to which "reality shows" with "water and plastic facts" matter more than reality itself. In our island reality, as i explain below, waters shape our *ways* and top our *worries*.

10. This, however, does not mean that islander critics are not concerned with the land and other solids. Land is precious in the islands, enough to be the site of tension and conflict (see essay by Neemia).

called upon to help in the creation of humanity (Gen 1:26). In this reading, humans are images of God *as well as* images of the land and of the waters.

In the case of the Yahwist story in Gen 2–4, the way that a mist/flow from the ground gave life to the plant world (Gen 2:6) and then presumably fed the four rivers that flowed into the known world of the time (Gen 2:10–14) will be celebrated in an islander reading. Both creation stories are water-founded, and they provide an alternative to the destructive forces of the waters in the flood stories (Gen 5–9).[11] The waters are both life-giving and life-threatening. In my islander mind, the upshot of the clash of creative and vicious waters flowing in and under the Genesis text is that the narrative has become wet, flexible, unstable, shifting, as well as powerful, substantial, crushing, and so forth. Genesis 1–9 is a wet narrative.

By their nature, biblical interpretations are fluid, so dominating and minoritizing readings can be resisted, protested, revoked, and alternated. The contributors to this collection fail in this regard, in part because we do not have access to all readings of the biblical texts on which we worked. We cannot protest readings to which we do not have access. Such is the upshot of reading in and from the so-called third world.[12] Nonetheless, the sea of readings in this collection is offered out of respect to the fluidity of readings. This of course applies to islander readings as well; islander readings are to be challenged and undermined. Failing to engage with the insights of subaltern people, maybe because they appeal to different languages and to other ways of thinking, has patronizing and minoritizing effects. Koloamatangi's essay is vulnerable in this regard; it has not been translated into English, and the introduction and inserts that i provide fail to capture the oral atmosphere in which his contribution was delivered and received with laughter and cheers. Orality (talanoa) too is a fluid apparatus.

---

11. I develop these alternative watery images further in my current project *Island Hermeneutics / ataMai Pasifika: Genesis 1–15* (forthcoming).

12. We will thus always fail, and so will readers who do not engage with our readings and the readings by other minoritized biblical critics. Our failure is unfortunate but expected, and it is not sufficient cause for disillusionment. Failure in the global optics—a contributor to the inferiority complex—should not be an islander's problem. To think that one can engage with all readings, on the other hand, as is expected of research students, is an illusion.

Limiting

Bodies of water are boundaries, but they are not barriers. Boundaries exist because there is a possibility that they could be crossed, physically and ritually (by observing cultural protocols). One may rightly argue that boundaries, especially the wet ones, are meant to be crossed. It is thus no big surprise that the fleeing mob of Israelites crossed the Sea of Reeds (Exod 14) and the river at Jordan (Josh 3). Boundaries invite crossing to the other side of rivers, lakes, and seas. Of course, not all island boundaries are watery, and not all watery boundaries are safe to cross. Some waters are too deep, have ripping currents, and/or are teeming with vile and hungry dwellers. Trauma is thus expected for the ones who cross those boundaries.

Given that boundaries are interwoven with cultural lore and protocols, which are believed to be broken when a fishing or travel party is not successful, trauma is also suffered by the boundaries. There are acceptable ways for breaking cultural lore and protocols, such as in the permission received through tulou, but i wish to emphasize here the islander conviction that boundaries (including water bodies) are not numb, unresponsive, or profane. Rather, boundaries are lively and aware of the kicks and dabbling of those who cross them. In this regard, boundaries also experience trauma.

With regard to islander criticism, biblical texts and interpretations are boundaries that invite crossing: to other scriptures, to other talanoa, and to other languages. But readers beware; these boundaries are hazardous, and crossing them may be traumatic. On the other hand, crossing them can also be healing, physically and intellectually (Brett 2016).

The essays in this collection cross both the biblical boundaries and the biblical texts as boundaries, and they engage something from the world of the Bible and with something in the island world of Pasifika. There is no uniformity in the approaches taken by the contributors, but the upshot is that biblical texts are no longer left to have dominion (as the first missionaries to arrive preferred) over the minds and tongues of Pasifika islanders. As a whole, this collection talks back both to biblical texts and traditions (e.g., essays by Ma'ilo and Song) as well as to cultural biases (e.g., essays by Mariota and Foi'akau). What this collection fails to address is how islander criticism causes trauma to the biblical texts (qua boundaries), given that boundary crossing (reading) is traumatic to those who cross (readers) as well as to the boundaries (texts) themselves.

Sustaining

As islanders are sustained by the riches and produce of saltwater and freshwater, so are biblical texts and interpretations understood to contribute toward nourishing and sustaining islander living (in both the spiritual and physical aspects). This is a fundamental missionary position which continues to bear fruits in evangelical communities throughout Pasifika. In fact, evangelicalism is alive and strong in the public square as well. Hardly any public event in Pasifika begins without some evangelical form of prayer, with the business and civil sectors churning to the tunes of retribution and prosperity (especially with Christian, but also with Hindu, Muslim, and Buddhist groundings).

The appeal of evangelical thinking is a challenge but also an opportunity for islander criticism. It is a challenge because evangelicalism builds theological walls around the Bible and around hallowed religious and cultural traditions, exempting them from critique and protest. In this regard, biblical texts and interpretations become authorized, uncontested barriers. On the other hand, the opportunity in evangelicalism is found in the way it takes the Bible seriously and holds it up as food for the soul. Biblical texts and interpretations are for consumption. And like food, some of the biblical texts and interpretations are unhealthy and toxic. They can make people sick (see Num 5:11–31) or die (like the countless number of Canaanites, Egyptians, Moabites, Philistinians, and Midianites, who were slaughtered in the cause of Yhwh-God and Israel-Judah, and the many victims of the Christian Crusades).

Unfortunately, Pasifika islanders are known to prefer unhealthy food (with ten in the list of top twenty obese nations being from Pasifika [Smith 2017]). While that is not the true reason why we embrace the Bible, it makes the point that we have a liking for unhealthy feed (read: Bible). What remains is for us all to make the leap into realizing how some biblical texts and interpretations are unhealthy and toxic. Literary critics and novelists like the Samoans Albert Wendt (see the essay by Ma'ilo) and Sia Figiel (see my "Wet Bible" essay) have made this leap. One of the tasks available for islander critics is to engage the literary creations of our own people so that we are sustained by the sons and daughters of our waters. The essays by Ma'ilo and myself take two steps in this direction.

Fluid, limiting, and sustaining are qualities of saltwater and freshwater that can be seen in biblical texts and interpretations when biblical criticism is islandly contextualized (see also Havea 2016).

Ways

Being contextualized in and oriented toward waters, the ways of islanders are consequently fluid, limiting, and sustaining. Two islander ways have received some attention from islander biblical critics—preference for oral modes of being and bondage to relational (kinship) island responsibilities. These two ways manifest in different forms and multiply into different formulations in the different island groups.

The oral-preferring cultures of islanders are at the bottom of the devotion to talanoa (story, telling, conversation), to the workings of language, to the limitations and politics of translation (Ma'ilo 2015), to the maneuverings of creolization (Spencer Miller 2015), and to biblical psalms and religious songs (Macaskill 2015; Middleton 2015). Islander critics thus deal with biblical texts that show evidences of oral preferences (such as psalms, songs, proverbs, and wisdom sayings; see essays by Koloamatangi and Afutiti), and we are moving toward reading other biblical texts to be containing the rhythms and beats of oral cultures. It helps in this move to avoid the temptations of biblicism, which are *limiting*, but to be *sustained* in the ways that biblical texts dance at the thresholds of translation and creolization. There are thus aspects of dancing (not simply as entertainment, but also as engagement and protest) with biblical texts that are, but have not been articulated, in islander criticism.

Dancing is groovy and bodily, and so should be the reading of biblical texts. In this way, the aim of islander reading is not to divide, claim, and control a biblical text but to dance with it. To tease the text so that meanings leap in front of one's eyes. Dance with the stories of Miriam, for instance, and one might think that she was not the unnamed older sister who spoke to Pharaoh's daughter in Exod 2:7. Miriam's stories make good sense if she was a younger sister of Moses because younger sisters, in my islander experience, are the ones who come out celebrating their older brothers' successes (Exod 15). Unless Miriam's song was an attempt to steal the limelight from Moses, which would explain her courage to speak against Moses in Num 12. Younger sisters and older brothers do not always hold back. And in a man's world, throwing a younger sister outside of the camp was not such a big issue. In this islander reading, Miriam could have been a younger sister, so Moses and Aaron would have at least two sisters. Dancing with Miriam's talanoa has thus produced another offspring.

Like dancing, one needs at least one partner in order to function in oral-preferring cultures. I do not advise being oral on one's own. Orality works when one is in a relationship, which could be with other relatives (which Nāsili Vaka'uta [2015] calls *fale-o-kāinga*) or with strangers (see essays by Foi'akau and Neemia). As i indicate above, orality invites one to relate to others, and relating is sustained by reciprocity. The three—orality, relationality, and reciprocity—are like strands in a weaving. They hold each other in place. To weave those into a mat on which to hold a feast is an island thing.

Our oral and relational ways are evident in all of the essays in this collection. What is not spelled out herein is the place of negotiation, one of the objectives of being oral and relational in islander criticism. Talanoa is not just for entertainment or for wasting time but for negotiating responsibilities, relations, and bond(age)s. There are several reasons for the failure to locate negotiation on the mat of orality, relationality, and reciprocity: Pasifika critics are too proud to negotiate, assume that negotiation is an indication of failure, think that negotiation is a foreign practice from bargaining cultures, and do not all see the Bible as a site for negotiation. In practice, however, even if it is not spelled out this way, islander critics are already negotiating with language, text-preferring cultures, colonial legacies, Jewish-Christian biases, and Western-defined academic barriers. Weaving metaphors, i offer a two-sided plea for islander critics: to weave negotiation into the fabric of islander criticism and to produce islander readings that would grease the pumping of protest. Doing these would sustain islander communities no matter where they are.

How might islander readings protest, for instance, the occupation of West Papua by Indonesia? At least this way, as an example: Jonah's protest against God for letting Nineveh off the hook (Jonah 3–4) applies also against the United Nations, Australia, and neighboring nations for ignoring the genocide of over 500,000 black native West Papuans, which lets the Indonesian government off the hook. To protest on behalf of West Papua invites one to protest also on behalf of other occupied islands in Pasifika and the Caribbean groups and in Palestine and beyond.

I have identified two islander ways—oralizing and relating—that are already explained and evident in readings offered by islander critics and that have called for the articulation of three more—dancing, feasting, and negotiating.[13] Imagine that the reading of biblical texts is an event to which

---

13. Feasting and dancing were themes for the Islands, Islanders, and Bible group at the Society of Biblical Literature in 2010 and 2011, but those papers have not been published.

islanders welcome fellow readers to come, talanoa, relate, dance, feast, negotiate, and protest. What else could make the event island'er? Laughter, of course. Humor is an islander thing as well. How would such an imagined event disturb, traumatize, heal, mend, and/or release biblical texts?

Worries

Hakuna matata, which means "no worries," is not all that one finds at island shores. Islanders are still laid back and full of laughter, but we also have worries concerning our water world and our cultural (compare to "traditional") ways. These worries make us tight in some ways.

Climate change (global warming) is, alongside poverty, a big problem for many of the smaller island nations. The scientific and political debates on climate change do not help us face the rising sea level, the droughts, the more frequent and more intense storms, the diseases and famines due to the desperate state of the environment, or those leaders who are uptight about the security of their southern borders at the expense of being neighborly. "Who is responsible for climate change?" is a question for privileged thinkers. "Why should we pay for the sins of the world?" is the critical question in the interest of islanders. In other words, climate justice is the gist of our protest.

The drive for climate justice brings to the surface the fact that climate change, to use a common island image, is only one of the ships that has wrecked on our shores. There are other shipwrecks that need to be floated and removed. Take the case of the low-lying Pasifika island groups of Tuvalu and Kiribati, the highest points of which are around four meters (thirteen feet) above sea level. Both of these island groups are projected to be the first to disappear in the rise of sea level. When the islands become uninhabitable, the islanders will be resettled somewhere else. What will it mean for those resettled islanders to be Tuvaluans or iKiribati[14] when there are no islands of Tuvalu and Kiribati? Climate change is threatening

---

14. It will not be the first time that islanders from Tuvalu and Kiribati are resettled. In 1945, islanders from Banaba (in Kiribati) were resettled to the island of Rabi (in Fiji) because their home island had been destroyed by phosphate mining. This resettlement was organized by the British Empire, the colonial power over both Kiribati and Fiji at that time. In 1947, islanders from Vaitupu (in Tuvalu) were relocated to the island of Kioa (also in Fiji) because the island was threatened by coastal erosion and polluted water wells. These relocations were in response to ecological challenges,

the islands, the islanders, and their ways, but there is another shipwreck on their shores.

Tuvalu and Kiribati used to be ruled as one group called Gilbert and Ellice Islands, which was a British protectorate from 1892 and colony from 1916 until the British evacuated in 1942 because of the (inappropriately named) Pacific War. Troops from the island of Japan had occupied the Gilbert/Kiribati islands, and the British authorities fled back to their island home. Two foreign islands were in conflict over the waters of Pasifika. United States troops started arriving to Ellice/Tuvalu in 1942 and built airstrips with sand and stones dug up from the womb of the island. Any visitor to Tuvalu will not miss the deep trenches throughout the capital island of Funafuti, dug up to build US airstrips in its war against Japan. And any visitor to Kiribati and Tuvalu will not miss the rusting machineries of war that the Japanese and US troops left behind.

With new names at independence, Tuvalu in 1978 and Kiribati in 1979, it became easier to overlook the havoc that the Japan-US war brought on the shores and waters of both island groups. This affected the rest of Pasifika because we are *wansolwara* ("one saltwater") people. The devastation of war includes the aftermath of the testing of atomic bombs in island waters. France and the United States were the key culprits in Pasifika, with their atomic tests in the waters of Bikini and Moruroa. Climate change has become confronting in recent years, but the destructions of war on island space and livelihood happened much earlier. In one way, climate change has distracted the global optic from seeing the aftermaths of war in Pasifika. In another way, climate justice cannot be secured only by seeking to lower methane and carbon emissions but also by accounting for the ecological devastations caused by war and other hostile acts. Climate justice is essential because we humans are lousy at protecting the wellbeing of the planet that we occupy.

With the placard of climate justice i return, in closing this reflection, to the garden story (Gen 2–3). Imagining the garden as an island, i protest against the fuss that some readers express toward the expulsion of the man and woman instead of celebrating the reason for it: "to keep the way to the tree of life" (Gen 3:24). At least one tree is protected, and that would help secure the wellbeing of the garden. The exclusion of the man and woman

---

and the next resettlement will undeniably be due to climate change (as the Carteret Islands in Papua New Guinea, relocated to Bougainville in 2009).

would have reduced the worries of the caretakers and inhabitants of the garden-island. Thanks to the tree of life, the garden was safeguarded for the sowing of imaginations (pun intended).

We may never be rid of all our worries, but climate justice is an opportunity to account for our waters and our ways. In the waters and ways of islanders, there are many corners. And many twists and turns.

Islandering Biblical Scholarship

We can no longer simply say that islanders are simple people or that islander criticism is a simple exercise. Islander criticism involves many twists and turns, engaging with which requires the islandering of biblical scholarship.

This collection of essays comes as a companion to the *RumInations* volume (Havea, Aymer, and Davidson 2015), with markers for issues that need further conversation (e.g., essays by Black and Raymond). One of those issues is the relation between biblical scholarship and the churches, a relation that is usually perceived to be limiting and coercive for both in the eyes of many traditionalist scholars. But this is a critical relation with respect to the place and impact of the Bible in the South Pacific.

The *sea of readings* in this volume ripple from, and towards, Pasifika societies and churches. The readings are critical of the Bible, of biblical interpretations, and of the churches, thus indicating that engaging with churches should not be naïve and simplistic. Neither the churches nor biblical scholarship, in Pasifika and beyond, is pure or innocent, given that both have a fair share in limiting and coercing peoples and cultures. In this respect, i imagine that when biblical scholarship and churches reengage, the attention will twist and turn from the *reception of the Bible* to the *rejection of the Bible* also. Looking forward, this is another "corner" that islander criticism could add to the ongoing conversations around context and biblical scholarship. When will we read "rejection history" (by readers who refuse to be cornered by the Bible) within the "reception history" of the Bible?

Works Cited

Bailey, Randall C. 2015. "Writing from Another 'Room-in-ating' Place." Pages 217–25 in *Islands, Islanders, and the Bible: RumInations*. Edited by Jione Havea, Margaret Aymer, and Steed Vernyl Davidson. SemeiaSt 77. Atlanta: SBL Press.

Bailey, Randall C., Tat-siong Benny Liew, and Fernando F. Segovia, eds. 2009. *They Were All Together in One Place? Toward Minority Biblical Criticism*. Atlanta: Society of Biblical Literature.

Boer, Roland. 2015. "Sand, Surf, and Scriptures." Pages 165–75 in *Islands, Islanders, and the Bible: RumInations*. Edited by Jione Havea, Margaret Aymer, and Steed Vernyl Davidson. SemeiaSt 77. Atlanta: SBL Press.

Brett, Mark G. 2016. *Political Trauma and Healing: Biblical Ethics for a Postcolonial World*. Grand Rapids: Eerdmans.

Charles, Ronald. 2016. Response to *Islands, Islanders, and the Bible: RumInations* at the Islands, Islanders, and Scriptures session of the Annual Meeting of the Society of Biblical Literature. San Antonio, November 21.

Davidson, Steed Vernyl. 2015. "Building on Sand: Shifting Readings of Genesis 38 and Daniel 8." Pages 37–55 in *Islands, Islanders, and the Bible: RumInations*. SemeiaSt 77. Edited by Jione Havea, Margaret Aymer, and Steed Vernyl Davidson. Atlanta: SBL Press.

Hamilton, Scott. 2016. *The Stolen Island: Searching for 'Ata*. Wellington: Bridget Williams.

Havea, Jione. 2008. "*'Unu'unu ki he loloto*, Shuffle Over into the Deep, into Island-Spaced Reading." Pages 88–97 in *Still at the Margins: Biblical Scholarship Fifteen Years after "Voices from the Margin."* Edited by R. S. Sugirtharajah. New York: T&T Clark.

———. 2016. "Reading Islandly." Pages 77–92 in *Voices from the Margin: Interpreting the Bible in the Third World*. Edited by R. S. Sugirtharajah. 25th Anniversary Edition. Maryknoll, NY: Orbis Books.

Havea, Jione, Margaret Aymer, and Steed Vernyl Davidson, eds. 2015. *Islands, Islanders, and the Bible: RumInations*. SemeiaSt 77. Atlanta: SBL Press.

Kinukawa, Hisako. 2015. "The Island of Tyre: The Exploitation of Peasants in the Regions of Tyre and Galilee." Pages 135–45 in *Islands, Islanders, and the Bible: RumInations*. Edited by Jione Havea, Margaret Aymer, and Steed Vernyl Davidson. SemeiaSt 77. Atlanta: SBL Press.

Ma'ilo, Mosese. 2015. "Celebrating Hybridity in Island Bibles: Jesus, the Tamaalepō (Child of the Dark) in Mataio 1:18–26." Pages 65–76 in *Islands, Islanders, and the Bible: RumInations*. Edited by Jione Havea, Margaret Aymer, and Steed Vernyl Davidson. SemeiaSt 77. Atlanta: SBL Press.

Macaskill, Grant. 2015. "Gaelic Psalmody and a Theology of Place in the Western Isles of Scotland." Pages 97–113 in *Islands, Islanders, and the*

Bible: RumInations. Edited by Jione Havea, Margaret Aymer, and Steed Vernyl Davidson. SemeiaSt 77. Atlanta: SBL Press.

Maude, Henry E. 1981. *Slavers in Paradise: The Peruvian Slave Trade in Polynesia, 1862–1864*. Stanford, CA: Stanford University Press.

Mein, Andrew. 2015. "The Wrong Kind of Island? Notes from a 'Scept'red Isle.'" Pages 185–97 in *Islands, Islanders, and the Bible: RumInations*. Edited by Jione Havea, Margaret Aymer, and Steed Vernyl Davidson. SemeiaSt 77. Atlanta: SBL Press.

Middleton, J. Richard. 2015. "Islands in the Sun: Overtures to a Caribbean Creation Theology." Pages 115–34 in *Islands, Islanders, and the Bible: RumInations*. Edited by Jione Havea, Margaret Aymer, and Steed Vernyl Davidson. SemeiaSt 77. Atlanta: SBL Press.

Premnath, D. N., ed. 2007. *Border Crossings: Cross-Cultural Hermeneutics*. Maryknoll, NY: Orbis Books.

Rees, Anthony. 2016. Response to *Islands, Islanders, and the Bible: RumInations* at the Islands, Islanders, and Scriptures session of the Annual Meeting of the Society of Biblical Literature. San Antonio, November 21.

Rubenstein, William B. 1999. "The Myth of Superiority." *CC* 16:599–625.

Smith, Oliver. 2017. "World Obesity Day: Which Countries Have the Biggest Weight Problem?" *Telegraph*, October 11, 2017. https://tinyurl.com/SBL0695a.

Spencer Miller, Althea. 2015. "Creolizing Hermeneutics: A Caribbean Invitation." Pages 77–95 in *Islands, Islanders, and the Bible: RumInations*. Edited by Jione Havea, Margaret Aymer, and Steed Vernyl Davidson. SemeiaSt 77. Atlanta: SBL Press.

Vaka'uta, Nāsili. 2015. "Island-Marking Texts: Engaging the Bible in Oceania." Pages 57–64 in *Islands, Islanders, and the Bible: RumInations*. Edited by Jione Havea, Margaret Aymer, and Steed Vernyl Davidson. SemeiaSt 77. Atlanta: SBL Press.

Wilson, Andrew P. 2016. Response to *Islands, Islanders, and the Bible: RumInations* at the Islands, Islanders, and Scriptures session of the Annual Meeting of the Society of Biblical Literature. San Antonio, November 21.

ISLAND TWISTS

Island Prodigals:
Encircling the Void in Luke 15:11–32 with Albert Wendt

Mosese Ma'ilo

Oceania is a *sea of stories* that flows way beyond the horizons of our *sea of islands*, which is the more appropriate designation that the late Epeli Hau'ofa (1994) gave our *moana* (deep ocean) region. I am here referring to the wealth of *talanoa*, legends, myths, and traditions of Oceania. Stories drifted along the islands, and islands were connected by stories (of creation, of the *tatau*/tattoo, of Lata/Rata, of Tagaloa/Tagaroa, of the fine mat, of chiefly links, and so on) and histories (of navigation, of colonization and decolonization, of rival mission societies, and so on). Our sea of stories has intensified to embrace the Bible, with poetry and novels written by islanders themselves.

The growing native literature has influence on the way islanders do politics, play rugby, make love, worship, paint, and nurture our sons and daughters, both in the islands and in diaspora. Island novelists, social scientists, dancers, painters, and biblical interpreters have a common ground in the way we retell island stories. Storytelling is one of the marks of being islanders, of being colonized and de-colonized, and of being re-presented, as well as of resistance, of intellectual and spiritual emancipation, and of complying with the winds of change … through it all, our tongues never cease to tell and retell our sea of stories. Islanders connect when we read *Call It Courage* (Sperry 1940) or *Sons for the Return Home* (Wendt 1973) and when we watch the Laughing Samoans or *Once Were Warriors* (Tamahori 1994). This sea of stories provides islanders with the confidence, courage, and liberties to rise and break, like ocean waves, our views in and of a changing world around us.

The Bible story (through the lenses of Oceania literature) is now part of Oceania's sea of stories; the Bible is no longer the *absolute story* (as missionaries wanted our forebears to think). Bible stories are foreign, from a different world, time, and space. They have been translated or retold with island languages, so they have become some of our stories. Island readers retell Bible stories "island style" because "Bible as the *only* story" leaves us with a void, a silent incompleteness in understanding who we are as islanders. Today, the sea of stories produced by island writers assists us to encircle our search and struggles for some structure of meaning, whether in reading the Bible or other pieces of literature.

Our task, as island biblical scholars (see Havea, Aymer, and Davidson 2015), is to encircle the void created by reading the Bible as the absolute story (see also Ma'ilo 2011). How? By retelling biblical stories as our stories—by reworking biblical stories with our indigenous references, symbols, values, languages, and literature, to reconstitute the biblical stories as changing but changeless island literary and hermeneutical designs.

Talalasi Reading

Talalasi ("big telling" or "telling big") is a Samoan device for telling and retelling stories and histories (see also Vaai 2016). In practice its weight rests on the proverbial saying, *E talalasi Samoa* ("big/many tellings of/for Samoa"). Orators use this saying to express the legitimacy of many tellings and their standing on equal platform of authority during exchange of oratorical speeches. As Albert Wendt concedes with reference to literature, "novels are about other novels, stories are about other stories, poems are about other poems. The changes come about in the way you tell them" (Ellis 1997, 88).

Talalasi simply means many/big tellings. While talanoa is the act of telling and sharing stories, talalasi is when the same story is told and retold in different ways and from varying perspectives. The telling may be influenced by the social, political, or economic background of the storyteller to suit the interests of her or his respective area or traditional constituency.

The finest obsession of talalasi is that no telling is absolute, for there is a certain amount of competitiveness involved. One telling fills the voids and cracks in the other tellings, and orators master the differences. No telling is concluded, per se, without the others. Talalasi is concerned about both story and the ongoing life of the story. It therefore assigns a continuing search and struggle for meaning while it also unsettles dominance and paternalism in the way stories are told, received, and interpreted. Talalasi, as it were, "blows" (expands, explodes) the story up, and this is expected in formal Samoan settings when skilled orators engage.

Which/Whose telling matters more? Is it the historical fact or the retelling? Is it the *tala* (story) or the talalasi? Samoan orators and storytellers believe that historical facts or data cannot be told without a certain element of narrativity. Therefore, the talalasi matters more than the tala (actual happening or original story) because the ongoing life of the story depends on the retelling. Similar to what Fisch (1998, 4) contends, the retelling includes "the potentiality for change inherent in the process of recapitulation." Talalasi in that regard is the experiencing afresh of a historical experience (by a new generation) in the name of relevance and is therefore a method of reading.

Talalasi Reading Is Biblical

The Hebrew Bible is full of telling and retelling of stories. The well-known Documentary Hypothesis on the different sources that constitute the mislabeled five books of Moses speaks to the multiplicity of tellings (sources) that were later blended to form a single story (Pentateuch). As a result, we have two tellings of the creation of humanity in Gen 1:27–28 and Gen 2:18, 21–22. The exodus is supposed to be a historical event, but readers were mandated with the task of retelling the experience of exodus to the children and grandchildren of Israel, as in Exod 10:2 and Exod 13:8. Things happened in the history of Israel, one could say, in order to be told and retold. In the spirit of talalasi, on the other hand, things became history for Israel in the process of their being told and retold.

The early Christian church provides us with at least four gospels, which are different tellings of the Jesus story. They do not demean the historical or actual event (if anyone knew what that was) but give meanings to it according to the interests and needs of the dissimilar contexts and reading situations of the early church. We therefore learn from the Bible that talalasi achieves two roles concurrently: one is the appreciation of the fundamental human need for originality, and the other is the resemblance or storyline for deepening of meanings. Bible writers were champions of such an enterprise.

Talalasi: Novels and Biblical Narratives

This is no place for a full analysis of the impact of biblical narratives on novels, but it is worth noting the powerful presence of the Bible's narratives and themes in the established canon of English and American novel genres from Bunyan to Hardy and Melville. According to Fisch (1998, 8), the biblical influence is manifested in three ways, "first, as authorizing the moral code by which the characters are perceived and judged; second, as undergirding the plot structure; and third, as the model for a particular kind of narrative realism." Fisch is correct when he boldly states that "The novel was ... the literary instrument of the new Bible-reading, Protestant middle class" (9). I add that the impact of the Bible is still reflected in the current generation of novels. While the Bible reflects the voice of the common person against the established Judaism and Roman formal religions during the early church, the novel is the voice of the common person against the elevated and hierarchical voices heard in the romances and the epics (Fisch 1998, 9). In other novels (and it is the same with island novels), the moral code, plot structures, and narrative realism of biblical narratives are in attendance in some way.

Sons for the Return Home echoes the biblical story of Luke 15:11–32 with Wendt's exceptional creativity not only in the most crucial components of the biblical story, as this chapter exposes, but because the author himself declared that his reading was confined to the Bible (Sharrad 2003, 8). Wendt also penned other literary works using biblical symbols, like "The Second Coming" and "A Second Christ," despite his having rejected the church (Sharrad 2003, 44). Most literary critics of Wendt's novel may have overlooked or downplayed the Bible's influence on his masterpiece, *Sons for the Return Home*. For this chapter, *Sons for the Return Home* is a most ample commentary on Luke 15:11–32, written from a contemporary point of view.

Sons for the Return Home: Experience of an Island Prodigal

The experience of leaving and returning home is universal. The story of the Prodigal Son in Luke 15:11–32 is popular, and there is no need to repeat it here. It is the iconic biblical story of leaving and returning home in the context of the Roman Empire. It represents the Bible and its Greco-Roman background. It is well commented upon by biblical scholars from a variety of perspectives in both the Christian West and the non-Christian worlds.

R. S. Sugirtharajah's (2003, 37–50) appropriation reflects what happens when the prodigal "travels outside its natural Christian habitat and falls into the hands of interpreters—especially expositors who belong to other religious traditions and writers of secular fictions."

Wendt's *Sons for the Return Home* (hereafter referred to as *Sons*) is chosen based on its unique perception of the theme of leaving and returning home, island style.[1] It is a novel that reflects the experience of the writer himself. Albert Wendt is a Samoan-born author. He became a member of an island immigrant colonial minority to New Zealand in the late 1950s. He moved back to the islands, and the novel was written in Samoa between 1969–1971, while his memories of New Zealand were still fresh and vivid. *Sons* is a straightforward story, written in a form that is not of mainstream standardized prose. It is the first Samoan postcolonial novel. When the book came out in 1973, it invited a mixture of criticisms from New Zealanders and mainstream literary critics as well as from Oceania politicians and church leaders due to its prose and parading sexuality (Sharrad 2003, 39–57). Fiji's parliament denounced it as pornography, and Samoans were outraged for its filthy language and for showing Samoa in a bad light to the outside world. But *Sons* is a Pasifika islander's genius talalasi, from island perspective, of the richness and complexity of the theme of leaving and returning home.

Nevertheless, these two stories (biblical Prodigal Son and Wendt's *Sons*) represent the reality of our changing world and a changing Oceania. I discuss *Sons* as a retelling of the Lukan story from the point of view of an islander of the 1970s, and that retelling is still relevant for today's islanders in Samoa and in the Pasifika diaspora. Provided below is a brief summary of *Sons*'s plot for the purpose of this essay, as summarized by Paul Sharrad (2003, 40–41):

> A Samoan family seeks wealth and education in New Zealand, land of material plenty but suspect for its secular values and the seductiveness of the *palagi* (Samoan for European, the Māori term for which is *pakeha*)[2] way of life. Father finds a job in a factory and becomes a deacon in the

---

1. *Sons for the Return Home* is the first novel ever written by a Samoan writer in the English language. It is also available as a film.
2. Palagi and pakeha refer to the same subjects—Europeans and their descendants who settled in Aotearoa, Samoa and other Pasifika islands. In the following discussion, I use palagi when the setting is Samoa and Samoans and pakeha when the setting is Aotearoa and Māori.

local Samoan Church, while mother holds the family together around the home. Youngest son is groomed as the one most likely to succeed: he is a skilled rugby player and is academically gifted (contrary to white expectations of Islanders). We meet him at university in the first chapter, where he is accosted in the cafeteria by a white girl trying to be friendly. She persists in the face of his taciturn reserve, and they become lovers.

Their carefree romance is offset by the attitudes of their families: by white prejudice among her circle of friends and former lovers; by the self-protective circle of the Samoan community and by the shared realization of the Māori history of dispossession. The girl discovers she is pregnant, makes her peace with her father (who, while a superficially typical pakeha settler-capitalist, has himself left the family farm and forsaken a Māori lover because of family prejudice) and goes to her boyfriend's mother for support. Ironically, she looks up to the Samoan woman as a warm, more forceful, presence than her own neurotic mother palely loitering among her cultivated flower garden. But her boyfriend's mother is horrified that she will be unlikely to have her boy as a success-story exhibit to take home and that she will be cursed with "half-caste" grandchildren.

The pregnant girl does not want her boyfriend to feel pressured into a wedding (her own birth having been the reason for her parents' less-than-ideal marriage), so she travels to Sydney and has an abortion. This she comes to regret, and she moves on to London to "sort herself out." Her boyfriend still loves her but is hurt by her decision. His father, already disappointed that his son will not follow his grandfather as a healer (the boy has dropped medicine to do a degree in history), can offer little comfort. In despair at losing the girl, the son takes it out on her former lover (a typical upper-class white racist) by beating him up, and returns with the family to the long dreamed of and highly romanticized Samoa.

All along, he has sought or felt driven to stand aside from the crowd, and in the collective, parochially complacent, village world the son feels even more alienated. He does find his grandfather's grave, a lone circle of stones in the bush, and achieves some sense of connection with tradition and with his father as they recover the story of this feared pagan isolate who had "removed the center of his circle" by killing his beloved wife, performing an abortion on her in suspicion of her being unfaithful.

After a fairly sordid time in the more urbanized Apia, the youth resolves to return to New Zealand. His mother, glorying in the modern palagi amenities brought back from the years away, triumphantly tells her prized son that he cannot go back to his girlfriend. Realizing that she has persuaded the girl to have the abortion, he ritually slaps her in renunciation of his connection and we see him finally suspended between the two countries, flying back to Wellington.

Wendt retells Luke's prodigal in the concrete life of islanders in the seventies and the driving force of the Commonwealth Literature of the sixties and seventies that fought for decolonization (Ashcroft 1981, 26–27; Sharrad 2003, 39–57). The prodigal is a complex phenomenon in *Sons*. It is about islanders struggling to find a place for themselves in the colonial and postcolonial contexts of Samoa and New Zealand. *Sons* is a realistic retelling of the biblical narrative, and Wendt left no stone unturned in the most gripping parts of the Lukan story. Wendt trails the plot structure of Luke 15:11–32 while his originality is reflected in the voices of island characters. Therefore, the moral code, plot structure, and narrative realism of the biblical story is maintained, and Wendt's retelling is at home (Oceania) as compared to the Western interpretations of Luke 15:11–32.

Island Prodigals: Families, Sons, and Daughters

There are two lines for interpreting the prodigal in the novel. First is an island immigrant family, a prodigal from the perspective of the village and island protocols. The family's decision to leave their home(is)land and move to New Zealand resembles the decision of the younger son in Luke 15. In island life, decisions concerning members of the family belong to the parents and the family as a whole. A young son does not decide on his own what to do or where to go. Wendt retells/replaces the individualism of the biblical prodigal with an island perception of an immigrant family, whose decision to migrate to a distant land for greener pastures in the early seventies was done by the elders in the interest of the family.

Second, *Sons* went further by creating a prodigal son within a Samoan immigrant or prodigal family to re-establish the biblical plot structure with the logic of individualism. The writer himself (Wendt) was a son of the immigrant colonial minority in Aotearoa New Zealand. He experienced how immigrant families faced unexpected problems when their children grew up and were instantly caught between two different cultures in their new home. This is a unique retelling of the biblical plot structure where a prodigal family (island perspective) produces prodigal sons as a result of their decision to leave the islands (home) and move to distant lands. This is one of *Sons*'s contributions to the retelling of Luke 15. Realistically, island young people who migrated with their families to New Zealand in the seventies did not have a say in the decision-making. But this did not mean that they migrated against their will. In the eyes of most young Samoans in the seventies, there was something attractive in the opportunity to migrate to a palangi country.

The pakeha family in *Sons* is originally from England, the center of empire that turned Aotearoa into a colonial space (New Zealand) in the eighteenth century. Wendt may have had in mind the English prodigals of that time who (were) moved from the center of empire for distant places (in the empire-building process), with reference to the English literature of Jane Austen and her companions. Cleverly juxtaposed in the plot structure, two families (Samoan and English) turned out to be both immigrant prodigals in Aotearoa New Zealand, the land (fished up by Maui) of the indigenous Māori. The two young lovers (Samoan son and English daughter) became prodigals, and they went back to their respective roots (London and Samoa) at the end of the story.

Wendt's idea of immigrant families enriches the biblical story. *Sons* reached out to several realities of island migration and colonial movements that created prodigals in both the empire and the islands. Colonialism, as identified by most of Wendt's literary critics, was at the backdrop of global and local movements, of discovery and rediscovery, of prodigal sons and daughters, migration and change, discrimination and misunderstandings that re-created both the empire and the islands in the early nineteenth century. The relationship of the two lovers (Samoan son and English daughter) in the novel wisely recapitulated the ambivalent relationship between the colonizer and colonized and how they learned, enriched, and were enriched by one another.

The purpose of most islanders who migrated to the distant land of New Zealand in the sixties and seventies was to come back to the home (is)land, one day, with riches. This desire is the bare consequence of colonialism: mimicry and desire for economic equality. Likewise, the purpose of English families who followed the footsteps of empire was to dig for riches in the treasure islands and other colonial spaces. New Zealand was therefore not viewed as a permanent home for both prodigal families and their prodigal sons and daughters. Rather, New Zealand was a land of milk, money, and honey, and islanders (of the older generation) like the protagonist's parents only wanted to acquire wealth and education for their sons. This drive is concrete and appealing to the natives of Oceania, to both appreciate (as benefactors) and critique (as subalterns) the benefits of colonization.

The Distant Land

The Bible never relates the name of the distant land in the story. The land is only referred to as a distant land, where the son squandered his property in dissolute living (Luke 15:13). The distant land could have been a country either under colonial rule by the Roman Empire or at the center of the empire itself. The distant country was struck by a famine, and the son began to be in need. No one gave him anything. The biblical author represents the distant land as hostile, to be in complete contrast to home. An indicator of the author's negative perspective of this lack appears in the subtle suggestion that to be struck by a famine indicates a curse as a consequence of sinfulness. Unfortunately, the distant land is barely featured in the story and is consequently silenced and represented as the Other.

The foreign land in Wendt's story is New Zealand, a dreamland for Oceania islanders of the 1950s and 1960s. Wendt exposed the shortcomings of the dreamland in a way that was common to the Commonwealth and postcolonial writers of the time. *Sons* is set in the context of New Zealand, which was "founded on a black-white dichotomy, exposing racist and colonialist discriminations and charting the main character's path towards iconoclastic self-possession in a complex and conflictual world" (Sharrad 2003, 43–44). The distant land (New Zealand) is a beautiful but conflicted colonial space that hosted both the colonizer (English family of the girlfriend) and the colonized (Māori and Islanders), including the protagonist's immigrant family. The distant land is set up in the novel as a land of opportunities for both colonizer and colonized. Such is a common expectation in the islands concerning New Zealand.

Wendt provides further observations about places and (is)lands. He uses the perceptions of the indigenous Māori to unveil the injustices of colonization and the dispossession of the Māori in their own backyard by the pakeha (white, European). There is more to the distant land than what is indicated in the Lukan prodigal. The overt sexuality in the novel may be taken as Wendt's exposition of the unexplained "dissolute living" in the Lukan story (Luke 15:13). Sex is liberated into a form of self-expression and spontaneity as in Wendt's generation of the 1970s in New Zealand, a place of immoral sexual values—homosexuality, gang rape, and premarital licentiousness. This is obviously written from the viewpoint of Samoan parents and churchgoing islanders, permeated by Victorian missionaries in the South Seas.

However, the view of the distant land in *Sons* is much more realistic than the Lukan representation. The author of Luke seems to distinguish between the distant land (immorality) and Israel (purity) as the perfect place. I return to this distinction later, but it is important to note how Wendt changed that perspective in the novel. He provides a more balanced view of places, where both islands and New Zealand have their advantages and disadvantages for young people.

Island Pigs versus Biblical Pigs

The pigs in the Lukan story symbolize impurity and contamination. The protagonist turned out to be a servant of impurity as a consequence of spending lavishly. From a Jewish perspective, he became impure by feeding the pigs. But it was by feeding the impure animals that a certain human being (Luke's prodigal son) came to his senses and thought of doing the right thing.

Sons's portrayal of pigs is quite interesting. Instead of representing them in a more sophisticated way, as a symbol of island economic prosperity, the pigs became a diehard memory for island kids. The killing of a pig in Samoa was the only event stored in the memory of the island prodigal son (in New Zealand) for many years, and he worked to perfect that memory "until every detail was fixed and final" (Wendt 1973, 78). The killing of the pig in Samoa became memory because of its violent performance. He was forced to be part of the ritual by his uncle, but he eventually came to appreciate the experience later. The ritual is a violent image of island culture, but the novel also presents it as an ambivalent (for a young kid) treatment of their pet animals. That pig was killed and roasted for the last feast they had in the island with their extended family before leaving for New Zealand the next day.

The next time the memory of killing the pig reappeared to the island prodigal son (in New Zealand) is significant. Just before the weekend when the Samoan family would return to the islands, the prodigal son beat up a pakeha man in the pub toilets. It was revenge, for he was the white guy who humiliated the island prodigal in front of his girlfriend. While he was washing the blood off his clothes and from his bruised knuckles, he suddenly became aware of his reflection in the mirror above the sink. "As he gazed into his face, into the staring eyes, he remembered how, as a child in Samoa, he had watched and then participated in the killing of that boar. It had been a terrifying beautiful ritual" (Wendt 1973, 167). What a way to conclude with the kid's experience of killing island pigs. While the biblical pigs teach humans to come to their senses, island pigs teach island boys to become men, violent men. Violence is universal. The island prodigal son's mother's representation of the islands as a pure and perfect place was just a representation. There is violence in the islands.

The Return

Wendt described the return of two prodigals, the Samoan son and the English daughter. The son returned with his family to the islands with wealth from New Zealand. The pakeha girl returned to London, torn apart (inwardly) after her abortion in Sydney. The two returns, the Samoan son with pride but the English daughter with shame, indicate the complexity of return (featured in the title of the novel) in Wendt's view. This complexity is relevant especially for the younger generation of islanders in diaspora.

The return is one of the central themes of the Lukan story. However, Western commentators of Luke 15 fail to see the complexity of the son's return in the light of the returnees of the postexilic era. But what I am arguing here is that the idea of a return is universal with its plethora of motives and complexities. The return of the Samoan family was a dream come true to the parents but not to their son. The younger generation of islanders in New Zealand and beyond faced the same crisis. Sometimes, they are expected to return against their will. Some of them, like Wendt's prodigal, were expecting the return of a runaway from personal struggles and oblivions. They may have expected that they were returning to an "island in the sun." The return to the islands in *Sons* is not so much a return to a missed culture or to a beloved country. Rather, return to the islands functions as an economicly driven optimism for the parents and as a desire for a trouble-free world for the son. The return is not even about "coming to his senses," as in the Lukan story.

What Is Home?

The younger son in New Zealand was only able to conjure images of Samoa (home) through his mother's memories and representations. The protagonist left Samoa as a young kid, and he only remembered how he participated in the slaughtering of a pig, as mentioned above. Home in *Sons* is a complicated search (opposite of home as portrayed in the Lukan story), and it is one of Wendt's valuable contributions to island postcolonial thinking. Home signifies paradox and contradiction, as indicated in the son's or the protagonist's search for a homeland. Right from the beginning, the novel develops the notion of home and brings the idea to its conclusions in the final lines.

In the first few chapters, *silence* is a recurrent word, and it is variously "hostile, sympathetic, critical, awkward, fragile and healing" (Sharrad 2003, 50). This silence helps develop the two vital elements in *Sons*, "the politics of self-transformation" and the "philosophy of possibility" (Ashcroft 1981, 24). Silence indicates the failure of language to express the deep-seated contradictions in the heart of the son's search, and W. D. Ashcroft (1981, 24) rightly articulates, "The discovery of silence as the ultimate direction of language … turns the boundaries of time and space inside out. The circle of the self becomes boundless because it becomes the circumference of that silence." While *silence* becomes a tool of self-transformation, the place of home in such search for meaning becomes fluid and opens up new beginnings, beyond island horizons. The prodigal's return with his parents to the dream home(is)land, Samoa, has an ironic connection to his roots. He observed how his own grandfather (who committed suicide) conducted an abortion and killed his wife, thus breaking his own family lines, just like the English girlfriend who opted for abortion in Sydney.

Samoa was no longer his dream home(is)land. Island life is no longer paradise. There is no island homecoming. Where is the true home(is)land? To the writer of Luke 15:11–32, homeland is where security and plenty are found, usually associated with the Promised Land. Everyone else is Other. The prodigal in *Sons*, on the other hand, remained a permanent outsider to the end. Writing out of misery, Wendt seems to declare that "he cannot find the home(is)land that he cannot cease to yearn for except as an Oceania that is succumbing to the rot of colonialism and capitalist greed" (Wendt 1976a, 49–50; 1976b, 28). However, the islander prodigal in *Sons* maintained his self-respect, integrity, and confidence in his decisions. He did not want to be turned into a domesticated islander.

At the end of the novel, the islander prodigal was on the plane back to New Zealand, the colonial space. And while he was in the air, he thought:

> He didn't know why he was going back (NZ), but even that didn't seem important any longer …
> He had nothing to regret, nothing to look forward to.
> All was well.

He was alive; at a new beginning. He was free of his dead. (Wendt 1973, 216)

Talalasi Encircles Voids of Who We Are in Biblical Stories

We have shown the biblical prodigal in the sea of stories and what that could offer to modern Oceania readers. Exemplifying the nature of the ocean, talalasi is fluid, enriching and giving spaces for change and progress. Talalasi exposes injustices of colonial racism and misguided notions of island paradise in the sea of stories. Big tellings, talalasi, allow balance and fairness in terms of representation and self-determination.

Sons, a novel from a son of Oceania, encircles the void of who we are as island sons and daughters in Luke's Prodigal Son. The novel retells the biblical worldview of leaving and returning home in a more realistic fashion to islanders of today and tomorrow. After all, to be excluded or to be forced into a story (like Luke 15) without our own telling and experiences is itself an indication of a void to be encircled. Turning to Oceania retellings fills such emptiness in our continuing search and struggle for new beginnings. Island is and is not always home(is)land. The idea of home is fluid and complex. Island as home(is)land is where we begin anew.

Ua lava na tala, e talalasi Samoa! So the tala completes, a Samoan talalasi!

Works Cited

Ashcroft, W. D. 1981. "The Place of the Spirit: Albert Wendt's *Sons for the Return Home.*" *NLR* 9:24–33.

Ellis, Juniper. 1997. "'The Techniques of Storytelling': An Interview with Albert Wendt." *ARIEL* 28.3:79–94.

Fisch, Harold. 1998. *New Stories for Old: Biblical Patterns in the Novel.* New York: St. Martin's.

Hau'ofa, Epeli. 1994. "Our Sea of Islands." *CP* 6.1:148–61.

Havea, Jione, Margaret Aymer, and Steed Vernyl Davidson, eds. 2015. *Islands, Islanders, and the Bible: RumInations.* SemeiaSt 77. Atlanta: SBL Press.

Ma'ilo, Mosese. 2011. "The Challenge and Contribution of Postcolonial Theory to Theological Hermeneutics in Oceania." *Pacific Journal of Theology* 46:34–54.

Sharrad, Paul. 2003. *Albert Wendt and Pacific Literature: Circling the Void*. Manchester: Manchester University Press.
Sperry, Armstrong. 1940. *Call It Courage*. New York: Macmillan.
Sugirtharajah, R. S. 2003. "Son(s) Behaving Badly: The Prodigal in Foreign Hands." Pages 37–50 in *Postcolonial Reconfigurations: An Alternative Way of Reading the Bible and Doing Theology*. London: SCM.
Tamahori, Lee, dir. 1994. *Once Were Warriors*. Fine Line Features.
Vaai, Upolu Luma. 2016. "A Theology of Talalasi: Challenging the 'One Truth' Ideology of the Empire." *PJT* 55:1–19.
Wendt, Albert. 1973. *Sons for the Return Home*. Auckland: Longman Paul.
———. 1976a. "Towards a New Oceania." *MR* 1.1:49–60.
———. 1976b. "In a Stone Castle in the South Seas." *MR* 1.2:27–29.

Wet Bible: Stor(y)ing Jonah with Sia Figiel

Jione Havea

> Thus I became a madman.
> And I have found both freedom and safety in my madness; the freedom of loneliness and the safety from being understood, for those who understand us enslave something in us.
>
> —Gibran, *The Madman*

The big fish would have been gutted, having to spew up his snack from three days earlier. And Jonah would have been soaking wet, with a thick coating of fish slime, when he walked up the streets of Nineveh. Or did he freshen up before he entered Nineveh? The fish spewed Jonah directly onto land (Jonah 2:11), so he would have landed with the kind of wetness one expects of someone who was thrown overboard during a storm and who then reclined in prayer for three days and three nights in the belly of a fish. In the fish's belly, Jonah was protected from the wind and the waves. In prayer, he was stopped from fleeing. Prayer has a way of calming both the mind and the body when trouble is all around. Prayer allows one to relax. Discharge. Calm. Infuse. Like a fresh sardine soaked in a spicy marinade for three straight days and nights, the prayerful Jonah would have been wet to his bones. That is how i[1] imagine his body and his story. That they were both. Wet.

An earlier version of this essay was presented as "Faka(l)ongo e Folofola: Silencing/hearing Jonah with Sia Figiel" at the meeting of the Oceania Biblical Studies Association at Piula Theological College, Samoa, September 11, 2015. This "wet" version benefited from the careful reading and provoking feedbacks from Sia Figiel and Philip Culbertson.

1. My usual explanation for using the lowercase is that i also use the lowercase with "you," "she," "they," "it," and "others," and i do not see the point in capitalizing the

Wetness

Islanders love stories. We live for stories. And the wetter the stories, the better. Not all stories, however, are wet in the same way. Or wet at the same place(s). Some stories become wet in their telling and wetter in the minds of their listeners.[2] On the other hand, some tellers have the gift to transform stories. To dip them in water, soak them, wash them, spin them, rinse them. And hang them up to dry. All in the same sitting. But listeners have the capacity to throw those stories right back in the water after they had been dried and just as easily soak them up all over again. Drip.

Pasifika (Pacific, Oceania) islanders tell and hear stories from the realms of wetness, being surrounded by the *moana* (deep sea). Wetness in our oceanic world has an attitude in its taste and in its texture. Salty. Wavy. Sandy. Before Disney's 2016 cultural appropriation of *Moana*,[3] an animation that appealed to only one corner (so-called Polynesia) of our "sea of islands" (Hau'ofa 1994), the deep sea was already called moana. Colorful. Alive. Powerful. Deep. Wet.

Wetness should not be romanticized, especially given that rainfall is not constant on the islands and that the sea level is rising up island borders. We have dry spells, and many Pasifika islands are projected to drown not too far from now in the whitewash of climate change. Romanticizing wetness in our oceanic world does not help. But stories are like winds in the sails of romantics, from Pasifika and beyond. Stories wet the mind and stroke the soul.

The story of Jonah is wet in several ways. It involves a character who drifted away from God's direction, who got dumped into the sea, who got swallowed by a big fish, and who found the people and animals on the other side of the sea to have fluid minds and will—the marks of a wet

---

first person when she or he *is* in relation to, and because of, everyone and everything else. My i is a relational subject. This time, i add the madman's confession: "The 'I' in me, my friend, dwells in the house of silence, and therein it shall remain for ever more, unperceived, unapproachable" (Gibran 2002, 11).

2. I imagine in the case of the native Samoan women who were Margret Mead's sources for *Coming of Age in Samoa* (1928) that some of them would have had fun fooling the naïve white American researcher. Their fun is an example of the working of island humor. See also Mosese Ma'ilo's discussion of *talalasi* in the previous chapter.

3. Because someone else had copyrighted *Moana* in Germany when the Disney animation was dubbed into German, the name of the main character and of the movie was changed to *Vaiana*. This is cultural appropriation times two.

story. Jonah's story is also dirty, slimy, and smelly, as things tend to be in the belly of ships. From the belly of the ship to the belly of the sea, then to the belly of a fish, then to the belly of an empire, and lastly onto the mount at the hinterland, the belly of the land. There is nothing romantic about such places. And the narrator did not say if he scrubbed up after the fish spit him out onto the shores of Nineveh. Unquestionably, Jonah's story is a wet one, with the propensity to disgust its listeners who would find it challenging because of its content, both admirable and vexing all the same.

Jonah is one of the better known biblical figures among Pasifika islanders. We hear his name at church and at community events, and we think that we understand his story. For some, the story is so fabulous that it is quite ridiculous—bordering on unbelievable. It is a fishy story (pun intended), and Jonah is like a madman (also in the way that Kahlil Gibran [2002] characterizes one). This is the kind of story by which legends are made.

Many islanders have not even read the biblical story but draw upon what they hear at Sunday School, at village grounds, and through bantering with friends and relatives. In oral-preferring cultures, stories slip through the fingers of textuality and the confirmation of scripturality. Stories are slippery. Wet. And conjure the pleasures of orality.

For many Tongans, Jonah brought bad luck to the sailors and to the other travelers on the boat (Jonah 1:3). In the face of trouble, Tongans usually ask, "Which one of us is Jonah?" The assumption is that if "Jonah" is identified and removed from the situation, then trouble will go away and then things will settle down. In this regard, Tongans are sympathetic towards the sailors who had to endure an unexpected storm. Like a bushfire that has been intentionally set, God cast the storm upon the sea. Simply because of Jonah. Identify Jonah, therefore, and dunk him. Trouble is expected consequently to go away.

At the same time, most Tongans are not ready to un-identify with Jonah and the people of Israel and Judah (qua people of God). So, there are warm and cold feelings with regard to Jonah: warm toward his courage to walk away from God (as indication that he did not want Nineveh to be saved), but cold toward the trouble he brought upon the sailors and the other travelers.

Stor(y)ing

Pasifika islanders think they understand Jonah's story, but many have not even read the biblical version. How can those islanders think that they understand the story? i raise this question not because i want to privilege the biblical text over or against the musings, meanderings, and ruminations of native peoples.[4] i am not one of those biblical critics who is obsessed with the so-called correct interpretation. Rather, my interest is with how readers and tellers *story* and/or *store* Jonah. We actually do both—storying and storing (stor[y]ing). In the process of storying, we also store Jonah (story, character), and vice versa.

Stor(y)ing is the English version of a play in my native tongue, Tongan. Two Tongan words, differentiated by one letter, refer to different actions: (1) When one listens to or hears a story, one *fakaongo* the details of the story. (2) When one silences the story, or stops its telling, one *fakalongo* (*whakarongo* in Māori) the teller and the story. Different words, different impacts. But the two words can intersect seeing that one needs to silence/fakalongo oneself in order to hear/fakaongo the story, and one needs to hear/fakaongo alternative stories in order to effectively silence/fakalongo an unwelcomed story. Two words, differentiated by the insertion of the letter "L." I use the Tongan construction interchangeably with the English one: fakaongo/story, fakalongo/store, and faka(l)ongo/stor(y)ing.[5]

I come to the story of Jonah this time (see also Havea 2011; 2012; 2013a; 2013b; and 2016, which together may suggest the obsession of a storyweaver) with the overlapping movement of storying and storing, of fakaongo and fakalongo, because i find both in the story as well as in its interpretation. God called Jonah to announce (which is also fakaongo in Tongan) words to (or against) Nineveh (Jonah 1:2; 3:2), and in the end, God wanted Jonah not to grieve (Jonah 4:4; 4:9). Relax. Which is one way

---

4. In the world of stories, understanding is available to those who are willing to be attentive (to listen closely) and to reflect. Understanding is not the privilege of readers only. Understanding involves under-standing, in the sense that one stands under the story that one thinks one understands.

5. My playing with words here gives expression to the fluidity, the wetness, of language and meaning (see also Havea 2005) and to the workings of island humor (sometimes perceived as trickery)—which undercuts while completely serious—in my thinking. When i play with the English language, it is about resisting a colonial language; when i play with the Tongan language, it is also about embracing the powers of orality.

of saying, be silent. Whakarongo. Shut up. After Jonah delivered God's words to Nineveh, God snubbed him and disregarded his death wishes (Jonah 4:3; 4:8). The supposedly prophetic character who was pushed to speak is literarily silenced; the one sent to announce (or to preach, *fai lauga* in Samoan) does not get the kind of audience for which he was hoping. Jonah preferred an unyielding, unrepenting Ninevite crowd as well as a firm, unchanging God. When Jonah complained (*launga* in Tongan), God gave him a scolding (Jonah 4:10–12). God preferred that Jonah be silenced (fakalongo).

The story of Jonah is accordingly an appropriate site for unravelling the workings of faka(l)ongo/stor(y)ing, and this is where i find the insights and teases of the Samoan novelist Sia Figiel engaging. I engage Figiel on three points: the practice of *su'ifefiloi*, the (non)place of the past (read: tradition) in day-to-day plotting, and the affirmation of the communal "we." I focus on ways in which these three points—around the spheres of orality, temporality, and subjectivity—help make the story of Jonah wet.

Su'ifefiloi

Figiel (1999) uses a traditional Samoan storytelling form, su'ifefiloi, in her novel *Where We Once Belonged*.[6] This novel explores the legacy of colonialism in Samoa through the story of a young woman named Alofa Filiga. The story is set in Malaefou ("new field"), suggesting a new beginning, at a new location, from where the narrator (through the voice of Alofa) looks back to *where we once belonged* before the arrival of the Christian mission and Western cultures. Figiel's point is clear: Samoa has changed, for better and for worse, due to the arrival of the *pālagi* (white Europeans) and their consumerist cultures. Consumerism drives people into their individual shells, withdrawn from the "we-ness" of community and relatives (*aiga*). I return to this "we" two sections down but here briefly fakaongo Figiel's methodological nudging.

Su'ifefiloi is the art of weaving a mixture of different flowers and leaves to form a long *ula* (*lei* for Hawai'ians) or necklace. Similarly, songs and stories are woven together to form one long narrative which we hear a lot from native orators in village greens (*malae*). Orators weave stories that

---

6. Figiel has several other works and has explored "wetness" in relation to the body, mind, and culture, but i limit myself in this essay to *Where We Once Belonged*.

come from different places and times. These stories may not have anything (in terms of their origin or plot) to do with each other, but the orators weave them together and consequently create a new story (see also essay by Ma'ilo in this collection). This new story is like a mat that has been woven with many strands. The strands do not have to be from the same material, but the process of weaving sheds their differences and makes them into one mat. Tight. Yet, unravel-able. The appropriate site for su'ifefiloi is therefore Malaefou—new malae,[7] new site, new beginning, new *talanoa*.[8]

Su'ifefiloi is story-weaving, linking different stories in a fluid (oceanic) process through which stories fly together into the unknown (cf. Brett and Havea 2014). Su'ifefiloi for Samoans is similar to *talanoa fakatatau* for Tongans in that it creates something new from the mixture of different elements; it is a communal act that is initiated by a singular singer, weaver, or storyteller (see Havea 2008). Thus, it compels a community to engage, interact, exchange, and intersect. Both are about people giving wings to stories so that they (the stories and the tellers) may fly, fly into the unknown (Tongan: *puna ki he ta'e'iloa*).

Could the book of Jonah have been the product of a process similar to su'ifefiloi? When this kind of query is raised by traditional biblical critics, they quickly notice the different forms and genres—this short novella is composed of a prose and a poetic prayer. The poetic prayer (Jonah 2) is most likely from a different place and time, and most critics assume that the prose (Jonah 1, 3–4) is one whole unit. The poetic prayer was inserted, as if it was woven, into the prose. The prose thus provided the frame for the poetic prayer, which was most likely from an earlier time.

What if the prose consists of several stories from different times and places, so that there were separate stories that a narrator wove together (e.g., Jonah 1 woven with Jonah 3–4)? If this was the case, then the narrator

---

7. In Te Reo Māori, a new *marae*. Readers who are familiar with Māori cultures will understand that the marae is the center of Māori communities. In this regard, the idea of a new malae/marae is critical in the eyes of traditionalists.

8. For the sake of ones who do not understand the lingo, talanoa is a word used in several (but not all) of the native Pasifika languages; it refers to the (three in one) triad of *story*, *telling*, and *conversation*. In the world of talanoa, *story* dies without *telling* and *conversation*; *telling* becomes an attempt to control when one does not respect the *story* or give room for *conversation*; and *conversation* is empty without *story* and *telling*. In talanoa cultures, there is no separation between story, telling, and conversation. They interweave in the one word, talanoa.

has done such a great job that we have been fooled into thinking that we have only one story in the prose.

Two elements in the prose suggest separate stories: first, the difference in the portrayal of the natives of Nineveh in chapter 1 (wicked natives) compared to chapters 3-4 (compliant natives); second, Nineveh is portrayed as consisting of only humans in chapter 1 but includes humane animals in chapters 3-4. The shift in the temperament of the natives and in the composition of the city suggests two different stories, especially seeing that Jonah and God did not shift in the story. Jonah did not go to Nineveh at first because he expected God to change God's mind (Jonah 4:2), and Jonah was right because God changed God's mind as expected (Jonah 3:10). God acted as expected. Foregrounding Nineveh in reading the prose suggests that two stories have been woven together: Jonah 1 with Jonah 3-4. This suggestion is made not on historical grounds but on the intermingling of su'ifefiloi.

There are other characters in this story—God and the sailors—so it is possible that we have four stories woven together here: the story of Jonah and God, in two parts (Jonah 1 and Jonah 3-4); the story of the sailors (Jonah 1:4-16); and the story of the people of Nineveh (Jonah 3:3b-10). The two-part story of Jonah and God is the metanarrative into which the story of the sailors and the story of the people of Nineveh are woven. This is a su'ifefiloi suggestion which—to borrow from Albert Wendt, also a Samoan literary critic (see also essay by Ma'ilo in the previous chapter)—shows that "novels are about other novels, stories are about other stories, poems are about other poems. The changes come about in how you 'tell' them" (Ellis 1997, 88).

I can also come to this suggestion from the other direction, echoing the popular query among feminist critics: in whose interests do we read the story of Jonah? The majority of biblical scholars read on behalf of Jonah and God (whose interests are favored, in different ways, by the metanarrative), and consequently in the interests of Israel and Judah, so the sailors and the people of Nineveh are seen as simply serving the interests of the Jonah-God exchange. The opportunity provided by su'ifefiloi is the possibility that this biblical narrative is the weaving of multiple stories, and this would not be a controversial suggestion in the ears of source and tradition critics.

Su'ifefiloi also provides an opportunity to read the same narrative in the interests of different, including minoritized, characters. The Jonah narrative reads differently when read in the interest of the sailors, in the interest of the moana/sea, or in the interest of the people of Nineveh.

When one reads the prose in the interest of the sailors, one would be led to sympathize with the working class and their duty of care, with the vulnerability of travelers and migrants, with the openheartedness of non-Hebrews, with the soundness of the vessel (the boat was fresh), with the bearing of the burden for others, and so forth. The story of the sailors is one of duty, service, safety, and survival (Havea 2016).

When one reads on behalf of the sea/moana, one learns to relax the vigor of anthropocentrism in order to appreciate the gifts and forces of the sea/moana, the courage and freedom that come with moana/sea orientation, and the availability of rescue in the depths of the ocean (see Vaka'uta 2014; see also Kunz-Lübcke 2016). It is worth noting here that the storm was not self-inflicted by the sea/moana but hurled upon the sea by God. The story of moana is about being troubled (in this case, by God) and finding resolution within (the sea/moana). And it is also about being wet.

When one reads on behalf of the people of Nineveh, one learns to love foreigners and the people for whom one does not usually care (see Lindsay 2016). In the interest of people like the Ninevites, the implication of the story is really simple—love your enemies! Nineveh was the capital of Assyria, one of the empires that occupied the land of Palestine in the biblical past. To read in the interest of Nineveh is like asking Samoans, Figiel's people, to read in the interest of their worst enemies (who might be Tongans, my people)!

The spirit of su'ifefiloi encourages readers to story/hear/fakaongo the characters and stories that have been silenced/fakalongo/stored because of the interests of Jonah, Israel, and God. Su'ifefiloi gives, in the end, an opportunity for readers to wet the story of Jonah. Up to this point, i have only storied/heard/fakaongo the silenced/fakalongo/stored voices in the prose of Jonah.[9] Awaiting another opportunity is the examination of stor(y)ing in the poem and in the ecological dimensions of the novella.

The Passed

There is a longing for the past in *Where We Once Belonged*, but Figiel does not fetishize precolonial Samoa. There is something worthwhile in the past, and there is also something maddening in clinging to the past. This is

---

9. These voices are in the text, but some are more pronounced than others. I resist labeling these as "foreign voices" because that would give the impression that i prefer the "native" or "local" voices of Jonah, God, Israel, and Judah.

the case with the character of Siniva, Alofa's aunt, who returned to Samoa in 1972 with both a bachelor's and a master's degree in history. Siniva succeeded in pālagi education, focusing on the history of her native home. She was certified in a pālagi system to cling to the past of her native people. Siniva returned to Samoa and called for a privileging of the old religion and the ancient cultures of Samoa. She even refused to eat imported pālagi foods, both the physical and spiritual types:

> Each prayer to Jesus means a nail in our own coffin. Each time we switch something ON (radio, lamps, TV, ignitions …) means a nail in our coffin. And agaga [spirit] as we once knew it dies in our still biologically functionable bodies, full of junk food … darkness-food … white-food … death food. (Figiel 1999, 238)

The community ignored Siniva, and she became blind and eventually committed suicide. She died clinging to a dream of a past imagined to be pure, unaffected by pālagi coercions: a past *where we once belonged*. In the spirit of su'ifefiloi, i turn to look for evidence of clinging to the past in the Jonah narrative.

Sailors

The sailors did not cling to their past, for at the end of their story they shifted and so worshipped the god of the Hebrews (Jonah 1:16). Similar to Ruth (cf. Ruth 1:16–17), the sailors let go of something (but not everything) from their tradition and the past of their people as if they too were ready to enter and occupy a malaefou. This move is problematic. While clinging to the past is maddening, uncritically endorsing a foreign culture is also problematic. No one lives in the past; also, no one lives in isolation (from others as well as from the past). Similar to the sailors, Pasifika islanders are affected by the cultures—religious and otherwise—that land on our shores (in the case of sailors, on their deck), and it is unwise to assume that pālagi and Christian cultures are always healthy for us.

In the case of Pasifika islanders who reside in diaspora, they face two challenges: whether to submit to the dominant cultures where they now live, and how to affect the pālagi cultures where they raise their "fresh off the boat" families. The sailors let go, gave up, what was dominant (but not necessarily everything meaningful) for their people. This is difficult for the first generation of Pasifika islanders in diaspora. They are not ready to make a clean break from their island customs, and they tend to be more traditionalist than the ones at the home island. The story of the sailors is challenging for islanders at home and over the seas. On the other hand, the story of the sailors is a lesson for dominant societies—it is not suicidal to give up the past and the traditions of one's people.

The sailors were not suicidal at all. They wanted to survive, and they even refused to throw Jonah overboard as he had instructed. Their response to Jonah's instruction to throw him overboard was to row even harder toward shore (Jonah 1:13). When they could not succeed, only then did they throw Jonah overboard, against their better judgment. This would have troubled them greatly. That the sailors were non-Hebrews does not mean that they did not have any values. Their willingness to let go of aspects of their tradition and their past was in response to a troubling experience. Trauma. Indeed, it takes a disturbing experience to come to terms with the devastation of clinging to the past.

Given their placement in the margins of society and of the book of Jonah, the sailors may not have had much investment in their cultures and religions. Letting go of elements of their past would have therefore been easy for them. They were sailors; what else should we expect? Sailors are people of the sea, and no one expects them to be "wrecked" upon some tradition or past. Right?

Nineveh

In the case of the people of Nineveh, they had no problem un-clinging from their past. Despite the greatness of the city, the living creatures in Nineveh were of one accord (Jonah 3:5–9). Jonah barely started to preach (only four Hebrew words) when the people of Nineveh put on sackcloth and repented, together with their king, nobles, and animals. Their repentance is a sign of their willingness to un-cling; to repent so easily is testimony to their character. They were wise people. They knew what was good for them, and they acted accordingly.

The people started to un-cling, and the king joined them (Jonah 3:6). On the one hand, we can tell who the real leaders of the city were—the people, rather than the king. On the other hand, we can see what tends to happen when the people lead—there is sparing and survival. The un-clinging was the people's movement. In comparison, the king's leadership was probably what led to God sending Jonah in the first place to speak against Nineveh.

But the king is not a dud; he ordered that the beasts too should fast and put on sackcloth (Jonah 3:7–8). Readers make light of this move—how ridiculous of the king of Nineveh to issue such an order! Absurd. Comical even. Besides, what possible change could the animals bring? Improbable. But in the king's order is a critical move if we read the story in the interest of the people of Nineveh. There is an inclusive spirit in the Ninevite community. As indicated above, the natives of Nineveh consist of complying humans and humane animals; the will of the beasts has a place in the sparing of Nineveh. In other words, Nineveh was spared not only because of the king, and not only because of the repenting people, but also because of the fasting and sackclothed beasts. The story of Nineveh problematizes prejudices against beasts and beastliness.

Jonah

Jonah, on the other hand, was not ready to let go of the past. He was not ready to let go of his expectation of God, that God would pardon Nineveh. Also, Jonah was suicidal: first on the boat, when he instructed the sailors to throw him overboard (Jonah 1:12), and later outside of the city, when he twice demanded that God let him die (Jonah 4:3; 4:8). In clinging to the past, Jonah withdrew. Inwardly. To himself. Away from Nineveh, that great city which God had spared. Jonah wanted to be alone, a move that draws me back to Figiel.

The "We"

The politics of identity have made minoritized biblical scholars critical of colleagues who use the personal pronoun "we." Are women included in the "we" of male scholars? Are black, brown, and shaded women included in the "we" of white feminists? Are queer folks included in the "we" of straight authors? Are indigenous queers included in the "we" of the others? Is it responsible to speak with and for "we" anymore?

There is no anxiety with those questions in *Where We Once Belonged*, in which Figiel seeks to reclaim the collective Samoan "we." With the arrival of Christian missions alongside Western consumerist cultures came individualistic tendencies over and against the communitarian ways of precolonial Samoa. Alofa resisted the drive toward individualism, which she saw at school in an exercise that their teacher Miss Cunningham required of the students—each student was to write about her or his individual experiences. This exercise required Alofa to think *as if she was alone*, which did not work for Alofa:

> You were always with someone.... Nothing was witnessed alone. Nothing was witnessed in the "I" form—nothing but penises and ghosts. "I" does not exist, Miss Cunningham. "I" is "we" ... *always*. (Figiel 1999, 136–37; emphasis original)

For Alofa, the narrator who speaks on behalf of Figiel the author, the "I" is always a "we."

This is where the story of Jonah differs from the stories of the sailors and of Nineveh. Jonah's story is about his "I" whereas the stories of the sailors and of Nineveh are about a collective "we." In the case of the story of Nineveh, the collective "we" includes the beasts. Seeing that God's final words in the story refer to the beasts, is it not wonderful that God (at the end of the story) has learned something from Nineveh?

> Then the LORD said: "You took pity on the plant, for which you did not toil nor did you make it grow, which one night came into being and the next night perished. Should I also not take pity on Nineveh, the great city, in which there are many more than one hundred twenty thousand people who do not know their right hand from their left, and many beasts as well?" (Jonah 4:10–11, my translation here and below)

I attribute God's concern for the beasts at the end of the story to the influence of the order given by the king of Nineveh in 3:6–10:

> The word reached the king of Nineveh, who rose from his throne, took off his royal robe, covered himself with sackcloth, and sat in ashes. And he caused it to be proclaimed and published throughout Nineveh: "By the counsel of the king and his nobles: Neither man nor beast, neither cattle nor sheep shall taste anything; they shall not graze, neither shall they drink water. And they shall cover themselves with sackcloth, both man and beast, and they shall call mightily to God, and everyone shall repent of his evil way and of the dishonest gain which is in their hands. Whoever knows shall repent, and God will relent, and He will return from His burning wrath, and we will not perish. And *God saw their deeds*, that they had repented of their evil way, and the *Lord relented concerning the evil that He had spoken to do to them*, and He did not do it. (emphasis added)

In-deed, Nineveh (king, nobles, people, and beasts) influenced the action of God. In this reading, God repented not because God was compassionate, gracious, and slow to anger (Jonah 4:2). That is how the stories of God and Jonah (the metanarrative) want us to understand. According to the story of Nineveh, on the other hand, God repented because of what Nineveh did. Nineveh, that great city, repented; God responded by also repenting. For this reading, two conclusions could be entertained: first, in their exchange, Nineveh entered into the "we" of God; and second, God entered the "we" of Nineveh, where people and beasts matter. God is alive and *enter*taining.

In the talanoa of Nineveh, the God of the Hebrews is not angry, distant, or mutable. Rather, God is alive and *affecti*onate. As well as flexible. Variable. Unreserved. The actions and hopes of the people of Nineveh indicate that in their hearts, the being and economy of God have not been worked out. God was still a work in progress. God was fluid. The fluidity of God allows for different kinds of relationship and for alternative ways of facing threats and woes. A fluid God does not need to resort to revenge and violence in order to resolve differences and tensions. A fluid God is not bound by hard-and-fast doctrines (e.g., of discovery and impartiality) and theologies (e.g., of retribution and monotheism). A fluid God is open for negotiation and repentance. A fluid God is repentant, and in the story of Nineveh, repentance is life-giving. A fluid God has time and space for foreigners and the diselected to be included in its "we."

These assertions may find support from among process theologians, for example, but such is not the drive of this essay. I am not interested in lodging some theological prolegomena on the natures of God. Rather, my drive is to invite appreciation for how the "we" of Nineveh has room both for the God of the Hebrews and for a different set of expectations about God and other divine beings. I presented God entering the "we" of Nineveh as indicative that, appealing to an island image, God was fluid. We-t.

Jonah, on the other hand, refused to enter the joint "we" of Nineveh with God. Jonah removed himself to sulk from a distance. Alone. He preferred to be in the midst of dryness. On his own. For his own. Isolated. Madness.

Sea of Stories

Su'ifefiloi imagines that the biblical texts were once wet, and stories welcomed other stories into their fold. There are several stories in the prose of Jonah, and it matters which/whose story one privileges in one's reading.

Like the major narratives in Genesis, Exodus, and Numbers, Jonah, too, is a sea of stories.

Su'ifefiloi moistens the seams of biblical texts so that i can weave realities of Pasifika islanders with the novella of Jonah. I started to do this by appealing to the weaving of a mat as the principal metaphor, but another form of weaving is also appropriate for su'ifefiloi—the braiding (*fi*) of an ula/lei or of a rope. This essay has accordingly shown how Pasifika wisdom and realities can strengthen the biblical account of Jonah. In Tonga, the final stage of braiding a rope involves soaking the rope so that the fiber of the cords would cling to one another. Wetness makes the rope strong. And by transference, su'ifefiloi climaxes at wetness.

This reading is under the influence of Figiel. I drew upon the spirit of su'ifefiloi to help me story/fakaongo the sailors and Nineveh who tend to be fakalongo/stored because of readers' interest in God, Jonah, Israel, and Judah. I offer this reading with an invitation: let us seek and engage the wisdom of the native writers of Pasifika, and let us cooperate in the stor(y)ing of scriptures.

Works Cited

Brett, Mark G., and Jione Havea, eds. 2014. *Colonial Contexts and Postcolonial Theologies: Storyweaving in the Asia-Pacific.* New York: Macmillan.

Ellis, Juniper. 1997. "'The Techniques of Storytelling': An Interview with Albert Wendt." *ARIEL* 28.3:79–94.

Figiel, Sia. 1999. *Where We Once Belonged.* New York: Kaya.

Gibran, Kahlil, 2002. *The Madman: His Parables and Poems.* Mineola, NY: Dover.

Hau'ofa, Epeli. 1994. "Our Sea of Islands." *CP* 6.1:148–61.

Havea, Jione. 2005. "Stor[y]ing Deuteronomy 22:13–19 in Missionary Positions." *BCT* 1.2. DOI 10:2104/bc050003.

———. 2008. "'*Unu'unu ki he loloto,* Shuffle Over into the Deep, into Island-Spaced Reading." Pages 88–97 in *Still at the Margins: Biblical Scholarship Fifteen Years after "Voices from the Margin."* Edited by R. S. Sugirtharajah. New York: T&T Clark.

———. 2011. "The Dilemma of Monotheism in Jonah." Pages 9–14 in *I believe in God.* Edited by William W. Emilsen. North Parramatta: UTC Publications.

———. 2012. "First People, Minority Reading: Reading Jonah, from Oceania." Pages 176–85 in *The One Who Reads May Run: Essays in Honour of Edgar W. Conrad*. Edited by Roland Boer, Michael Carden, and Julie Kelso. New York: T&T Clark.

———. 2013a. "AdJusting Jonah." *IRM* 102.1:44–55.

———. 2013b. "Casting Jonah across Seas and Tongues: A Transnationalizing Reading." Pages 25–36 in *Babel Is Everywhere! Migrant Readings from Africa, Europe, and Asia*. SIHC. Edited by J. Kwabena Asamoah-Gyadu, Andrea Fröchtling, and Andreas Kunz-Lübcke. New York: Lang.

———. 2016. "Sitting Jonah with Job: Resailing Intertextuality." *BCT* 12.1:94–108.

Kunz-Lübcke, Andreas. 2016. "Jonah, Robinsons, and Unlimited Gods: Re-reading Jonah as a Sea Adventure Story." *BCT* 12.1:62–78.

Lindsay, Rebecca. 2016. "Overthrowing Nineveh: Revisiting the City with Postcolonial Imagination." *BCT* 12.1:49–61.

Vaka'uta, Nāsili. 2014. "A Tongan Island Reading of Jonah as Oriented toward the Ocean." Pages 128–29 in *Global Perspectives on the Bible*. Edited by Mark Roncace and Joseph Weaver. Boston: Pearson.

Native Texts:
Samoan Proverbial and Wisdom Sayings

Levesi Laumau Afutiti

How might Samoan proverbial (*alagaupu*) and wisdom sayings (*muagagana*), like other traditional (ancient and modern, scriptural and oral) wisdom sayings, be utilized in biblical exegesis? This is a critical question given that many Samoan preachers and readers do not use Samoan proverbs nor wisdom teachings in their preaching and interpretation.

This chapter (1) explores the form, function, and significance of Samoan proverbial and wisdom sayings; (2) posits a basis upon which these sayings may be included in biblical interpretation, for they could present the biblical message in meaningful ways for Samoans; and (3) demonstrates how Samoan wisdom proves useful for interpreting Mark 1:16–20.

Samoan Text

As with other languages, Samoans regard their language, with reference to its wisdom sayings, as a repository that contains their cultural and traditional values. Samoan cultures and traditions are embedded in proverbial and wisdom sayings, making those a Samoan text.

The Samoan language carries traditional cultural values. Considering Samoa's oral tradition, language has been the primary means of transmitting norms and values as "word of life." Through speaking and hearing, language helps give birth to one's self-understanding, chiefly because language molds one's worldview and disposition. The Samoan language nurtures one's life as a Samoan (Aiono 1996, 21–27). In other words, the Samoan language has served as an *oo* (receptacle) for storing Samoan values, for use in later occasions (1).

Oo is the place where the water of the Pesega river disappears. Pesega is a village near Apia, at the center of which lies this river. The river is usually dry. But whenever it flows, it is quite dangerous. The river flows toward the sea, but only a small amount of water goes into the sea; the rest disappears as it sinks into what is called oo (an unfilled hole underground). The water goes to the oo, and as soon as rain stops in the mountains, the river dries up again. This experience has been related to similar occurrences in life through the saying *E tetele a Pesega, ae matua a i le oo* ("Although the Pesega flows strongly and hastily, the water rests at oo"). From this saying, one could say that language is a kind of oo. In spite of foreign changes that affect Samoa, the Samoan language is oo—a reservoir in which resides people's identity, traditional norms, and values (Aiono 1996, 1–2).

Samoan language, according to Laumau Faavaoga Salamina, a Samoan orator from the village of Puleia Savaii, is *O le ato-ponapona a le atunuu* (*o le ato* means "the basket," *ponapona* refers to the joint segments of the kava plant, and *atunuu* means "country").[1] These ponapona joints are the parts of the kava that Samoans plant, for they contain the life of the plant. Hence the phrase *O le ato-ponapona a le atunuu* refers to "the country's basket that holds her nature, life, and identity." Language is that basket. Language as a basket refers to its function as a carrier; the ponapona is the identity and worldview inherited from past generations. Since this basket is filled with Samoa's teachings and experiences through her interactions with God and nature, the Samoan language carries "the established twofold Samoan philosophy" (Aiono 1996, 10–11): first, the way to communicate, both through worship and in lived experience; and second, the philosophy of creation. Within these teachings and philosophies are the proverbs and wisdom sayings.

Proverbs and Wisdom Sayings

Understanding alagaupu and muagagana may be gained through examining each term. The word alagaupu has two connotations. First, alagaupu is the combination of three words: *ala* (way, event, or story), *ga* (from which), and *upu* (word or words). Alagaupu thus means "the way, story,

---

1. The kava plant is what we call in Samoa 'ava. Its roots are used to produce chiefly drink used in cultural ceremonies or matai's meetings. Its stem, with its segmented parts like a sugarcane stem, can be cut in segments (pieces) and planted to produce new kava plants.

or event from which words came." This echoes another saying, *O le tala e maua aiupu* ("the story on which words are found"). This saying suggests that there is a story or event behind each proverb (Schultz and Herman 1985, vii). Second, alagaupu can also divide into two words: *alaga* (to call or convey) and upu. Here, alagaupu refers to words (sayings, texts) that convey something important. The first connotation points to the world from which a saying arose, while the second connotation emphasizes what the saying conveys (means) in the present world. Together, alagaupu is about an old saying having a present (relational) meaning.

Muagagana is the combination of *mua* (first, best, excellent) and *gagana* (language) (Schultz and Herman 1985, vii). The construction suggests that wisdom sayings use choice language. The muagagana are the wisest sayings of Samoans, from their life experiences and interactions with nature. Muagagana express ethical and philosophical insights gained experientially, gleaned from natural events. An example of muagagana is *E a le una e tausili, ae tigaina ai fua le atigi* ("It is the shelly crab that contends, but the whole shell suffers"). This saying refers to the crab that stays in a shell; whatever it strives for, its shell suffers from crashing into rocks and obstacles on the way. This muagagana means that those who strive for power and live selfishly cause their relatives and friends to suffer the consequences.[2]

Muagagana are sayings that people create from their experiences of everyday life. Alagaupu, on the other hand, are sayings formulated as messages from events in history. Their origins can be traced by rediscovering the stories upon which they are based. For example, the alagaupu *O le a ou nofo atu ma tui atu le mulipapaga ina iatupu olaola le malo* is derived from an event in history. The story concerns one of the districts of the island of Upolu named Aana, whose representatives travelled to the island of Savaii to ask the prophetess Nafanua to give them authority to lead and control Samoa. Nafanua was not merely a prophetess but was also the greatest warrior who held all of the leading titles of Samoa, the *Tafaifa*. Nafanua finally agreed to give them what they wanted, with the prophetess' final

---

2. Another common muagagana is *E sau a le fuauli ma le palusami eiloga a ona toa le moa* ("Taro and palusami have completely filled and satisfied the desire of hunger"). *Fuauli* refers to taro, and *palusami* is the traditional food made of taro leaves and coconut cream. Taro and palusami are traditional Samoan foods that can satisfy a Samoan's appetite. Fuauli and palusami satisfy hunger, physical and spiritual. People use this saying in appreciation of a satisfying speech!

words now utilized as a proverb: *O le a ou nofo atu ma tui atu le mulipapaga ina ia tupu olaola le malo* ("I will stay but will pray for the successful establishment of the malo [country] in days to come"; Peseta 1984, 115). This alagaupu was Nafanua's blessing for Aana. But it is used nowadays as a blessing and assurance for those who leave the homeland to pursue greater avenues in sports, education, and work, for the benefit of the whole community and the country. This blessing is an assurance for those who leave, that behind their endeavors are the prayers of those who are aware of what they are doing.

Another popular alagaupu is *Ua patipati taoto aao o le alii o Feepo* ("Chief Feepo clapped his hands lying down"; Saipele 1994, 20). There was a blind old man named Feepo who lived on the island of Savaii. He had only one son named Atiogie, who liked playing the game of *malofie* (fighting with clubs). One day, Atiogie asked his father if he could take part in the game. The father agreed, and his son went and played. Atiogie fought well and won every game. Every time the good news of Atiogie's game reached his father, Feepo joyfully clapped his hands while lying on his bed, for he was blind. People use this saying to refer to the parents or relatives of someone who is successful and to encourage those who will participate in a game, study, or competition. "Go with understanding that Feepo is clapping while you fight." This alagaupu brings to mind "A wise child makes a glad father, but a foolish child is a mother's grief" (Prov 10:1).[3]

Alagaupu and muagagana are commonly used by Samoans in everyday life. Using these sayings in an address serves not simply to play with words but rather to stress the message that one gives. In this regard, the intended message is most suitably conveyed by a proverb or a wisdom saying.

Functions of Samoan Proverbial and Wisdom Sayings

Proverbs and wisdom sayings are in the form of teachings, reminders, or encouragements. They are taught in formal settings (e.g., schools) and in the social life of the people. In schools, children are taught the Samoan language in order to know how to read and write. In the upper primary level (classes 6 to 8), children are introduced to proverbs and wisdom sayings so that they can understand what they hear at home or in villages.[4]

---

3. Unless otherwise stated, all biblical translations follow the NRSV.

4. I experienced this in my twelve years teaching in Samoan government schools, 1977–1988.

Parents also teach children the meanings of wisdom sayings. Families customarily gather every evening for devotions. Parents use this gathering to teach the children. They scold ones who misbehave and give advice for better conduct and success. They use Samoan proverbs and wisdom sayings, together with biblical sayings, to stimulate the minds and hearts of children into deeper understanding.

The common sayings include (1) *E pala le maa ae le pala le tala* ("the stone can decompose but not the story"). This muagagana demands good, positive stories from their children, for bad ones bring shame. This saying is a reminder to children to be careful and behave well. (2) *E uo, uo, foa* ("a friend could bring pain into one's life") is often related to Jesus and his disciples. Jesus called them his friends, but one of them betrayed him. Others hid themselves, as they were afraid. (3) *Ua fanau e le toa le ofaofa* ("courage has given birth to cowardice") is a challenge to children to be courageous, honest, and faithful like their parents. This proverb is often related to the biblical saying, "Figs are not gathered from thorns, nor are grapes picked from a bramble bush" (Luke 6:44; see also Jas 3:13).

Parents use Samoan sayings at home, and they relate them to biblical stories and teachings. These sayings function to safeguard children and their families from shame—the greatest pain in Samoan culture—and to instruct them in the paths to success. They serve the same purpose as Prov 13:18: "Poverty and disgrace are for the one who ignores instruction, but one who heeds reproof is honored" and Prov 19:20: "Listen to advice and accept instruction, that you may gain wisdom for the future." Like the Samoan sayings, these biblical proverbs encourage young people to follow the instructions of their elders in order that they may succeed in life.

In the Extended Family

An extended family meets when the *matai* (head, chief, heir, title holder of a family) calls a meeting, for example, to prepare for a special occasion or to resolve a tension. The matai uses proverbial and wisdom sayings in his or her advice, encouraging family members to safeguard the family from shame and guilt.

The Samoan village setting includes several families, each with a matai (chief), *faletua ma tausi* (wife of matai), *aumaga* (untitled men), and *aualuma* (village ladies). These groups have regular meetings concerning their roles for the benefit of the village. In addition to group meetings there is the *fono* (village meeting) at the beginning of every month.

Proverbial and wisdom sayings are used in these events. In the village fono, wrongdoers of the past month are fined as a way of disciplining them and their families. Apart from the fine (typically pigs or cartons of tinned fish), the matais usually ask the wrongdoers to sit in the middle of the meeting house, where they are disciplined through scolding by high chiefs. Those speeches include proverbs and wisdom sayings. Proverbs and wisdom sayings discipline people to conform to the expected standards. The sayings, as "word of life," challenge people to remain in love, unity, and sincerity. They promote ethical living and mold people's lives into maturity and harmony.

In their book *Proverbial Expressions of the Samoans*, E. Schultz and Brother Herman (1985) classified the sayings in terms of the different events from which they originated: fishing (9–29); hunting (30–39); manual work inside and outside the house (40–52); food and preparation (53–62); games, dances, and feasts (63–71); and land and sea travel (72–80). There are expressions of respect and courtesy, denial and refusal, joy and contentment, respect and courtesy in the form of self-abasement, encouragement and persuasion, repentance and remorse, love and sympathy, warning and appeasement, and others. These sayings take the form of prophecy or admonishment, which bring understanding to those who use and hear them.

As prophecies, the sayings are used as figures or metaphors to substitute for a longer, more direct explanation. For example, *Ua faiva ese lo Pepe*[5] ("Pepe is having an unexpected catch") is commonly used when someone meets unexpected fortune while his or her thoughts and actions are directed to something else (Schultz and Herman 1985, 34). Once these words are heard, the meaning automatically comes to mind that one is facing something unexpected.

The origins of many proverbs are lost, but these proverbs exist as a result of continued use in oration amongst Samoans. These sayings function metaphorically without one having to dig deep to get to their origins

---

5. *Ua faiva ese lo Pepe* is derived from the task of catching pigeons in the old days. Pepe was the man catching pigeons at a narrow neck of the land near Puipaa in Faleata, Apia. There was another man who tried to catch pigeons from the other side. While the other man tried to catch one, a pigeon flew away, skimming over the water where Pepe hid. Pepe tried to catch this pigeon. At this same moment, a fish (*malauli*) jumped out of the water. With one swoop of the net, Pepe caught both the pigeon and fish. The neck of the land is now called *tiapepe*.

or to have any historical certainty about what prompted them. The meaning is implicit in the saying. For example, *E lutia i Puava ae mapu i Fagalele* ("distress at Puava, but rest or comfort at Fagalele") is a common saying used as exhortation for people in hardship (Schultz and Herman 1985, 79). Although one is at Puava, one hopes for happy arrival at Fagalele. Most people use this proverb without understanding how it came into being.[6]

Sayings are related to other sayings. For instance, *E lutia i Puava ae mapu i Fagalele* is related to *E leai se mea lelei e maua ma se filemu* ("good thing is not found without suffering, or beyond suffering is the good thing"). Orators use one saying to conceive (explain, understand) another saying, even though the sayings come from different times and settings. Orators also "ping pong" sayings in their speeches and responses.

Objections to the Use of Samoan Proverbial and Wisdom Sayings

The alagaupu and muagagana have teachings for ordinary people. The resemblances between Samoan texts and biblical sayings lend authority to the Samoan proverbs and wisdom sayings as God's gifts for Samoa (Aiono 1996, 11). Yet, they are not used in biblical exegesis by Samoan preachers, for varied reasons. First, alagaupu and muagagana are part and parcel of the Samoan oratory language, and this language is specific for the matai. This language is for the *malae* (meeting place) but not the church. Seeing the world and the church as separate arenas, enforced by the Samoan theological intelligentsia (church leaders), has limited the use of traditional wisdom sayings.

A church minister is not allowed to hold a matai title because he (women are not ordained in the Methodist and Congregational churches of Samoa) is supposed to be a servant, although ministers are regarded as of the highest rank in village settings. The church should not be affiliated with *faiga faanuu* (village traditions) or *faiga faamatai* (matai's traditional ways), which are considered to be worldly. The church, in other words, is independent from the culture. Its mission is to evangelize the village people but not to affiliate with the village systems whose authorities are the matais. In the village *malaefono* (meeting place), the matais play their

---

6. Puava is a cape between Papa and Falealupo, Savaii, and Fagalele is a bay beyond Puava on the Falealupo side. Because of the cross-currents, it is dangerous to sail past Puava, but in the protected bay of Fagalele the seamen find rest (Schultz and Herman 1985, 79).

part for the village. The church is the malaefono of the minister. Although each entity (church, village) needs the advice of the other, church and village matters are not meant to interfere with each other. So, the oratory language which includes alagaupu and muagagana is not taken into the deeper consideration of the church.

The second factor that accounts for the limited use of alagaupu and muagagana by some ministers is that they do not understand these sayings. Many pastors are young or have come from overseas (e.g., New Zealand, Hawaii, Australia, or the United States). In recent years, 40 to 50 percent of the students who entered Malua Theological College were from overseas, and more than 50 percent of that group had no knowledge of Samoan traditions, alagaupu, or muagagana. Pastors from this group see no problem with knowing nothing about Samoan traditions and sayings. They do their work apart from such understandings of traditional teachings, and they rely on the Bible as the only word of God. For this group, traditional sayings should not have a place in biblical exegesis.

Some of the pastors who are not opposed to using alagaupu and muagagana use them as phrases to introduce their sermons but do not use them in their exegetical work. This attitude derives from the way they were taught and learned traditional exegetical methods. Since those traditional methodologies are confined to the boundaries of biblical texts, they are taken as the only appropriate means for interpretation. This disallows any reader from discovering how God reveals Godself in the reader's world, in which one learns from his or her language and traditional teachings. This (disallowed, Samoan) language, with its cultural teachings, must have a place in exegesis so that the exegete, together with the Samoan readers and hearers, all participate in the interpretation.

Pastors are misled by their reliance on the Bible as the only word of God. The consequence of this perspective is negative attitudes toward traditional proverbs and sayings. They consider using alagaupu and muagagana in sermons as collecting rubbish, *O le lauga taetae lapisi* ("the collecting rubbish sermon").[7] Hence, the preachers who utilize the alagaupu and

---

7. *Lauga taetae lapisi* is a common response by preachers whom I interviewed in December 1999, on the island of Savaii. They call these sayings rubbish, for they are humans' words. They fear these sayings might allegorize the word of God. In addition, sayings are rubbish because they are already known to people, and there is no freshness within them for people to hear again.

muagagana tend to be village matais who became pastors and who show off by using what they know about the knowledge of matais.

The objections to the use of alagaupu and muagagana represent a sincere concern of some Samoan pastors to safeguard the Bible, which they regard as the word of God. They search for the true meaning as if it was lost or unknown in the text. These pastors are steeped in the traditional methodologies of biblical exegesis in which they were trained, and they find meanings to use in preparing their sermons. If they are gifted with such traditional knowledge formed from nonlocal sources, what else do they need?

Despite the concerns for the sacredness of the Bible as the word of God and for church and worship to be distinctively separated from worldly things, the fact is that most ministers regard alagaupu and muagagana as rubbish. These attitudes deny the relevance of these common Samoan sayings.

Answers to the Objections[8]

The fact that proverbial and wisdom sayings are important in Samoan culture is one obvious reason that they could be used in preaching. Because preachers see them as unbiblical, it is helpful to note how the Bible itself uses wisdom sayings from the general culture in the proclamation of its message. Utilizing proverbial and wisdom sayings in a rhetorical sense is neither new nor unbiblical.

Many of the wisdom sayings and proverbs in the book of Proverbs resemble teachings of, and may have been borrowed from, other cultures (Carr 2011, 408–410). As Daniel Smith-Christopher suggests, "there are interesting other possibilities when noting that the book of Proverbs includes aspects of Egyptian wisdom, which may represent a kind of *philosophical creolization* that signals an openness to the value of other's thoughts and traditions" (2015, 211, emphasis original). Put directly, the Hebrew Bible exhibits cross-cultural borrowing and appropriation.

In the New Testament, Paul for instance states that "'in him we live and move and have our being'; as even some of your own poets have said, 'For we too are his offspring'" (Acts 17:28). Here, Paul upholds and utilizes familiar and understandable sayings. Paul appeals to readers'

---

8. This response intends to convince Samoan readers of the importance of incorporating Samoan sayings in biblical interpretation. Readers in other lands may do the same with their native wisdom teachings.

own poets. Thus, Paul's Aeropagus speech shares presuppositions with the Greeks (pagans). The strategy of his speech is to establish an area of common understanding and then move into the alternative truth of the gospel. Paul was trying to establish a common basis on which he could build his case (Powell 1991, 99). In so doing, "Paul effects this fusion of horizons between the pre-comprehension of his listeners and the new meanings he offers by using symbolic language and polyvalent terminology" (98). I. Howard Marshall (1980, 288–89) and Johannes Munck (1967, 171) claim that Paul took from Epimenides of Crete these sayings in which Menos of Crete addressed his father Zeus and attacked the Cretan belief that Zeus was buried on the island. Menos had said, "They fashioned a tomb for thee, o holy and high. The Cretans, always liars, evil beasts, slow bellies! But thou art not dead; thou art risen and alive forever; for in thee we live, and move, and have our being" (Marshall 1980, 288–89).

Paul appropriated Greek poems and expressions of Stoic philosophies and applied them to God. Paul used the Greek thought of the divine nature of the person to express that the human is the image of God and that God is the source of one's life (Marshall 1980, 289). J. W. Packer (1966, 148) adds that the phrase "we are also his offspring" is a quotation from the stoic poet which exemplifies Paul's skill in using his Greek material to suit his audience. Paul was confident in utilizing Greek and Jewish sayings and expressions to convey his Christian message to his audience and readers. He knew the Christian message and theology and retold those using expressions and sayings with which his audiences were familiar. In light of the book of Proverbs and Paul, why should there be a problem with using Samoan proverbial and wisdom sayings? It is biblically sound to posit that traditional sayings are in the framework of God's acts through preaching to nurture life. In this sense, our Samoan proverbial and wisdom sayings have authority, for they too are God's gifts to nurture God's people.

Using Samoan Proverbs and Wisdom Sayings: A Demonstration

Samoan proverbial and wisdom sayings, like other traditional sayings, are God's gifts. In this section, I briefly demonstrate how Samoan sayings could be interwoven with biblical texts. Samoa has no wisdom literature like that in the Bible, but we have wisdom teachings. In the first subsection, some of the Samoan wisdom sayings are juxtaposed with biblical teachings that illuminate the wisdom in the Samoan *alagaupu* and *muagagana*. Through this comparative study I affirm that wisdom is not limited to the biblical wisdom literature. Then in the second subsection I use a Samoan text—*Fili e le tai e agavaa* ("let the sea determine who are the skillful persons"; Brown and Penisimani 1914, 18)—to develop a sermon on Mark 1:16–20.

Samoan and Biblical Sayings in Contact

E a sipa le lamaga ae gase ai fua malolo ("It is sipas' lamaga, but malolo is killed"; Brown and Penisimani 1914, 32). The *lamaga* (night fishing with torches) was for the fish sipa but it also killed the fish malolo. This proverb is similar to another proverb, *Ua lavea fua lava Foaga ae lei fai misa* ("Foaga is injured, but he was not involved in the fight"). Both sayings apply to those who face undeserved suffering, like Luke 23:41: "And we indeed have been condemned justly, for we are getting what we deserve for our deeds, but this man has done nothing wrong."

E sau a le fuauli ma le palusami e iloga a ona toa le moa ("Fuauli [taro] and palusami have completely filled and satisfied the desire of hunger"). The saying refers to Samoans' best and favorite food, but it could also reflect a longing for God as we find in Ps 63:1, 3: "O God, you are my God, I seek you, my soul thirsts for you; my flesh faints for you, as in a dry and weary land where there is no water.… Because your steadfast love is better than life, my lips will praise you."

O le ia paulia i le tai masa ("a fish stranded in the ebb tide"; Brown and Penisimani 1914, 20). This saying applies to those who live far away from home, where they usually get support. This is similar to Lam 1:6: "From daughter Zion has departed all her majesty. Her princes have become like stags that find no pasture; they fled without strength before the pursuer."

Lutia i Puava ae mapu i Fagalele ("distress at Puava but we shall rest at Fagalele"). An encouragement not to fail in Puava but to have courage for hope lies at Fagalele. Compare with Jas 1:12: "Blessed is anyone who endures temptation. Such a one has stood the test and will receive the crown of life that the Lord has promised to those who love him."

O le funafuna gutulua ("the funafuna with two mouths"; Brown and Penisimani 1914, 11). *Funafuna* is a sea cucumber, and this phrase is often given to an undecided person who has two mouths or tongues. Compare Jas 1:8: "For the doubter, being double-minded and unstable in every way, must not expect to receive anything from the Lord." See also Jas 3:10–11:

"From the same mouth come blessing and cursing.... Does a spring pour forth from the same opening both fresh and brackish water?"

Ia o gatasi le futia ma le umele ("let the futia [the sinnet ring] and the umele [the stand for the bamboo fishing-rod] go together"; Brown and Penisimani 1914, 20). That is, let your words go together with your actions. See Jas 2:17: "So faith by itself, if it has no works, is dead." See also Jas 2:26: "For just as the body without the spirit is dead, so faith without works is also dead."

Na tagisia e Laulu se vaa ia goto ("Laulu cried, for a canoe may sink"; Brown and Penisimani 1914, 20). Laulu greedily wanted more fish to fill his whole canoe. When it was filled, it sank. It is a warning against greed and lust, as we find in Sir 14:9: "The eye of the greedy person is not satisfied with his share; greedy injustice withers the soul."

O le fetalaiga e malu ae ivia ("speeches that are gentle but bony"; Brown and Penisimani 1914, 24) refers to soft sounds that are harsh, something that sounds good but is really evil. See Prov 5:3–4: "For the lips of a loose woman drip honey, and her speech is smoother than oil; but in the end she is bitter as wormwood, sharp as a two-edged sword." See also Rev 10:10: "So I took the little scroll from the hand of the angel and ate it; it was sweet as honey in my mouth, but when I had eaten it, my stomach was made bitter."

Ua ou nofo atu fua pe tautala atu fua, ao au o Ae[9] ("I am sitting or talking before you, but I am Ae"). These are words of confession used to express how guilty one is. "I am very guilty, I am Ae (I am wrong)." See Sir 4:26: "Do not be ashamed to confess your sins, and do not try to stop the current of a river."

O le maualalo a tavai ("the short height of the tavai"; Brown and Penisimani 1914, 11). *Tavai* is a forest tree which is extremely short. However, pigeons like resting on the tavai instead of the taller trees. This saying is used to refer to those who humble themselves. See Luke 14:11: "For all who exalt themselves will be humbled, and those who humble themselves will be exalted"; Jas 4:6: "God opposes the proud, but gives grace to the humble"; Jas 1:9: "Let the believer who is lowly boast in being raised up";

---

9. *Ae* is the name of the person who committed wrong. He was loved by one of the chiefs who allowed him to ride back to his home on the chief's turtle, with the understanding that if he arrived, he would send the turtle back. However, when Ae arrived home, he ate the turtle. When he was brought before the chief and asked where the turtle was, Ae just said, *Ou te nofo atu fua ao au o Ae* (Brown and Penisimani 1914, 6).

and Sir 11:1: "The wisdom of the humble lifts their heads high, and seats them among the great."

The examples above illustrate that there are points of contact between Samoan wisdom sayings and biblical texts. Those points of contact are opportunities for intertextual and cross-cultural readings.

Weaving a Samoan Text with a Biblical Text

When we talk about *tai* (tide or sea), we talk about *faagatama i le tai* (games, like canoe and fautasi, in the sea).[10] So the saying *Fili e le tai e agavaa* ("let the sea determine who are the skillful persons") means that the sea determines who is most skillful, according to their performances in the sea, whether in games or fishing.

In canoe or vaaalo racing, both paddlers have to work together. Both paddlers must be strong, be in one spirit, and be in sync with their tactics. The stronger one usually sits at the rear of the canoe, as her or his roles are both paddling and navigating the canoe. Deciding who sits at the back is done by the sea, based upon the experience of both paddlers.

In the celebrations of Samoa's independence in the 1980s and 1990s, the vaaalo races were dominated by the "Laulelei o Amoa," paddled by the brothers Iupeli and Simeona from Savaii, while the fautasi races were won by the "Laau o le Saualii" from the island of Manono. The sea decided that they were the best. The "Laulelei o Amoa" was paddled by brothers who, in one spirit, were in sync. And "Laau o le Saualii" was paddled by the people of the island of Manono who were in one spirit, one people, and one family that worked together to achieve their goal.

The saying *fili e le tai e agavaa* is also applied to *aloga atu* (fishing for tuna, bonito). Nowadays we use motorboats for catching tuna (*atu*), but in the 1970s and 1980s nearly every family had a vaaalo used for aloga-atu. Atu was a fish rarely found but important in Samoan society. Since each family had a vaaalo, each family had two or three relatives to go for aloga-atu. Catching atu is not easy, but it is an exciting experience that requires good paddlers.

In the deep sea, a flock of birds feeding on sardines signals a school of atu. Both fishermen need to paddle hard to reach that spot, dragging

---

10. *Fautasi* is a long racing boat paddled by twenty or more people. *Vaaalo* is the canoe that is paddled by two or three persons.

a fishing line tied to the end of a long bamboo (*launiu*). Both fishermen would paddle until the line is pulled by an atu; then the one at the back jerks up the bamboo in order for the atu to land in the canoe. Sometimes the bonito comes flying in the air and hits one of the fishermen. The more fish they catch, the more pain they get. But this pain is nothing compared to the excitement and satisfaction of catching fish.

When the canoes return, the partners who caught the most fish are regarded as the best fishermen of the day. Why? The sea has decided that they were the best. How? They caught more fish than the others. In their tireless paddling, they found the right spot. In their painful labor, they got more. In one spirit, they worked together and achieved their goal.

The Samoan sayings explained above could be used to find something meaningful in Mark 1:16–20:

> As Jesus passed along the Sea of Galilee, he saw Simon and his brother Andrew casting a net into the sea—for they were fishermen. And Jesus said to them, "Follow me and I will make you fish for people." And immediately they left their nets and followed him. As he went a little farther, he saw James son of Zebedee and his brother John, who were in their boat mending the nets. Immediately he called them; and they left their father Zebedee in the boat with the hired men, and followed him.

Mark provides no indication of the criteria Jesus used to choose his disciples.[11] He chose on his own initiative. However, we Samoans could conclude what appears clear to us in the text—Jesus chose his first disciples from the sea. *Ua uluai fili e Iesu mai le tai e agavaa.* Jesus chose people whom he found working together. And Jesus chose brothers—Simon and Andrew whom he found casting their net together, and James and John whom he found together mending their nets. Jesus chose those who have the sibling spirit that made them work and mend together. It is in and through sibling spirit that success comes. By virtue of that spirit, there is interdependency, love, sharing, suffering in hard times, and full commitment to God in order to succeed. The disciples must be ones who have such a spirit, which leads them toward partnership.

---

11. According to K. C. Hanson (1997, 100–101), the fishermen called by Jesus were peasants who, with their profession, were middle class, but they were also abused under an oppressive economic system.

In our games and life experiences, God has shown the way in which we can be harmonious. Why then do communities, villages, families, and churches collapse? Because we have a divided spirit, in which one wants to boss the others around. We spend a great deal of our time praying, but we do not show enough concern for others. We are good at learning, teaching, and preaching theology, but we have few people doing theology.

As the Pacific sea determines the best Samoans, the Sea of Galilee determines the disciples who lived theology. Jesus chose from the sea those whom he preferred. To them Jesus said, "Follow me."

Works Cited

Aiono, Letagaloa F. 1996. *O La ta Gagana*. Samoa: Lamepa.
Brown, George, and Penisimani. 1914. *Proverbs, Phrases and Similes of the Samoans*. Papakura: McMillan.
Carr, David M. 2011. *The Formation of the Hebrew Bible: A New Reconstruction*. New York: Oxford University Press.
Hanson, K. C. 1997. "The Galilean Fishing Economy and the Jesus Tradition." *BTBull* 27: 99–111.
Marshall, I. Howard. 1980. *The Acts of the Apostles: An Introduction and Commentary*. TNTC. Leicester: Inter-Varsity.
Munck, Johannes. 1967. *The Acts of the Apostles*. AB. New York: Doubleday.
Packer, J. W. 1966. *The Acts of the Apostles*. CBC. Cambridge: Cambridge University Press.
Peseta, S. Sio. 1984. *Tapasa o Folauga I Aso Afa* [*Compass of Sailing in Storm*]. Apia, Samoa: University of the South Pacific Centre.
Powell, Mark Allan. 1991. *What Are They Saying about Acts?* New York: Paulist.
Saipele, Nu'uiali'i Mulipola Ma'ilo. 1994. *Proverbs of Samoa*. Wellington: Australian High Commission.
Schultz, E., and Brother Herman. 1985. *Proverbial Expressions of the Samoans*. Suva: University of the South Pacific.
Smith-Christopher, Daniel. 2015. "Thinking on Islands." Pages 207–16 in *Islands, Islanders, and the Bible: RumInations*. Edited by Jione Havea, Margaret Aymer, and Steed Vernyl Davidson. SemeiaSt 77. Atlanta: SBL Press.

Ko e Punake mo 'e ne Ta'anga, pea mo e Folofola (Composer, Composition, and the Canon)

Tangikefataua Koloamatangi

Editor's introduction

This chapter is in the Tongan language, by the late Tongan composer and cultural performer Tangikefataua Koloamatangi. In the first part of the essay, Koloamatangi reflects on the intersection of the works of Tongan composers with the working of scriptural (canon) teachings. The works by Tongan composers Sione Tu'ifua, Vaisima Hopoate, Kuini Sālote III, Nau Saimone, Tu'imala Kaho, and Koloamatangi himself receive scripturalizing attention in the first part of the essay. Without claiming that scriptural texts shape the works by these Tongan composers, Koloamatangi celebrates their creative wisdom. It is indeed unfair to claim that the Bible controls the imagination of Tongan poets and composers. On the other hand, it is illusory to assume that there is no cross-feeding by poets and composers on biblical literature.

Koloamatangi shows that it is difficult to pinpoint the origin of inspiration and the points of contact between inspirations, wisdom, scriptures, and compositions in the works of creative artists. Composers compose with several networks of inspirations, using several strands of languages, and their compositions *hop and scotch* over myths, metaphors, imaginations, histories, and current and future realities. Compositions are meant to be worn like a garland so that their colors, beauty, fragrance, and feel (prickly at some places) may be appreciated and endured. When compositions are worn (pun intended), their authority (canonicity) is established.

In the second part of the essay, Koloamatangi names and presents four pillars for contemporary and future Tongan poets and composers to use in their composition to be effective in what they do: poets and composers need to be clear about, as well as submit to, their (1) goals (*taumuʻa*), (2) vibes (*ongo*), (3) lures (*ʻuhinga*), and (4) skills (*taukei*). Good compositions are intentional, emotional, alluring, and calculating. Without these pillars, one's composition will be weak, unsafe, and boring.

In a closing section, Koloamatangi adds two *fehihi* (cross-pieces that hold up the roof of Tongan houses) that bind his four pillars—*toumuʻa* (front, frontside, foreground) and *toumui* (back, backside, background)— to link the work of poets and composers onto the work of biblical authors, both of which call attention to the physicality and bodyliness of the arts of Tongan poetry and songwriting. In the Tongan setting, the *toumui* (back), even though it is often filthy and infested, is as important as the *toumuʻa* (front) because cooking, welcome, and hospitality extends from the *toumui* of homes. A singer or performer of Tongan poems and songs is thus invited to tune in to the *toumui* of the compositions and, in a similar way, so should readers of biblical texts tune into the (filthy and infested) backsides of scriptural texts. In this regard, Koloamatangi gives expression to the obsession of many biblical critics, whether they are historical, literary, ideological, cultural, queer, or post-something—they all assume that there is something at the underside of texts and at the underside of readings that needs to be brought out and engaged.

We first received Koloamatangi's contribution written in Tongan for an oral presentation at the meeting of the Oceania Biblical Studies Association at Tonga in 2012, and it is offered here in Tongan out of respect to the limits of translation and the untamability of orality. May it herein encourage biblical scholars to learn and respect the vibes and workings of native tongues and to learn the speak of the subaltern (local, common, native).

Whereas Afutiti (in the previous chapter) focuses on traditional (or ancient) proverbial and wisdom sayings (native texts), Koloamatangi is concerned with contemporary composers and compositions. Nonetheless, both authors wish that more attention be given to, and more value be recognized in, native texts. Native texts are scriptural, too. Canons.

* * *

Te u vavaku atu pē au ʻi heʻeku aʻusia´ mo ʻene mahino kiate au ʻa e kaveinga kuo ʻomi ke u fatongiaʻaki´.

ʻOku fai ʻa e fakafetaʻi ki he ʻEiki´ ʻetau aʻusia ha ʻaho pehe´ ni. ʻOku fuʻu mahuʻinga kiate au ke u tomuʻa kole fakamolemole atu. Pe ʻe fēfē kiʻi louloutoi ʻoku taʻotaʻo´, ko hoku ngataʻanga´ pē ia; pea neongo ko e taukovi ka ʻoku ou falala ki he toitoiʻanga ʻoku lelei. Ko e fakahohaʻa te u fai´ ʻoku konga ua.

1. Te u fakahoa ʻa e ngaahi potu folofola mo e ngaahi kongokonga taʻanga ʻa ha kau punake ʻe niʻihi.
2. Te u fokotuʻu atu ha nāunau ʻe ʻaoga ki he taʻanga ʻa e punake´.

Taʻanga mo e tuʻunga ʻa e folofola

Te u feinga ke feʻiloaki pe kāinga e taʻanga ʻa e niʻihi ʻo e kau punake´ mo e ngaahi potu folofola he tohitapu´.

Naʻe mahino ʻaupito ʻa e taʻanga´ ʻi he fonua´ ni mo hotau potu tahi ʻi he kuonga ʻo e fakapoʻuli´. Haʻu ʻa e kau misinale mo e kuonga fakalaka ʻo e sivilaise ʻa e Uēsite´ pea pulia atu ai e taʻanga fakahīteni ʻa e kau punake´. Ka ko e "hīteni" he lau mo e meʻafua ʻa hai?

> When missionaries brought Western civilization, the heathen works of our composers disappeared. But "heathen" in whose assessment and according to whose standards?

Naʻe hake mai ʻa e kau misinale fakamafola lotu´ ʻo taʻofi e ngaahi lea mo e haka ne ʻikai feʻunga mo taau mo e lotu faka-Kalisitiane´. Kimuʻa hono ʻomai ʻa e tohitapu´, ko e taʻanga mo e haka naʻe faʻu ʻe he kau punake´, ko ʻene mālie´ kapau ʻoku lahilahi ke fepaki mo e maama ʻo e tohitapu´.

Naʻe kamata e hake mai ʻa e kau misinale he 1790-tupu, ko e kau LMS ia. Ko e 1822 ko Misa Lole ia, pea hoko mai ʻa Misa Tōmasi mo Misa Haisione he 1826. Kuo ʻosi senituli ʻe ua hono ʻomi e lotu ki Tonga, pea ko e senituli ai pē ia ʻe ua e ʻomi e meʻafua fakaUēsite ke levaʻiʻaki e fatu ʻa e kau punake ʻo hotau fonua.

Naʻe haʻu ʻa e kau misinale pea ongoʻi leva ʻe he kau punake´ ʻoku ʻikai ke nau toe maʻu ʻa e tauʻatāina (pe faʻiteliha?) naʻa nau maʻu kimuʻa ʻi he teʻeki hake mai ʻa e maama ʻo e tohitapu´, kae fakangatangata ʻenau tauʻatāina´ ke hoa pea kāinga mo e tohitapu´.

> When missionaries came ... composers were limited to be appropriate and related to the Bible.

ʻOku lahi ʻaupito ʻi he ngaahi ʻaho´ ni e feinga ʻa e kau punake ʻe niʻihi ke hakaʻi mo tauʻolungaʻi ʻa e ngaahi talanoa mo e akonaki ʻoku hiki ʻi he tohitapu'. Ko e ngaahi founga mo e taumu'a 'oku fakahinohino 'e he tohitapu' 'oku ngāue'aki mo ia 'e he kau punake 'e ni'ihi ki he ngaahi fiema'u kehekehe. Hangē ko e founga fakatauhisipi 'a e tohitapu', kuo fai 'e he kau punake 'e ni'ihi 'a e ngaahi ta'anga fakatauhisipi, 'o lahi 'ene 'asi' 'i he Himi'.

'Oku ou to'o mai 'a e ngaahi konga ta'anga mei he fatu 'a e kau punake 'e toko ono (6), 'o fakakāinga ia mo e ngaahi potu folofola mei he tohitapu'. 'E 'ikai te u pehē ko e ngaahi potu folofola eni ne ne langa'i e fatu 'a e kau punake ni, ka 'oku ou mālie'ia 'i he'enau kāinga.

(1) Ko e taha 'o e kau punake 'iloa 'i he fonua' ni ko Sione Tu'ifua, ko 'ene hiva 'oku 'iloa ko e "Kapukapu e Vaha'akolo," pea ko e veesi 2:

> Kuo hopo 'a e fetu'u'aho'
> Ko e afo' ena kuo falō
> Ne sila'i 'i he funga Pouono'
> Tukufua 'a Ha'a Moheofo'

'Oku langa'i mai 'e he veesi ni 'a Luke 2:2—'E Tamai, ke tāpuhā ho Huafa', ke hoko mai ho'o pule' ..." Ko e lotu ia 'a e 'Eiki'.

Ko e fa'ahinga fakalāngilāngi 'oku fai 'e he tohitapu' ki he 'Otua', 'oku natula pehē mo e fatu 'a e kau punake'. 'Oku nau fa'u 'o fakalangilangi'i ha ikuna kuo lava, 'i he ako pe sipoti.

The praise that the Bible extends to God is similar to the praise composers give to achievements in life (e.g., education and sports).

---

(2) Ko e "Ise'isa" ko e hiva 'a Vaisima Hopoate, 'oku pehē ni 'a e tau 'o e hiva':

> 'Ofa hoto sino kuo vaivai
> 'I he anga 'eku 'ofa hono lahi
> Kafo e loto' ni mo e 'atamai
> Ifo 'a e mate' he nofo māmani

Ko e hahanu eni mo e to'e, pea 'oku si'i faka'ofa 'o hangē ko e tangi 'a e punake mo Sisū, "Ilai, Ilai, lama sapakatanai? 'E hoku 'Otua, 'e hoku 'Otua, na'a ke li'aki au kaehā?" (Saame 22 mo Mātiu 27:46).

(3) 'Oku ai e konga mālie he talanoa 'o Tevita, 'oku 'ia 1 Sāmiuela 17:48-49. "Pea 'iloange' na'e tu'u mai 'a e Filisitia', 'o laka mai ke ofi, ke fepaki mo Tevita, pea fakavave 'a Tevita 'o ne lele ki he matatau' ke fakafepaki ki he Filisitia', pea 'ai 'e Tevita hono nima' ki he 'angame'a' 'o ne to'o

mei ai ha maka 'o ne makataa'i 'o lave 'i he la'e 'o e Filisitia´, pea ngalo 'a e maka´ 'i hono la'e´ 'o ne tō fo'ohifo ki he kelekele´."

Ko Tevita na'e kei si'i, ka na'a ne fai 'a e me'a lahi. Ko e fa'ahinga me'a 'a Tevita na'e fai 'oku lava ke tau fanongo ki ai 'i he maa'imoa 'a Kuini Salote ko e "Lea 'a e Fuiva":

Tamaiki laka ta'ata'ofi pē
Kae tuku ke u toli e moto e siale´
Ke fungani'aki 'a e sisi maile´
Ko hoku teunga ki he fakatētē

Laka ta'ota'ofi pē, tamaiki!

(4) Ko e me'a tatau ne fakatokanga ki ai 'a Angakehe mei he Peauma'a´ mo e Funga Faka'ala´: "Oua te ke ngutu 'oho he 'oku kakai, he 'e pukepuke ka te ta fetaulaki."

"Watch your mouth, for it is crowded; they might stop us, but we shall confront."

---

(5) Ko e ngaahi potu folofola mo e ngaahi kongokonga ta'anga 'a e kau punake kuo u 'osi lave ki ai 'i mu'a´, ka ko e hā ha'aku´ ia tāheu? 'A au, ko au Taua … Ko e hā ha'aku lau 'a'aku?

'Oku ou fakakaukau ki he talanoa 'o Tevita, pea mahino kiate au na'e toe ke pehē ange 'a Tevita ki he Filisitia: "Mohe'uli, tuku ho'o kaemu'a pea ke tōtōmui hifo, 'oua te ke sekisekia 'i ho'o sio ki ho'omou tokolahi´ mo e sio 'a e kau Filisitia´. Mohe'u'uli!"

David could have said to the Philistine, "*Mohe'uli* (someone who slept without bathing), stop showing off; don't be arrogant seing that there are many of you. Mohe'u'uli!"

Kuo 'osi 'i ai pē fanga ki'i ta'anga na'a ku tātāsipa ai, pea kuo 'osi hiva'i 'e he Kalapu Huolanga´, 'oku 'i ai pē 'ene felāve'i mo e tohitapu´. Ko e taha 'o e fanga ki'i fakamuna´ ko e hiva na'a´ ku fa'u ki he "Pule Lelei," pea 'oku 'i ai hono ki'i konga 'i loto 'oku fakalea 'o pehē:

Kovināniti he talatala'aamoa´
Ko e hala ia ki he fonua e tala'ofa´

Ko 'eku fakakaukau´ ia. Ko e Fekau 'e Hongofulu´ 'oku tefito ai 'a e Pule

Lelei'. Ko 'eku fakakaukau', ko Mōsese, ko e taki mo e pule ia ki he fononga 'a Isileli ki he fonua e tala'ofa, pea ko 'ene fefolofolai mo e 'Otua' 'i he talatala'amoa' mo e Fekau 'e Hongofulu', ko e nāunau ia ki ha Pule Lelei mo e hala ki he fonua 'o e hone' mo e hu'akau'.

(6) He 'ikai te u lau kuo kakato, kae 'oua leva ke 'omai ha punake mo ha'ane faka'ingo'ingo he 'ofa'.

I can't say that it is complete, without referring to a composer's work on love.

Pea 'oku ou sio heni kia Sione 3:16—"He na'e 'ofa pehē 'a e 'Otua' ki māmani, ko ia na'a' ne foaki hono 'alo tofu pē taha ne fakatupu', koe'uhi' ko ia kotoa pē 'oku tui pikitai kiate Ia', ke 'oua na'a 'auha kae ma'u 'a e mo'ui ta'engata'."

Ko e afo tatau eni 'i he hiva 'oku hiki 'e he Lou'ilima Koula 'o 'Amusia-e-'ā' ko e "Lose Kolosi" pea ko e taha eni hono ngaahi veesi':
Si'a lose hina 'o ha ngouetapu
Tulutā ai ha 'ofa manatu
Kāpui leva 'a e fakakaukau
To'i pea manongi lose fakama'u

White rose in a holy garden
On which dropped longing love
In-closing all meditations
Leak and whiff, (en)closing roses

Mahalo kuo fe'unga e fakatokanga'i e ngaahi ta'anga 'a e kau punake 'oku ou pehē 'e au 'oku kāinga mo e ngaahi potu folofola, 'i he 'uhinga, founga pe taumu'a. Pea 'oku ou kole fakamolemole atu kapau 'oku 'ikai ha'anau vāvāofi pe kāinga 'i he ngaahi konga ta'anga 'a e kau punake 'oku ou lave ki ai 'i mu'a', mo e ngaahi potu folofola 'oku ou to'o mei' he tohitapu'.

Pou 'e fā ke ta'anga 'e he punake

Kuo pau ke ta'anga 'e he punake' 'a e fu'u pou 'e fā (4). Hei'ilo koe, pe ko e hā e lahi ho'o pou 'e langa'aki ho fale ko e punake', ka ko e tui 'a e motu'a' ni, na'e kau mo e fu'u pou 'e fā ko eni' 'i he langa fale 'a e ngaahi mo'ui na'a nau hiki mo fokotu'utu'u e tohitapu'.

'Oku tau'atāina ki he lahi e pou 'e takitaha fai'aki 'e ne langafale, ka ko au mo hoku vaivai´, kuo pau ke ma'u 'e he punake´ 'a e ngaahi fu'u pou ko eni´, pea 'oku ou tui na'e tatau mo kinautolu na'a nau tohi 'a e tohitapu´.

1. Ko e taumu'a

Ko e hā 'a e taumu'a 'o e ta'anga 'a e punake´? Ko 'e ne fa'u ta'anga´, faiva ke hiva'i pea haka'i, ko e faiva ki he hā? Hilifaki kalauni? Tali hā'ele mai ha tu'i? Kuo pau ke fa'u 'o fakatatau ki he taumu'a´.

Ko e hā nai 'a e taumu'a 'a Mātiu 'oku hā he vahe 2 veesi 8? "Pea ne fekau ke nau ō ki Petelihema, 'o ne pehē, 'Mou 'alu 'o 'eke fakatotolo ki he tamasi'i´; pea ka mou ka 'ilo ia pea tala mai koe'uhi´ ke u 'alu mo au 'o hū 'iate ia.'"

Ko e hā 'a e taumu'a 'a Mātiu? Kuo mahino 'a e taumu'a ia 'a Hēlota mo e māmani´ ki he Pilinisi 'o e Melino´, ke tamate'i 'oku kei valevale, ka ko e hā 'a e taumu'a ia 'a Mātiu? Ko e taumu'a 'a Mātiu´ ke fakamahino ko e tala'ofa 'a hotau 'Otua´ na'e pau ke ha'u. Ko e tamasi'i falengāmamahi, ko e hau ta'eliua pea 'e hilifaki hono uma´ 'a e pule ki he tūkuifonua´.

2. Ko e ongo

Na'e lahi 'aupito e ngaahi ta'anga ko e ngaahi 'anitema 'a e kau punake 'iloa 'i he mamani kuo u 'osi fa'a toutou hiva ai. Haniteli mo e "Haleluia´" mo e ngaahi hiva kehekehe pē.

Ko e taha 'o e ngaahi ta'anga 'iloa´ ko e "I will sing to you God a new song." Na'e liliu 'e Simi Taumoefolau ki he nota mo e lea faka-Tonga, ko e *Taumaiā*, pea fuofua hiva'i 'e Kolomotu'a 'i he sivi hiva 'o e Senituli 'o e Konisitūtone 'i Pangai, 1975. Na'e 'ikai te u lava 'o ta'ofi hoku lo'imata´ he'eku a'usia 'a e ongo ko ia ne hanga 'e he lea 'o e hiva´ mo hono fasi´ 'o fakaafe'i 'a e fiefia na'e ma'upu 'i loto he'eku mo'ui 'i he taimi ko ia´.

Lyrics and rhthyms invite pleasures that boil within to flow out.

Kapau kuo u māfana au na'a´ ku hiva 'ata'atā pē, huanoa 'a Simi Taumoefolau na'a´ ne fai 'a e hiva´ mo liliu ki he faka-Tonga´. Pea 'e fēfē nai 'a e tokotaha totonu 'oku 'a'ana 'a e ta'anga´? He 'ikai te u toe veiveiua ke u fakahā 'i he fakamatala´ ni na'e a'usia 'e he kau tohi 'o e tohitapu´ 'a e fa'ahinga ongo ko eni´. Ko hono fakamo'oni´ 'oku te'eki ke lāfua'a ha potu folofola ia, pe kuo kakā 'a e tohitapu´.

'Oku kei mahu 'a e folofola', pea kei ma'u mo e fāngota 'a e kau faka-mafola 'o e ongoongo lelei'. Kei ma'ui'ui mo fefafa 'a e kau 'evangeliō fakama'unga 'i he tohitapu' mo polo'uto 'a e fua 'o e tohitapu' ... ko e fakamo'oni ki he mā'olunga mo e māfana 'o e ongo na'e ma'u 'e he kakai na'a nau tohi 'a e tohitapu'.

'Oku ou tui ta'etoeveiveiua 'oku 'alu hake mei loto 'a e fa'ahinga ongo kuo pau ke a'usia 'e he punake' pea toki lava ke hoko 'ene ta'anga' ko e ta'anga 'oku mātu'aki mahu'inga, ma'u 'a e 'uhinga mo e taumu'a 'oku mātu'aki mālie, manakoa pea toe faingata'a ke mole mei he manatu', mohu akonaki, hoko ko e ako'anga mo e fa'ifa'itaki'anga he to'utangata mo e to'utangata, mo e kuonga ki he kuonga.

3. Ko e 'uhinga

Ko e fo'i 'ilo pe ko e a'usia mālie eni hono ngāue'aki 'e he kau punake' pea mo hono toe ngāue'aki 'i he tohitapu'. Te u talanoa atu pē au ko e Tonga au, mo'ui'aki 'a e tō'onga mo e 'uhinga fakaTonga, fakataha mo hoku ngata'anga', pea 'oku angamaheni'aki hono ui 'e he kau punake tokolahi e 'ilo pe a'usia ko eni' ko e *heliaki*.

Ko e hiva 'a e punake ko Tu'imala Kaho ko e "Si'i lose hina 'o Kahala" ko e heliaki 'a e punake' ki he'ene tama na'e luva ai 'e he 'ea fika ua ki he taloni 'o e Pule'anga Tonga' hono pito'ingalau', ki he fika tolu' 'a eni 'oku taloni he 'aho' ni', Tupou VI, koe'uhi' ko hono loto mo 'ene manako, ke hoko 'a e Si'i Lose Hina 'o Kahala' ko hono fakamokomoko.

Na'e 'ikai faingata'a ke pehē mai 'a e punake' ... "Si'i heilala mei he Kolokakala." 'Ikai! Na'e taki 'e he punake' 'a 'ene talanoa' ki tu'apule'anga. Heliaki ki he lose' ko e 'akau muli; pea ko Kahala, ko e potu muli! Ko e ki'i heliaki si'i, ka ko e 'uhinga' 'oku hangē ha 'oa 'oku fiu hono 'a'au ke hā hake hono talafau'. Hangē ha moana' e 'uhinga'.

Ko e talanoa fakatātā 'e fiha 'i he tohitapu' 'oku tata'o ai 'a e 'uhinga 'oku lahi mo mālie? Fēfē talanoa 'a Netane kia Tevita hono fakamālohi'i 'e he tokotaha na'e lahi 'ene fanga sipi' 'a e tokotaha na'e taha pē 'ene ki'i sipi' (2 Sam 12)? Na'e hanga 'e Netane 'o fakatātaa'i 'a e tu'i' ki he taha fai fakamālohi. Ko e ngaahi talanoa fakatātā mo e heliaki 'oku fonu he me'a ko e 'uhinga.

Parables and *heliaki*[1] are filled with the stuff of meanings.

---

1. In Tongan poetry, *heliaki* is the art of musing on a different subject (e.g., rose, a

4. Ko e taukei

Ko e faʻahinga aʻusia ʻo e *ʻilo*ʹ mo e *mahino*ʹ ʻoku hulu ange ia ʻi he angamaheniʹ, pea hoko leva ʻa e tokotaha ko iaʹ ko e taukei. Ko e taʻanga ko ēʹ ʻa e punake ʻoku ne maʻu ʻa e taukeiʹ, he ʻikai te te fiu kita he fanongoʹ. Pe ko e malanga, ʻoku kehe pē ʻa e tōtōkaki ia ʻa e taukeiʹ, pea mo ha toe faʻahinga malaʻe pē. ʻOku manumanumelie ʻene meʻa kotoa ki he sioʹ mo e fanongoʹ, pea naʻa mo hoto lotoʹ kuo kau mo ia hono toʻo ʻe he taukeiʹ.

Ko e tohitapuʹ ʻoku ou matuʻaki fakapapauʻi ʻi he fakamatalaʹ ni, ko e haʻi ama ʻeni ʻa e kau taukei he toutaiʹ, he kuo laulaui toʻutangata ʻoku teʻeki ai mofisi ha ama pe ʻe malala ha foʻi ama. ʻOku kei hoko e tohitapuʹ ko e ama tūhulu mo e ama takiloa ke huluʻaki e fakapoʻuliʹ, ke ʻilo ʻe he tangataʹ mo e fefineʹ ʻa e ika mo e fingota ʻe fai ai ʻa e hūkiaʹ mo e konāʹ, mo e ika ʻoku ʻaonga ki heʻetau fononga'. Kapau naʻe ʻikai maʻu ʻe he kau toutaiʹ ni ʻa e taukeiʹ, ʻe fēfē nai ʻa e ongoongo leleiʹ?

Naʻe pehē tofu pē mo e kakai naʻa nau tohi ʻa e tohitapuʹ. Naʻa nau lea mo hiki tohi mei he aʻusia, mo e moʻui kuo fonu he kelesi. Naʻa nau taukei he tala ʻo e fonuaʹ, mo hono tukufakaholoʹ. Naʻa nau taukei mo maheni mo e ʻātakai ʻo naturaʹ pea mo e faʻahinga kakai kehekehe. Pea naʻa nau taukei ʻi tahi, taukei he fonuaʹ, he ʻatāʹ, naʻa mo lolofonua, kuo pau ke taukei kae toki lava ke te aʻusia ʻa e faʻahinga pōtoʻi ko eniʹ.

The authors of the Bible [if they were like native poets] must have mastered the seas, the land, the skies, and even the underworld; they had to master those in order to gain the wisdom necessary for their task [i.e., to compose texts that are full of meanings].

Ko e fehihi

ʻOku ou loto ke fokotuʻu ha foʻi fehihi ke pouʻaki e fale ʻo e punakeʹ, pea hangē ko ʻeku lave ki muʻaʹ, takitaha tauʻataina ki he lahi ʻete pou fehihi ki hoto fale, kae ʻoua muʻa naʻa liʻaki ʻa e ongo ʻakau ko eni ʻe ua (2) mei he taʻanga fehihi ʻoku tau fai'.

Ko e ongo ʻakauʹ ni ʻoku ou ui ʻe au ko e *toumuʻa* mo e *toumui*. Ko e angamaheni ʻo e ʻapi kotoa ʻoku ʻi ai e hala ki ai, pea ko e konga koē ʻo e ʻapiʹ ʻoku taupotu ki he halaʹ, ko *toumuʻa* ia. Ko e feituʻu ia ʻoku faingofua ke sio

---

foreign flower) in the place of the real subject (e.g., a daughter who caused the second son of Tonga's king to give up his right to the throne) of one's composition.

mo vakai mai ki ai e kakai´, pea ui leva ʻa e feituʻu ʻoku tuʻu ai ʻa e ngotoʻumu´ mo e tofunanga´, tau atu ai mo ha pasikala maumau, ko *toumui*.

ʻOku ou mahuʻingaʻia ke tokanga ʻa e punake´ ki hono *toumuʻa*´. Tokanga ki heʻene teuteu´! Tokanga ki hono teuteu´, tokanga ki hono fōtunga ʻoku hā mai ki he kakai´. Kuo´ u ʻosi ako faiva ʻi he punake naʻe taʻetokanga ki hono toumuʻa´. Kuo ʻai ai ʻe te fiu feinga ke puke ʻa e haka´, pea mo ʻe te toe fakaʻamu ke maʻu mai ha ʻea ʻoku lelei´. ʻOku mahuʻinga ke sino lelei mo moʻui lelei ʻa e punake´.

A composer should have a good and healthy body.

Kuo´ u ʻosi fetaulaki au mo e faingataʻa ko eni ʻa e taʻetokanga ki he toumuʻa´. ʻOku ʻi ai ʻa e ngaahi haka mo e ngaahi ngaue fakapunake ʻoku ʻikai ʻaupito te u lava ʻe au ʻo fakahoko fakalelei, pea ʻoku ʻi ai mo e ngaahi konga ʻe niʻihi ʻoku ʻikai ke lava ia. Ko hono tupuʻanga´ ko ʻeku fuʻu sino´ mo ʻeku mahamahaki´.

ʻOku ʻi ai ʻa e foʻi haka ʻoku puna ki muʻa ʻo hekeheka he ʻateʻi vaʻe´ pea musu, pea puna ki mui! Koeʻuhi´ ko ʻeku taʻetokanga ki hoku toumuʻa´, kuo ʻikai toe lava ia.

Ko e taʻu 2005, kuo u lolotonga fokoutua he falemahaki´. Ne fanongo e Tokoni Pule ʻo e Kolisi Kuini Salote´ kuo u kamata ke ako tuʻu mo ako ʻalu, pea aʻu ange ʻa Mele Taulanga: "Taua! Ko ʻemau fanongo eni kuo ke tuʻu´, pea kuo mau loto ke fai ʻa e māʻuluʻulu ʻa e Kolisi´." Naʻa ku kole ange ki he Tokoni Pule´ ke kumi ā ha taha he kuo´ u mahamahaki. "ʻIkai te mau tali mai kia koe." Naʻa´ ku loi ki he toketā´ ke u ʻalu ʻo ʻeveʻeva. ʻAlu au ki Kuini Sālote ʻo ako māʻuluʻulu!

Naʻa´ ku faingataʻaʻia, kei tete ʻa e vaʻe´, teʻeki ke u lava ʻo tuʻu lelei, faingataʻa ʻeku mānava´, hifo mei´ he meʻalele ki he meʻateke! Ko e hā hono ʻuhinga´? Ko ʻeku taʻetokanga ki hoku toumuʻa´. ʻOku fuʻu mahuʻinga ke moʻui lelei ʻa e punake´, ʻo tatau pe mo hano fiemaʻu ha kau fakamafola ongoongo lelei ʻoku lelei honau toumuʻa´. Honau sino hā mai´, fakaʻofoʻofa, talavou, teuteu lelei mo matamata lelei. ʻOku maʻu hala ʻa e faʻahinga ʻe niʻihi, ko e kau tufaki ʻo e ongoongo lelei´ ʻoku fakaʻofoʻofa ʻa e mafahifahi ʻa e kili´ he ʻunoʻunoa´ mo kiʻi fakalālāfuaʻa. ʻOua! Tokangaʻi ʻa toumuʻa!

Many get it wrong, that it is charming for bearers of good news to have cracked skin and be dull. No! Take care of your frontyard!

Fakamolemole kae tātā'i faka'osi 'a e ki'i fo'i fehihi ko eni´; ko e *va'a toumui´*. Ko e konga eni he 'api´ 'oku fa'a tuenoa hono tokanga'i´, koe'uhi´ ko e tātāitaha hono 'alu'i´, na'a mo kinautolu 'oku 'o nautolu 'a e 'api´, 'oku nau fa'a ma'u taimi lahi pē ke nofo 'i fale, pe ko falefakatolo, pea mo e konga ki toumu'a´, kae 'oua pē na'a fei'umu Sāpate pe tunu puaka ki ha fatongia. Hangē 'oku angamaheni 'oku ngali pē 'a e toumui´ ia mo e feliha'a´.

Kapau te tau ta'etokanga ki hotau toumui´, 'e kina'ia 'a e kaungā'api´ 'i he'ete 'ā puaka´ pea mo 'e te tutu'angaveve´. Hoko leva hoto toumui´ ko e 'apitanga 'o e lango´, namu´, kumā´ mo e mongomonga´. Ko 'eku tēpile na'e ngaahi ki he konifelenisi´, ko e feitu'u eni na'e ngaahi mei ai´. Na'a mo e me'akai 'oku ou ma'u he 'aho kotoa pē´. Ko e tēpile 'oku´ ou fakaafe'i ki ai ha kau fakaafe, ko e toenga kai ia 'a e lango´ mo e mongomonga´ mo e kumā´ mei hoku toumui´.

Ko e hongofulu (10) he pongipongi Sāpate´: Ko au; ko e folofola himi 'uluaki 'o e pongipongi´ ni´. Ko au 'oku malanga´! Ko hoku toumu'a´ eni 'oku mou me'a mai ki ai´. Faka'ofo'ofa hoku teutu´, kote, hekesi, ta'ovala, 'ange'ange ia he malanga´, 'ā'ā lelei e Siasi´. 'Ikai 'aupito ke nau lavelave'iloa pe na'a´ ku 'i fē 'anepō. Ko e fo'i malanga´ na'e teu ia 'i Uafu 'Amelika. 'Oku ngata ho'omou 'ilo´ 'i hoku toumu'a´. Faka'ofo'ofa 'eku tu'u atu´, pea mo hono malanga. Ko e tēpile kuo u teutu ma'a e fanga sipi´ na'e ngaahi ia mei he toumui ta'emaau mo palakū, 'uli mo fakatupumahaki.

You only know my frontyard. Before you I stand beautifully, and I present well. What you see and hear was prepared in a messy and unhealthy backyard.

'Oku fu'u matu'aki mahu'inga 'aupito ki he punake´ ke tokanga ki hono toumui´, he 'oku faingata'a ki he kakai´ ke nau ma'u ha faingamālie lelei ke nau vakai fakalelei ki he toumui 'o e punake´, ki he KAKANO *'ene mo'ui'*.

It is important that a composer takes care of his backyard, for people are not able to see what's at her/his backyard, at the CONTENT/BODY of her/his life.

'Oku malava pē 'e he punake´ ke fa'u ha hiva ke fai ai ha vākovi, feke'ike'i ai ha to'utupu, ha 'apiako mo ha 'apiako. 'Oku ki'i faingofua ange hono tauhi 'o toumu'a´. Ko e kakano 'o e ta'anga 'a e punake´, pe 'oku kano kovi pe kano sai, 'oku fakatefito ia mei he toumui 'o e punake´.

Ko e taʻanga ko ē ʻa e punake ʻoku tonu ʻene moʻuiʹ mei lotoʹ, meʻa ko ē ʻoku ʻikai ʻilo lelei mo lahi ki ai ʻa e kakaiʹ, ʻoku fakafiefia, langa hake, fakatupu melino, pea fakalakalaka ki muʻa ʻetau moʻuiʹ.

Naʻe talanoa mai ʻe Peni Tutuʻila, naʻe folofola ange ʻa Kuini Sālote ke lele ange ki palasi, fekauʻaki mo ʻene teuteu ke hoko ko e punake ʻa e Kolisi Kuini Saloteʹ. Tō folofola ʻa Kuini ʻi he ngaahi meʻa kehekehe, pea ko e fakaʻosiʹ, "Peni! Tokanga ki he ʻapi ʻokuʹ ke ʻalu ki aiʹ, ko e lotoʻā sipi ia ʻa e Siasiʹ." Naʻe ʻikai foki ke sio ha taha ia ki he loto ʻo Peniʹ, ki toumuiʹ, pea ʻoua naʻa ngalo ko toumuiʹ ʻoku ʻi ai ho ʻutoʹ. Ko hai ʻokuʹ ne ʻilo mai ʻe te fakakaukau? Kovi pe lelei, ʻoku fūfūʻi ʻi toumui!

Don't forget that your backyard is where your brain is.

Ko e loloto ange ko ē ʻete vakili ʻa e tohitapuʹ, mo ʻilo ki aiʹ, ʻe moʻui leva ʻa e laumālie ʻo e kakaiʹ pea maama lelei e hala ke nau fononga aiʹ. He ʻikai foki ke toe hiki fakalahi ʻa e tohitapuʹ ia, pea ka fakavaivai ʻetau feinga ke ʻilo mo mahino ʻa e fuʻu tohiʹ, ko e hē ia ʻa e kau muimuiʹ. Tokangaʻi ʻa toumui he ko ia ʻoku fai mei ai ʻa e fafanga ʻo e fanga sipiʹ pea mo e mālie ʻa e taʻanga ʻa e punakeʹ.

Te u pehē ʻe au ʻoku māhanga pe ʻoku tuʻupau mo felāveʻi ʻa e punakeʹ mo e kau fakamafola ʻo e ongoongo lelei ʻi he tohitapuʹ ʻi he ʻikai malava ke hanga ʻe he kau punakeʹ ia ʻo tuʻuaki ʻa e fakaʻofoʻofa ʻo e ʻātakai ʻo e mamaniʹ pe ko e lelei ki he mamaniʹ ʻa e melinoʹ, pe ko e fiefiaʹ, ke takitaha taʻaki ʻe he punake ʻa e haohaoa mo e fakaʻofoʻofa ʻa e fakatupu ʻa e ʻOtuaʹ. ʻOku tau moʻunofoa kitautolu hono viki pē ʻa e meʻa naʻa tau ngaahi. ʻOku ʻangeʻange ia he kau talaki e folofolaʹ. Ko Tongaʹ ni, ʻoku toko tahakilutoluafe. Kakai tokosiʻi ʻi he kiʻi fonua siʻisiʻi, ka ʻoku kaka ki ʻolunga ʻa e fika ʻo e fakaʻotuamateʹ. ʻOku teʻeki ai ke lava ʻo fakamāsima fakalelei ʻa e kiʻi fonua tokosiʻi mo siʻisiʻi ko eni ko Tonga, tupu mei he ʻikai malava ʻe he punakeʹ ʻo viki mo tala ʻa e fakaʻofoʻofa ʻo e fakatupu ʻa e ʻOtuaʹ. Hangē ʻoku holo ai pē ʻa e mālohi, moʻoni mo e moʻui ʻo e tohitapuʹ.

Ko e tohitapuʹ, ko e kaveinga folau pe ko e feleoko mo e fakatolongaʻanga ia ʻo e tala ʻo e kau Kalisitianeʹ ki he moʻui taʻengataʹ. Manatuʻi ʻa e fuʻu ivi taʻemahakulea ʻoku nofo loto he tohiʹ ni.

Kuo pau ke tonu peaʹ te mātuʻaki talangofua ki he tuli kaveinga ʻa e kau kupengaʹ ni. ʻOku ʻulungaanga tatau pē ia mo e taʻanga ʻa e kau punakeʹ. Kuo pau ke te fuʻu matuʻaki maheni mo e siolotoʹ kae lava ke te fakaofiofi ki he kelesi mo e taʻemahakulea ʻi he tohitapu.

'Oku lava 'o tauhi 'i he fakatolonga'anga ni mo e feleoko ko eni´ 'a e tala 'o e fonua´, mo e tala tukufakaholo, ngaahi fekau mo e ngaahi faka'amu, pea 'oku tala pē 'akau´ 'i hono fua´. He 'oku 'i ai pē punake ia mo 'ene ta'anga 'oku hangē tofu pē ia ko e ngaahi potu folofola 'i he tohitapu´. 'Oku malave loto pea fakangalongata'a, 'o iku ki he mo'ui ta'engata´.

Some composers and compositions are like biblical texts. They inspire and are unforgettable, leading to eternal living.

Ko e fanga ki'i fa'u ia 'a kimautolu mo 'emau kau fie-punake 'e ni'ihi, 'oku mo'oni 'a e hiva kakala´: "'Oku hangē ha misi 'oku puli atu´, si'emau 'au'auhia vave 'i ho'omou manatu´!"

'Ofa atu!

ISLAND TURNS

Lifting the Tapu of Sex:
A *Tulou* Reading of the Song of Songs

Brian Fiu Kolia

I propose a *Tulou* hermeneutic as one of the ways of reading problematic texts, such as the Song of Songs (hereafter the Song), which Samoans and other Pasifika islanders avoid because of its carnal nature and sexual imageries. Because the topic of sex is *tapu* (taboo, sacred) in the Samoan context, the Song has not been engaged nor appreciated by Samoan readers. This nonengagement and unappreciation adds to the assumption from mostly nonislander circles that islanders cannot read and that they are too "naïve" and "simplistic" (Davidson, Aymer, and Havea 2015, 1). Such a colonial attitude was prevalent among early European missionaries, and as a result, many aspects of Samoan pre-Christian indigenous religion, which contained sexually charged stories, were whispered to later generations. These stories were whispered due to the tapu imposed on sex matters with the arrival of Christianity into Samoa (Efi 2014, 37).

In this essay, I appeal to key Samoan concepts to elaborate the importance of tulou in the Samoan context. The concepts of *fa'aaloalo* (respect) and tapu (sacred, taboo) are pivotal in understanding the context of tulou and its application. I define tulou as a construct of the terms *tu* (stand) and *lou* (pluck, bring down), and I use reader-response criticism as a theoretical framework for formulating my hermeneutic. The tulou hermeneutic informs my analysis of the Song, as I negotiate the Song from a humanistic point of view. I find in Samoa that the Song is whispered to the faithful without much attention to the sexuality expressed. I thus find that there is a need to lift the tapu and reread the Song from a different perspective. As such, a hermeneutic built on fa'aaloalo is ideal, given that fa'aaloalo is the foundation of the Samoan culture. Tulou is grounded in respect (fa'aaloalo), and it is with respect that I propose to read the Song.

Constructing a Tulou Hermeneutic

In Pasefika (Pacific, Oceania), tulou acts as a pardon, or excusing a person out of respect for infringing a tapu with regard to another person or group of people. Nations around Samoa have similar understandings of the word:

Tonga	*tulou*	excuse me
Fiji	*tilou*	excuse me
Rarotonga, Maohi	*turou*	expression of glorification to deities
Maohi Nui (Tahiti)	*turou*	expression of shame and humiliation
Hawaii	*kulou*	excuse me

The common feature among these meanings is a lowering of oneself. Whether this lowering involves excusing the individual for breaching tapu, self-humiliation, or adoration and glorification, the need to lower oneself is imperative.

By lowering oneself, "*Tulou* permits one to wrong another, respectfully" (Havea 2013, 296). *Respect* in the Samoan context is essential to "save face" (Vaai 2006, 178). Much of the concern of tulou is dealing with those people who have been offended when their space is crossed. An awkward situation becomes apparent. As Alessandro Duranti (1992, 667) indicates, "individuals find themselves standing and hence higher than those sitting, some of whom are probably of higher status." To amend this awkward situation, one crouches down (in respect) and says "tulou." There is no hesitation to say tulou because tulou, in most Polynesian contexts, is expected and compulsory. The action of bending down one's body conveys to people that one is remorseful for breaching the tapu. My only point of contention with Duranti's understanding of tulou is that while fa'aaloalo is mostly paid to those of higher rank, tulou is not reserved for those of higher rank. Tulou can be said and given to anyone and to everyone, regardless of status or standing.

Tu ae Lou

To date, Pasefika writers have not explained where the term tulou originates. As such, I explain the construction of the word in my own view as an Australian Samoan. The word tulou has evolved from its original meaning. But I imagine that it is like other Samoan words, which originated either from Samoan mythology or from observations of the land and ocean in everyday life (cf. Lefale 2010, 323–25). Penehuro Fatu Lefale, in his article about Samoa's weather and climate, explains how Samoans named elements of the cosmos based on what they resembled. For example, the Belt of Orion was named *amoga* (load) because it resembled a man carrying a load on his shoulders (323). Following this pattern of Samoan etymology, I construct an etymology of tulou.

The word tulou resonates with the practice of plucking breadfruits from a breadfruit tree and lowering the fruit down to ground level, as tulou requires a lowering of oneself in respect of the other. This imagery allows us to understand how tulou can be viewed as a model for bringing the horizon of the text to our own horizon.

To elaborate, tulou breaks down into two words, tu and lou: The word tu means "to stand" or "to stop." As such, tu defines the stand-point of the person. In the example of a breadfruit tree picker, the person at the bottom of the tree represents a position of humility: a position from where faʻaaloalo is derived. And the word lou refers to the plucking action (the stick used for plucking is also known as lou). When one uses a lou to pluck a breadfruit, she or he is not interested in the lower branches but the fruits in the higher branches. These higher breadfruits are plucked and brought down to the ground. Therefore, lou represents a descending action. To see this in the context of faʻaaloalo, the high point represents nobility while the low point represents humility.

When tu and lou are put together, tulou means *tu ae lou* ("stand then bring down"). The person acting out of faʻaaloalo becomes aware of a sacred space and is obliged to stand or stop. As the person stops, the person realizes that she or he is in a place of nobility and must descend to a low point of humility; one lou(er) oneself. The person brings herself or himself down to a level of humility and utters the word tulou to show faʻaaloalo.

Breaching Tapu with Tulou

When a person breaches tapu through tulou, she or he *claims* (as opposed to *seeks*) permission. A person who says tulou does not wait for someone to permit her or him to walk passed but simply says tulou and proceeds. Even if the seated people would not grant permission, per se, tulou is still reciprocated through a positive acknowledgment of the person. As a result, the reputation of the person saying tulou is complimented. Those who are seated often meet the one who does not say tulou with sneers of contempt and disapproval.[1]

For the people who are seated, there is a changed attitude when tulou is uttered. This change in attitude is similar to a *palagi* concept known as *schema*. The schema reflects a positive change in people, where a person "can deliberately confront [an] anomaly and try to create a new pattern of reality in which it has a place" (Douglas 2002, 48). This positive emancipation is what occurs to the people who are seated. What seemed rude is given a positive reality as those who are seated accept the need for the individual to cross their space.

Tulou as Hermeneutical Lens

Given the reciprocity of tulou, whose perspective in the tulou transaction is relevant for this hermeneutical exercise? Traditionally, tulou is given to other readers. For instance, in the traditional readings of the Song, one would tulou other readers by giving an allegorical interpretation so that the tension of speaking about sex in a mixed-gender audience would be reduced. The text itself was not granted the status of tulou, as readers prefer to avoid reading references to sex and would therefore fail to make meaning from the context of such sexual references. References to sexuality and eroticism were suppressed and not even mentioned.

Breaching Tapu

With a tulou hermeneutic, the reader approaches the text with the tulou mindset. The reader pays respect to the text. The sexual content in the text may cause shock and embarrassment to the Samoan reader, but through the tulou hermeneutic, she or he understands that the text exhibits its author's style, method, and message. With a tulou mindset, the reader becomes aware of tapu, but she or he must still cross that tapu space. Thus, the reader should not avoid the sexual content. The reader cannot avoid the text's eroticism. Engaging them is faʻaaloalo to the text, and making meaning of them is giving respect to the text. Through the tulou hermeneutic, the reader's mindset changes from the negative sense imposed by

---

[1]. This is based on the premise that people at Samoan cultural functions and gatherings are seated until the end.

tapu into a positive one constituting openness to talking about sex and sexuality. From this positive context, the reader can make new meanings.

Through the tulou hermeneutic, possibilities eventuate. The reader can appreciate the sacredness of sexual imagery. The tulou hermeneutic can also diverge into a discussion of human sexuality as part of being "made in God's image." This is a problem in the Samoan context because mentioning of the word *susu* (breast), for instance, in public is tapu. As a Samoan male reader, the disturbance is out of respect for my sister, not out of disgust. Tulou relaxes the Samoan cultural tapu and enables the text to speak and the reader to make new meaning.

In addition, a tulou hermeneutic gives fa'aaloalo to other readers. It acknowledges that the space between myself and Samoan female readers is respected. This space is *va tapu'ia* (sacred space), which implies a sacred relationship. The reason that the *va* (space) is *tapu'ia* (sacred) is to ensure one party in the relationship does not offend or hurt the other. The topic of sex, for example, stands to offend and breach the va.

So how can tulou respectfully breach va or tapu? This requires that the conditions of tapu be redefined. In dealing with a text that is considered holy, it is necessary to breach the tapu between readers. As Samoans acknowledge (at least on an ideological level) the holiness of the Bible, a reading which maintains the integrity of the text is appropriate. This way, one pays fa'aaloalo both to the text and to other readers.

Reading with the lens of tulou is an exercise in reader-response criticism. The reader undergoes a change through the tulou hermeneutic. Hans-Georg Gadamer is adamant that the reader makes a contribution to making meaning through what he terms the fusion of horizons. This implies that the horizon of the text and the horizon of the reader must fuse in order to come to an understanding. Gadamer (2004, 301) defines *horizon* as "the range of vision that includes everything that can be seen from a particular vantage point." In interpretation, each person has her or his own horizon, which is determined by her or his capacity to think. "Applying this to the thinking mind, we speak of narrowness of horizon, of the possible expansion of horizon, of the opening up of new horizons, and so forth" (Gadamer 2004, 301).

Tulou Horizon

Tu signifies the reader's horizon. The reader's horizon is constituted with human experience, and the context of fa'aaloalo is a human context. This is important to note because as Stanley Fish (1980, 173) states, interpreting "is constitutive of being human."

The faʻaaloalo context informs the interpretive decisions that one makes of and about the text. The meaning that is constructed does not constitute primarily a faʻaaloalo to the tapu, nor does it ignore the tapu. Out of faʻaaloalo for the text, the sexual content is not disregarded by concealing it through allegorical and christological understandings. The reader instead must search for meaning within the eroticism of the text.

This may seem difficult for the traditional Samoan reader. In order to talk about sex in the Samoan context, an Australian Samoan understanding can provide a platform. Being an Australian Samoan, I am part of a community that values our traditional Samoan customs and is open to incorporating values which are not prominent in the Samoan context but are prevalent in the Australian context, such as gender equality and freedom of speech. We are aware of the multicultural context, and in our bid to survive in the Australian context, there is a need for openness and acceptance of other views.

This awareness of the multicultural context harbors a reading which values the notion of faʻaaloalo while at the same time concedes the chance for modern Australian views to inform traditional Samoan understanding. The result would be a reading that confronts the sexual imagery through tulou. The text is interpreted out of the traditional perspective of faʻaaloalo but with a twist, as the attitudes toward sex held by many Samoans in the Australian context put sex in a positive light. When a sexual metaphor is read, the reader pays faʻaaloalo to the text. The tulou reading proposed below promotes faʻaaloalo to the text and frees the topic of sex from the tapu that holds back Samoan readers.

Tulou in Reading

I go back to the two words tu and lou. Tu (stand) defines the reader's standpoint. Meaning which seems impossible to create is made possible with the use of lou, in a similar manner as the hard-to-reach breadfruits are plucked with the lou and brought down to where one stands (tu). There are in lou both ascending and descending actions. The ascending of the lou to the breadfruit constitutes a plucking of the text from the high grasps (spiritualized interpretation) of allegory, which the reader brings down to tu (humanistic interpretation). The lou becomes an extension of the reader's horizon into the text while the descending of the lou corresponds to the bringing of the text to the reader's horizon. The lou allows for the horizons to fuse, to bridge the gap between reader and text.

If we apply this to the tapu on sex, we realize that the tapu may not be congruent with the current context. The reality is that we participate in sex, whether it is for pleasure or for procreation, in the context of marriage or not. This is the horizon of the reader; this is the reality from where meaning must be made. We cannot make meaning from an alternative reality, for the Song has sexual overtones and makes references to erotic love.

Tulou to Readers

As a male reader, how might I deal with a female reader, and vice versa? The awkwardness is felt when the opposite sex is present, for example, in a Bible study group or village meeting. This is because blood-related males and females are in *vā tapuia* (sacred relationship), and they do not discuss matters of the body in public. Sex is thus tapu in the sense that it is taboo, not allowed to be discussed in public for fear that one might insult the vā tapuia. In addition, there is a Christian tendency to think shamefully about sex and to reserve it for private conversations. Samoan churches still honor missionary teachings according to which sex is dirty and defiling. So, when Samoans need to talk about sex or the Song in mixed-gender settings, awkwardness is avoided with allegorical interpretation. Talk of sex is bypassed or spiritualized, and the Song's sexual character is neglected. As expected, the text plays second fiddle to theological interests. In the lens of tulou, this shows no fa'aaloalo to the text.

The tulou hermeneutic puts allegory aside, leading to an alternative way of paying fa'aaloalo to the reader. How, then, might a male reader pay tulou to a female reader, and vice versa? Through the tulou hermeneutic, the reader's attitude toward sex changes. Sex is no longer awkward but is appreciated. What was previously viewed as awkward can be seen as positive and adored according to the next context (Douglas 2002, 48). This new context is created by the tulou reading. When we create new meaning, we rewrite the text (cf. Fish 1980, 172), and as we rewrite the text, we rewrite the context. In rewriting the context, I say tulou to my parents and to Samoans of past generations because in negotiating with traditional Samoan culture, I bring my horizon as an Australian Samoan. I also say tulou because I bring values such as freedom of speech and gender equality, characteristics of the modern Australian context that challenge the *fa'a-Sāmoa* and its limitations.

A Tulou Reading of the Song

For this exercise, I choose to focus on Song 8:1 and 8:8. The challenge in 8:1 for Samoan readers relates to *feagaiga* (sacred relation between brother and sister, according to which the brother is responsible for his sister's safety and welfare) and the problem with lovers who call each other by sibling terms. The challenge with 8:8 is nudity, and a tulou reading helps construct alternative meanings to what allegorical readings present. I stand not to defy cultural customs but to maintain the sanctity of fa'a-Sāmoa in comprehending nudity in the text. At the outset, therefore, I must first say tulou!

It is important to point out that the traditional Samoan interpretive community is predominantly male, a reflection of the dominant male voice in traditional Samoan society. Being a Samoan male, I am located in this dominant male discourse; therefore, I say tulou, as some of my presumptions about the feminine voice in the Song may be misguided.

In this reading, I lou the text to my male Australian Samoan horizon. Through my Australian Samoan understanding of Samoan indigenous references and the theme of fa'aaloalo, I launch a bid to gain an interpretation of the sexual imagery for the Samoan context. Through the influence of my Australian context, I also make a case for bringing out the female voice which traditional Samoan society often subjugates.

As an Australian Samoan, and like many others, I have my own assumptions about the fa'a-Sāmoa and how these assumptions inform my own perspective. I thus perform a *negotiation of identities* "whereby individuals in an intercultural situation attempt to assert, define, modify, challenge, and/or support their own and others' desired self-images" (Ting-Toomey 1999, 40). As a result, I negotiate with the behavioral patterns of traditional Samoans and the context of Samoa in the pre-Christian era. My understanding of the fa'a-Sāmoa is not complete, so the need for negotiation is necessary. By doing this, I satisfy my curiosity in Samoan folklore and legends as well as the customs of my Samoan heritage. On the other hand, I am equally intrigued by how the text can inform my own cultural worldview. In this hermeneutical exercise, I present my tu (standpoint) on the text and the problems of interpretation that the text presents for my interpretive community. I then seek to reconcile these problems in interpretation through lou(ering) the text to my tu in order to make meaning.

"Like a Brother to Me": The Feagaiga Problem (Song 8:1)

Tu

One temptation for the Samoan reader in this passage is assuming that the brother of whom the woman speaks in 8:1 is someone in the feagaiga (between brother and sister) relationship. With this assumption, two things are likely to occur. First, any sexual activity suggested in the text is deflected because sex is not expected in a Samoan feagaiga. Second, if the text is unambiguous that sex occurred, it is avoided as an ambiguous moment in the text, and the sexual content is left aside with no interpretation. The problem of assumption hinders the ability to understand what "brother" could mean, which leads to the risk of avoiding interpretation altogether.

Duane Garrett and Paul R. House (2004, 247) explain that *"brother* and *sister* were common terms of endearment between lovers in the ancient Near East." This understanding is based on the context of Egyptian love songs to which the Song bore resemblance (Arnold and Beyer 2002, 192). "Brother" and "sister" were part of the language of foreplay, indicating interest from the opposite sex. This excerpt from an Egyptian love poem highlights the use of "brother" in expressions of sexual desire:

> My brother stirs up my heart with his voice, making me take ill.
> Although he is among the neighbors of my mother's house,
> I cannot go to him.
> Mother is right to command me thus:
> Avoid seeing him!
> Yet my heart is vexed when he comes to mind,
> for love of him has captured me. (Arnold and Beyer 2002, 192)

In the Samoan context, "brother" and "sister" are not used in such a manner due to the sacredness of feagaiga. The text becomes even more dubious through the yearning expressed in 8:1, "O that you were like a brother to me" (NRSV). The words connote a desire for an incestuous relationship. For the brother and sister even to be together is condemned in Samoan culture, as Raymond Firth (1970, 279) writes: "Those who call each other brother and sister cannot sit together, eat, walk or travel together." The importance of Firth's statement lies not in the actions banned but in the fa'aaloalo and care that siblings pay to each other. In the Samoan context, an interpretation that does not compromise the feagaiga is preferred.

In the phrase "O that you were like a brother to me," it is interesting to note the woman's use of כאח "like a brother." The fact that the woman says "like," as indicated by the prefix כ, rules out any incestuous sentiments. Michael V. Fox (1985, 166) states that the translation "like *a* brother" (rather than "like *my* brother") allows for the endearing sense of the word "brother" to be assumed.

Michael D. Goulder (1986, 61) reasons that the woman desires an open show of affection and freedom to love her man openly. Her feelings for him are strong, and she wishes for social recognition. The woman's desperation for her lover is more of a desire "for social recognition of their relationship," so that the two lovers can be with each other without restraint (Patmore 2006, 241).

Lou

The feagaiga is socially recognized in Samoan society, which is why siblings are careful of each other's space, because tapu ensures that feagaiga is sacred. From the Samoan perspective of tulou: how can we avoid the temptation to read this as a text which expresses incestuous love? As tulou calls for fa'aaloalo interpretation, we see a woman of fa'aaloalo who yearns for their relationship to be *like* a feagaiga—that is, to be recognized by the society. Recognition, in Samoan society, is not a simple matter of people accepting and moving on; rather, it is the recognition that the relationship is *sā* (holy) and that there is a communal responsibility to ensure the relationship is kept sā.

Another significant element of the feagaiga is the role of the brother as protector. The woman in her desire for sex does not show desperation but a desire for protection from her lover. The desire equates with a wish for her lover to protect her sexual loins so that she is not touched sexually by anyone besides her lover. This need for protection appears clearly in the declaration by the brothers that they will "build a wall" (8:9) to protect the woman, perhaps a reference to her chastity. In the Samoan context, the brother safeguards his sister from many things, and protecting her chastity would be among the main priorities. The woman in 8:1 thus asks her lover to be like a brother by providing protection for her.

Through the tulou hermeneutic, we see fa'aaloalo with the text here in the voice of women. Women are often subjugated in the Old Testament, and their voices are regularly suppressed (Schüssler Fiorenza 1995, xi). Athalya Brenner (1993, 15) argues that this is a product of androcentric readings of the biblical text, where "interpretation and teaching have been performed almost exclusively by males, and exploited to further the gender-specific interests of their dominant social group." Women whose voices had been suppressed in the Old Testament include, for instance, Tamar (2 Sam 13), who was raped by her half-brother in his quest for power. She dwelled "'desolate' in her brother's house," yet the father remained silent (cf. Fontaine 1997, 84). In the traditional Samoan context, it is easy to see the Song's female protagonist in a negative light due to her unconventional sexual desires. But in rereading the text through the tulou hermeneutic, we avoid succumbing to an androcentric reading.[2] A focus on the woman's desire for public show of affection is not ideal, but this reading endorses the feagaiga relationship. The woman does not ask for cultural constraints to be broken but for her relationship to be publicly endorsed under the constraints of her own context.

A tulou reading replaces the focus upon the woman as the central concern of the passage. She instigates the need to be protected for her own purpose rather than the brothers taking the initiative to contain an errant sister, according to traditional readings of the passage. She does not pursue her erotic desires directly but yearns for them. In her yearning, her desire is for her lover to do what a brother does, that is, to protect her. By instigating the call for protection, she upholds the integrity of the feagaiga. From a Samoan perspective, this is a display of great fa'aaloalo. In the eyes of Samoans, the woman could be seen as a *matai* (chief) because she actively promotes the ideals of fa'aaloalo. Her acknowledgment of her brother's role is seen as wise because she prompts her brother to act out of fa'aaloalo. This resonates with the *tōfā* (wisdom) of a matai who seeks to inspire others to acts of fa'aaloalo.

In the traditional Samoan context, it is assumed that protection of the feagaiga is the domain of the brother. But the text can speak to the Samoan context if Samoans are willing to be challenged by the text

---

2. The misunderstanding of the woman's yearning resonates with the misunderstanding of the needs of Australian Samoans. The community of Australian Samoans demand acceptance from other Samoans. Regardless of vocation, choice of career, sexuality, or choice of partners (e.g., Samoan or non-Samoan), the ultimate concern for the Australian Samoan community is that we are accepted by our elders (cf. Anae 2003, 89). While our Samoan parents may view our willingness to adopt the values of the modern Australian context as *fia-pālagi* ("want to be pālagi"), we identify with our Samoan heritage.

because, for an Australian Samoan, there is no reason why it should not also be the domain of the sister. The traditional Samoan reader may see the woman's yearning as acting out of rebelliousness, but the Australian Samoan can identify with the nature of the woman's desire. While her actions may seem carefree, the woman is also eager to have her relationship accepted. This displays fa'aaloalo because she wishes to maintain cultural constraints.

The dominant understanding of feagaiga is construed through male interests. In reading with an Australian Samoan perspective—which values Samoan tradition but also incorporates modern values, such as gender equality—I point to a glaring weakness with the traditional understanding of feagaiga (that only the brother displays fa'aaloalo by obliging to offer protection). The Song affirms that the sister can also show fa'aaloalo, for the call to be "like a brother" is acknowledgement of service that is not limited to the male gender.

No Breasts? (Song 8:8)

Tu

The sister's honor could be brought into disrepute in many ways, and in Song 8:8, talking of a girl's breasts is one example. In the Samoan context, this is an insult to the feagaiga relationship. How could the brothers see that she has no breasts? A male speaking of his sister's body this way is disrespectful in the Samoan context. To speak of nudity is disrespectful in the Samoan public. Since the arrival of the *pālangi* missionaries, adult women and men were required to cover up their private parts (including women's breasts). The mind of the Samoan reader is aware of this fact, and whenever nudity appears in the text, curiosity emerges also. Such curiosity seeks to dig for how the exposing of breasts, particularly those of a minor, could be deemed acceptable. First, before breasts are even mentioned in the verse, the text states that she is small. Fox (1985, 173) clarifies that small here does not refer to her size but to "her supposed sexual immaturity, as in mishnaic Hebrew, in which *qeṭannah* means a minor (less than 12 years old)." The explanation here permeates the understanding of "no breasts," as it indicates that the girl had "not yet reached the age of puberty" (Fredericks and Estes 2010, 412). The language hints also at the sexual activity of the girl, which at this stage is nonexistent. It is difficult for a Samoan reader who reads that the girl has no susu to envision her in a different situation than being naked. So how does one deal with this verse from a Samoan perspective?

Lou

From a tulou perspective, we pay faʻaaloalo to the text by comprehending the image of the girl with no breasts. Commentators have claimed that the girl's lack of breasts hints at her sexual immaturity and sexual inactivity. Yet in the pre-Christian Samoan context, sexual activity was associated with the genitalia. Tui Atua Tupua Tamasese Taʻisi Efi (2014, 55) writes that "according to Samoan indigenous traditions the reproductive and sexual organs of the human body underline human divinity and spirituality. They are the instruments for procreation and symbolise the power to make new life. Sex in this equation was the vehicle for procreation and as such a sacred act." The breasts do not suggest sexual activity or procreation as the "female breasts were not necessary for the conception of new life and so not afforded the same *tapu* as the genitals" (Efi 2009, 13). With this pre-Christian understanding of susu, I contend that the girl's sexual activity cannot be determined by her breasts because they are not considered sexual organs. From a faʻaaloalo mindset, the breasts are seen for their nurturing purposes. This formulates an alternative understanding of the image in 8:8, whereby the girl is seen as unqualified for motherhood. Her lack of breasts indicates that she is without child and does not bear the responsibilities of a mother.

In the context of chapter 8, verses 4 and 10 assist with this interpretation. The call for the daughters of Jerusalem not to stir up love until it is ready, or "pleased" in 8:4, points toward the youth of the girl. The word שתחפץ ("she/it is pleased") is in the third-person feminine, which means that "readiness" does not necessarily refer to "love" but could also refer to the girl. In this regard, the girl is young and has not reached the age of sexual maturity.

Furthermore, the word שלום ("peace") in 8:10 points to a context of prosperity and fertility. When 8:8 is read in this way, the breasts of the girl refer to fertility rather than sexual pleasure. A different picture of the girl is envisioned: she is without responsibility. She is exposed in a social sense, with an emphasis upon the fact that she is not a mother. In the context of the Song, she is not ready for love and had no experience of it. The rationale behind the question that follows, "What do we do to our sister on the day which she will be spoken of?" (8:8 NRSV) becomes clear in this reading. This is a question that stems from the knowledge that the girl is not yet nubile. As Tremper Longman III (2001, 216) stresses, "the brothers represent social restraint on the woman's love, and the time appears to be right that that restraint may be lifted." Thus, this verse can be read as a preparatory stage of the girl's life, where the brothers brace themselves for the day when she will no longer be under their protection. From a Samoan perspective, exposing the girl's nudity is acknowledgement of her lack of social status and responsibility.

To scrutinize where I tu, the text can inform our perceptions of nudity in that, in the anthropology of being made in God's image, we readers can no longer be quick to lay tapu on what is essentially God's creation. The text pushes Samoans back to the pre-Christian understanding of nudity as a celebration of life. Genitalia were viewed as organs for procreation and were celebrated in public cultural festivities with the anticipation of sex between lovers. Sex is life-giving. The men in the passage were bracing for this eventuality that, as life continues, the girl will soon become a woman. Her nudity is a sign of her growth and a sign of social status. It is perhaps time that our understanding of nudity resides on the notion that one day our own young will become adults.

The Need for Tulou

The Song deals with sexuality and erotic love, topics which are tapu (taboo, prohibited) in the Samoan public context. Evidently, there is a need for tulou in order for Samoan readers to deal with the Song. There is a need to breach the tapu on sex. This is where tulou enters the fray because tulou is grounded on fa'aaloalo—a perspective where tapu (sacred) implicates adoration and worship. This leads to approaching and reading the Song from a perspective that appreciates its sexual content.

In the Christian context, the Song has been read in light of the relationship of the church to God. Jill M. Munro (1995, 12) poses a key argument regarding this type of allegorical reading:

> The allegorical interpretation in its various forms is a venerable tradition which, so far from being cold and mechanistic, is extremely supple. Its strength lies in its capacity to stimulate the imagination to explore the very parameters of faith. In so doing it discloses the spiritual and theological depths of a particular worldview, Jewish and Christian. The disadvantage however is that the Song is in danger of becoming a code to be cracked, a means to an end, for the vivid imagery of the Song tends to

be subordinated to a general interpretation in the light of which the Song as an imaginative ensemble increasingly fades from view.

Munro's claim that the Song tends to be subordinated is precisely what is occurring in the Samoan context. What is clear in the Samoan context is that the source of awkwardness and embarrassment one feels when reading the Song stems from a history, thanks to the European missionaries, of restrained attitudes toward sex.

In response, the Samoan tapu—in the sense of prohibition—needs to be breached. But tapu—in the sense of adoration—also needs to be restored for the sake of making meaning, and this can be done through tulou. Tulou does not avoid the eroticism but instead asks critical questions while making meaning of it. I side with Munro that the text should not be treated as though it is a code. The imagery is vivid, and it needs to be engaged. According to the tulou hermeneutic, treating the imagery solely through allegory signals a lack of fa'aaloalo (respect, for the text).

Tulou can also have an impact upon social change because the protagonist in the Song is in a relationship that was not accepted. In my Samoan mind, this can mean one of three relationships: that she was in an extramarital affair, that she was in a same-sex relationship, or that she was unmarried and was having premarital sex. Premarital sex was a cardinal sin in the time of the missionaries, but such an attitude is obsolete for many Australian Samoans in the present time. There is also acceptance by Australian Samoans of people in same-sex and extramarital relations, in spite of our traditional Samoan heritage.

The Song challenges the Samoan public, offering to redefine Samoan attitudes toward sex and acknowledge the reality of the context in which Samoans live. The Song does this by accentuating sex as a profound expression of love when expressed according to the spirit of fa'aaloalo. Tulou is a necessary breach, so if premarital chastity is breached, may it be breached necessarily out of love and fa'aaloalo. I stress that this impact upon social change is not a changed view toward marriage but a changed outlook on how sex operates in the context of fa'aaloalo (respect, between two lovers).

Finally, the need for tulou is crucial in our reading of women in the Bible. Women are marginalized in the Bible, often presented and viewed as femme fatales or originators of sinful acts. Through the tulou hermeneutic, the female character in chapter 8 of the Song is seen as a heroine in the Samoan context, for she is the instigator of fa'aaloalo. She seeks protection and mature love. She is represented as a matai who seeks to maintain fa'aaloalo in society. Since the majority of matai are men, a representation of the woman in chapter 8 as a matai is subversive. This representation confronts the common attitude toward women in Samoan society as behind-the-scenes members who are spared from the tensions of decision-making and controversy. The woman in chapter 8 is venerated amidst the controversy, and it is her wisdom (*tōfā*) that leads to her call for protection.

Conclusion

The tulou hermeneutic meets the need to negotiate problematic texts. Such problematic texts had been dealt with in a manner that compromised the integrity of the text, as readers traditionally overlooked the issues and problems in the text in favor of passive (mostly allegorical) interpretations. As I have argued, there is a need to deal with these texts more carefully, and I have proposed a tulou hermeneutic that brings the text down (lou) from the high points of allegory and spiritualized readings, down to a humanistic reading that allows the reader to formulate questions of the text from his or her standpoint (tu).

I use the Song of Songs, littered with sexual imagery and erotic language, to illustrate how the tulou hermeneutic may work. I lou(er) the text from the high point represented by spiritualized readings in light of God's covenant with Israel and the church. I lou(er) the text to the reader's tu, representing the reader's human standpoint, where I make meaning in light of my human experiences as an Australian Samoan who perceives sex in the Song as a celebration of human life. As a result, the text is given its integrity and the fa'aaloalo that it had lost through tapu.

Works Cited

Anae, Melani. 2003. "O A'u/I—My Identity Journey." Pages 89–101 in *Making Our Place: Growing up PI in New Zealand*. Edited by Peggy Fairbairn-Dunlop and Gabrielle Sisifo Makisi. Palmerston North: Dunmore.

Arnold, Bill T., and Bryan E. Beyer, eds. 2002. *Readings from the Ancient Near East: Primary Sources for Old Testament Study*. EBS. Grand Rapids: Baker Academic.

Brenner, Athalya. 1993. "On Reading the Hebrew Bible as a Feminist Woman: Introduction to the Series." Pages 11–27 in *A Feminist Companion to the Song of Songs*. Edited by Athalya Brenner. FCB 1. Sheffield: JSOT Press.

Davidson, Steed Vernyl, Margaret Aymer, and Jione Havea. 2015. "RumInations." Pages 1–24 in *Islands, Islanders, and the Bible: RumInations*. Edited by Jione Havea, Margaret Aymer, and Steed Vernyl Davidson. SemeiaSt 77. Atlanta: SBL Press.

Douglas, Mary. 2002. *Purity and Danger: An Analysis of Concepts of Pollution and Taboo*. London: Routledge.

Duranti, Alessandro. 1992. "Language and Bodies in Social Space: Samoan Ceremonial Greetings." *AA* 94.3: 657–91.

Efi, Tui Atua Tupua tamasese Ta'isi. 2014. "Whispers and Vanities in Samoan Indigenous Religious Culure." Pages 37–76 in *Whispers and Vanities: Samoan Indigenous Knowledge and Religion*. Edited by Stephen L. Filipo, Naomi Fuamatu, Vitolia Mo'a, Tamasailau M. Sualii-Sauni, Upolu Luma Va'ai, Maualaivao Albert Wendt, and Reina Whaitiri. Wellington: Huia.

Firth, Raymond. 1970. "Sibling Terms in Polynesia." *JPolyS* 79.3: 272–87.

Fish, Stanley. 1980. *Is There a Text in This Class? The Authority of Interpretive Communities*. Cambridge: Harvard University Press.

Fontaine, Carole R. 1997. "The Abusive Bible: On the Use of Feminist Method in Pastoral Contexts." Pages 84–113 in *A Feminist Companion to Reading the Bible: Approaches, Methods, and Strategies*. Edited by Athalya Brenner and Carole R. Fontaine. Sheffield: Sheffield Academic.

Fox, Michael V. 1985. *The Song of Songs and the Ancient Egyptian Love Songs*. Madison: University of Wisconsin Press.

Fredericks, Daniel C., and Daniel J. Estes. 2010. *Ecclesiastes and The Song of Songs*. AOTC 16. Downers Grove, IL: InterVarsity Press.

Gadamer, Hans-Georg. 2004. *Truth and Method*. Translated by Joel Weinsheimer and Donald G. Marshall. 2nd rev. ed. New York: Continuum.

Garrett, Duane, and Paul R. House. 2004. *Song of Songs/Lamentations*. Edited by Bruce M. Metzger, David A. Hubbard, and Glenn W. Barker. WBC 23B. Nashville: Nelson.

Goulder, Michael D. 1986. *The Song of Fourteen Songs*. JSOTSup 36. Sheffield: JSOT Press.

Havea, Jione. 2013. "From Reconciliation to Adoption: A Talanoa from Oceania." Pages 294–300 in *Mission as Ministry of Reconciliation*.

Edited by Robert Schreiter and Knud Jørgensen. RECS 16. Oxford: Regnum.

Lefale, Penehuro Fatu. 2010. "*Ua 'afa le Aso* Stormy Weather Today: Traditional Ecological Knowledge of Weather and Culture, The Samoa Experience." *ClimC* 100.2: 317–35.

Longman, Tremper, III. 2001. *Song of Songs*. NICOT 26. Grand Rapids: Eerdmans.

Munro, Jill M. 1995. *Spikenard and Saffron: The Imagery of the Song of Songs*. JSOTSup 203. Sheffield: Sheffield Academic.

Patmore, Hector. 2006. "'The Plain and Literal Sense': On Contemporary Assumptions about the Song of Songs." *VT* 56.2:239–50.

Schüssler Fiorenza, Elisabeth. 1995. *Bread Not Stone: The Challenge of Feminist Biblical Interpretation: With a New Afterword*. 10th anniversary ed. Boston: Beacon.

Ting-Toomey, Stella. 1999. *Communicating Across Cultures*. New York: Guilford.

Vaai, Upolu Luma. 2006. "*Fa'aaloalo*: A Theological Reinterpretation of the Doctrine of the Trinity from a Samoan Perspective." PhD diss., Griffith University.

Moses, Both Hebrew and Egyptian:
A Samoan *Palagi* Reading of Exodus 2–3

Martin Wilson Mariota

This chapter offers a Samoan *Palagi* (lit. "sky bursters")[1] reading of Exod 2–3, a reading that negotiates the pains and joys, challenges and opportunities, of being both indigenous (Samoan) and foreign (palagi). This reading speaks for myself and for other Samoan Palagi (i.e., overseas-born Samoan) readers, as well as other readers who are subject to multiple discourses and who are positioned in between those discourses. Negotiation of meaning takes place at the in-between spaces where the boundaries are pushed to create new meaning. I argue that the in-between spaces (*vā*, in Samoan) are not places of marginalization or confusion but of empowerment. Reading Exod 2–3 with the Samoan Palagi lens highlights how Moses, like a Samoan Palagi character, pushes the boundaries of the Hebrew, Midian, and Egyptian discourses to renegotiate a new meaning and empower him to become a new type of leader for the exodus community. The empowerment factor is based on Moses's polycultural capital which gives him the ability to maneuver strategically back and forth between different discourses to renegotiate new meaning. This reading is drawn from my experience as a Samoan Palagi reader, which I explain below, and it may not be evident to readers who do not have polycultural awareness (even though no one, whether at home or in diaspora, reads in a monoculture). Notwithstanding, this essay comes as an invitation that we read for the polycultural constitution of Exod 2–3.

A Samoan Palagi reading of Exod 2–3, based upon a polycultural constitution, serves another important function—to inform contem-

---

1. *Palagi* used to be in reference to white Europeans (who first arrived on ships with masts that were seen to "burst the sky") but nowadays also refers to natives who behave as if they are white Europeans (see discussion of *fia palagi* below).

porary issues faced by second-generation Samoan Christians and their struggle to find a place in the Samoan church in Aotearoa New Zealand. The Samoan Palagi reading provides a critical service since most Samoans look to the Bible for direction and inspiration in their search for identity as Christians in both Samoan and palagi (European, Western; the Māori word for which is *pākeha*) discourses. This essay, therefore, provides a basis for a responsible use of the Bible for ethnic Samoan Christians in Aotearoa New Zealand.

Growing up Samoan Palagi

My experience of the Samoan church life in New Zealand was filled with confusion. In my younger years, I could not speak the Samoan language and did not have a good understanding of the (traditional) Samoan culture. As a result, I could not fully engage with Sunday worship. My lack of understanding and my youth meant that I had no voice in the church, apart from the voice I used to recite Bible memory verses and sing hymns that I never understood. Some may consider my position as one that was seen but not heard. I felt more engaged with my English-speaking friends who were mainly of European and Māori descent.

This limited participation in the church was in no way an indication that I did not have a heart for the church in which I was raised or the Samoan culture with which it was fused. I often shared with other Aotearoa New Zealand-born Samoans in the Congregational Christian Church of Samoa (CCCS) that there is a need to bridge the gap between the elders (who are traditionalist in their minds and practices) and the youth (who are more palagi than Samoan). The proposed Samoan Palagi reading exercise is a step toward bridging the generational and cultural gap.

After graduating from university, working as a tax auditor for the Inland Revenue Department, and serving in a mainstream English-speaking Pentecostal church for three years, I was faced with a decision that would change my life and transform my perception of my position. With strong convincing from my parents, I decided to go to Malua Theological College in Samoa to follow the path towards becoming a CCCS church minister. After completing my four years of theological training in Samoa, I was called to lead the same church in which I was raised. The decision to lead my home church was made after the sudden passing of our church minister, Rev. Saniva Ngshiu. I had come full circle to end up on the other side, leading the church in which, formerly, I was only seen and not heard.

As a result, my experience in Aotearoa New Zealand and Samoa allows me to experience two worlds: the world of the palagi discourse, as reflected through my birthplace and upbringing in Aotearoa New Zealand; as well as the world of the Samoan discourse, as reflected through my ethnicity and theological training in Samoa. As an ethnic minority in Aotearoa New Zealand, I was able to mimic the New Zealand lifestyle and values and progress through the palagi education system. Through my theological training in Samoa, I have been enriched with a renewed understanding of Samoan discourse, a voice to speak in *fono* (meetings), and credibility with the elders. I have experienced firsthand the fluidity of being in between Samoan and palagi discourses and the empowerment received through building my capability in both discourses. This is the basis for my position as a Samoan Palagi and my interest in postcolonial studies, as they relate to my own situation of moving between discourses.

Two experiences awaken my own polycultural awareness: my experience of a church that sought to "grow" Samoa in Aotearoa New Zealand, and my experience of Samoa through the lenses of a theological institution. I became aware of my polycultural capital because I moved to Samoa and then back to Aotearoa New Zealand. Other Samoans who have made similar (re)migration journeys are also aware of their polycultural capital, and we share our polycultural awakening with overseas-born Samoans who have not made the journey. For us, it is easy to imagine that someone like Moses—an Egypt-born Hebrew who migrated to Midian, then remigrated to Egypt—could have polycultural awareness. The text does not confirm if Moses was ever aware of his polycultural capital, but the ease with which the text describes his cross-border movements suggests that there was no anxiety about his being formed in, and thus exhibiting, Egyptian, Hebrew, and Midianite cultures. Which capital belonged to which culture is difficult to determine. The point of my reflection here is to problematize the naïve assumption that Moses was only Hebrew, only Egyptian, or only Midianite. Rather, Moses was a mixture of several cultures. He would have been as much a palagi (in Egypt, in Midian, and among Hebrews) as we overseas-born Samoans are (in Samoa and in diaspora).

Samoan Palagi Reading

The Samoan Palagi reading methodology highlights elements in the narrative that push the boundaries of structures that are deemed to be stable. This reading reveals how meaning is constantly renegotiated through the characters that build their polycultural capital and therefore have the ability to maneuver strategically back and forth between different discourses. Building polycultural capital is based on how characters engage with the Other. The Samoan Palagi reading approach to the Bible uses three categories to analyze the text: *fa'asinomaga*, palangi, and polycultural capital.

Fa'asinomaga

One of the concepts of identity for Samoans is expressed as fa'asinomaga. This word is made up of two words, *fa'asino* and *maga*. The first word, fa'asino, is a verb meaning "to point" or "to direct" in regard to providing direction towards a specific path or destination. The word can also be used to describe the judging of others in a negative sense, such as *fa'asinosino lima*, which means "pointing the finger." The second part of the word, maga, refers to a position. Maga refers to the point where a road splits into two or more different roads. Maga also applies to the instrument used in Samoa to collect breadfruit, which is called a *lou* (see essay by Kolia in this collection). This is a long pole, long enough to reach fruits at high and hard to reach places, the top part of which is called a maga—it is v-shaped, similar to the shape of a road that has been split in two.

In the Samoan discourse, every member of an *aiga* (extended family) is bound to the *suafa matai* (chiefly title) and the *fanua* (land) (Macpherson 1999, 73). These are the first paths that direct a Samoan's identity construction. The term fa'asinomaga is linked to key components of one's ancestral and societal links in the Samoan discourse. A Samoan fa'asinomaga is a way to identify a person through her or his connection to the fanua and suafa matai.

A Samoan, therefore, stands at the maga (junction) of time and space connecting the past to the present and the future and is fa'asino (directed) to the different *auala* (paths, roads) that make up her or his identity construction. One path points to the fanua (land), and the other points to the suafa matai (chiefly title) of the aiga. These two are the foundational paths that ensure Samoans are genetically connected and geographically located. The suafa matai links each Samoan with a genealogy that traces the ancestors who connect the aiga of a *nu'u* (village) to the fanua.

The suafa matai of each aiga and nu'u is acknowledged through formal salutations called *fa'alupega*. These salutations are used to address representatives of a nu'u or aiga at formal gatherings. This poetic greeting incorporates the major suafa matai from a particular nu'u, in order of rank. The intention behind using fa'alupega is to acknowledge formally the history and political structure that make up the unique identity of a nu'u.

These two paths are not the only auala that contribute to the Samoan identity construction. Instead, identity is developed from the many auala that one takes and eventually fa'asino to one's place in the aiga, nu'u, *lotu* (church), and wider *sosaiete* (society). Therefore, the maga is the "third space" where one stands in the junction of multiple auala that fa'asino to the different discourses.

The following questions guide the reading of the biblical narrative through the fa'asinomaga lens: Who determines the links to fanua and suafa matai? How does the dominant discourse fa'asino the auala that develop identity and place in society? Who does this fa'asino benefit? Are there any alternative fa'asino? Does fa'asinomaga exclude those who have never been to the fanua (like Samoans born in Aotearoa New Zealand or in the Pasifika diaspora) or who are unaware of the suafa matai that links them to the fanua?

Palagi

The term palagi has many nuances, and its application is flexible. Palagi or *papalagi* can be literally translated as "sky-bursters," and it had a divine connotation among the twentieth-century writers. Bear in mind that palagi came with Eurocentric overtones and that the Polynesian history was dictated and developed by European romanticism. There is, nonetheless, no conclusive evidence that the Polynesians considered the first European visitors to be divine beings. A reason for this misconception of self-bestowed divinity is due to the misinterpretation of the *lagi* element of *pa-lagi*—which could also be translated as "horizon," "cloud," or "sky"—as if it only means "heaven." Serge Tcherkēzoff (1999, 417–19), on the other hand, suggests that lagi refers to "sky" rather than "heaven" since the Polynesians did not believe that the sky was the place where the gods dwelt. The idea of the gods dwelling in the sky appears to be a Christian extension of the original meaning of *lagi*.

The misinterpretation of lagi to mean heaven seems to have contributed to the colonial attitudes of the European settlers and their self-indulgent belief of superiority and self-validated divinity. The meaning of palagi in this colonial context carries connotations of superiority and dominance in the eyes of the colonizer. Palagi carries connotations of Eurocentric dominance as well as references to a divine state of being. Palagi has become a term which Samoan discourse has categorized as *otherness* for its symbolism of independence and self-gain, which do not coincide with the values and communal living of the Samoans. The application of palagi not only refers to those who are physically and ethnically of European descent, but it also refers to a state of being, which includes those who are not European by descent but conduct themselves or carry traits of the "white man" (the so-called *fia palagi*).

The palagi concept gained its meaning from a Samoan perspective of otherness in the context of Samoan discourse, but its modern use is not limited to those of European ancestry. The phrase *fia palagi* (*fia* is an adjective meaning "wanting to be like" or "trying to be like") applies to ethnic Samoans who favor the "white man's" lifestyle or culture instead of traditional Polynesian modes of speech, dress, housing, and interpersonal relations. Ethnic Samoans seen and charged as fia palagi find the designation derogatory or a form of mockery (Tiatia 1998, 51). Melani Anae explains how the word palagi is used to refer to Samoans who were born and raised in Aotearoa New Zealand. In her studies, palagi, or otherness, is defined by birthplace and socialization experiences rather than physical attributes and ethnicity (Anae 1998, 355). This includes New Zealand-born Samoans who speak the Samoan language with a palagi accent. However, being called palagi is not a denial of Samoanness. Anae continues to explain that palagi was a term used to refer to anyone, including Samoans, who does things differently with respect to Samoan culture and traditions and to those who do not help or participate in the *faaSamoa* (the Samoan way of life). Being classified as palagi in the Samoan discourse expresses an attitude of indifference more than one of mockery (Anae 1998, 355).

This two-world ideology, where New Zealand-born Samoans are imperfect hybrids of the palagi and Samoan discourses, is prevalent in New Zealand society today. As imperfect hybrids, many New Zealand-born Samoans feel inadequate in both worlds and, to an extent, marginalized because of their limited experiences of the Samoan discourse (faaSamoa) as well as their being ethnic minorities in New Zealand (Anae 1998, 254). The continued interactions of Samoan discourse and palagi discourse have pushed the boundaries of both discourses, making what is palagi or other unclear. The possibility, therefore, exists for the second-generation Samoans to assert their Samoanness but at the same time be assigned by other Samoans as palagi based on their physical appearance or lack of participation and experience in the Samoan discourse. This blurred nature of the palagi concept describes characters that stand at the maga and strategically use their polycultural capital to push the boundaries of the discourses to which they are subjected.

The following questions guide the reading through the palagi lens: Who are the palagi in the narrative? How do they assert themselves? How are they assigned or categorized by others?

Polycultural Capital

The polycultural capital lens takes a strength-based approach to the maga position by focusing on the ability to navigate back and forth from different discourses (Mila-Schaaf 2010, 5). This lens traces the character development in the text and highlights the character's fa'asinomaga or the many auala that fa'asino the different discourses to which a character is subjected. Polycultural capital is the means or the ability of a character that stands at the maga to navigate strategically through several auala that fa'asino to different discourses. This ability renegotiates their fa'asinomaga and their place in the aiga, nu'u, lotu, sosaiete, and fanua.

Polycultural capital is associated with the ability to make contextually responsive and strategic cultural choices and identifications. The wider the variety of resources, knowledge gained as well as the experiences with the Other, the more auala become available. By emphasizing the many auala available through the polycultural capital that a character in the narrative builds, the position between discourses can be interpreted as one of empowerment rather than one of confusion and marginalization.

Fa'asinomaga focuses on different auala that fa'asino to the different discourses that make up a character's identity and place in society. Polycultural capital allows characters to open up new auala that fa'asino to new discourses. Polycultural capital equips the character with the ability to navigate strategically back and forth through these auala in a fluid movement to renegotiate a character's fa'asinomaga.

The following questions guide reading with the polycultural capital lens: Whose character development does the narrative privilege? What are the different discourses to which each auala is fa'asino for this character? What polycultural capital is gained through this character's development in the narrative? How does this character use her or his polycultural capital to navigate strategically through the different auala? How does this strategic movement renegotiate the character's fa'asinomaga?

Samoan Palagi Reading of Exodus 2–3

The Exod 2–3 narrative focuses on the character development of Moses, who stands at the maga. Throughout his journey, Moses's passion for the oppressed fa'asino him to several auala that develop his palagi character. Moses uses his polycultural capital strategically to push the boundaries of Hebrew and Egyptian discourses and renegotiate new meaning. The Hebrews are redefined from slaves to a community linked to blessings and promises, whereas the Egyptians are redefined from being the oppressors to becoming the oppressed.

Different Shades of Moses

At different points in the exodus story, other characters perceive Moses as an Egyptian rather than a Hebrew (Exod 2:19). Even when Moses asserts himself as a Hebrew, the Hebrews do not fully accept him. In mentioning his Egyptian connections and appearance early in his life, as well as mentioning his uncircumcised son and Midianite wife (see essay by Foi'akau in this collection), the narrative hints that the Hebrews may question his leadership due to his Egyptian ties. Questions regarding Moses's Hebrew commitments continue in the book of Numbers. For example, Aaron and Miriam question the exclusivity of Moses's role as divine mediator due to his marriage to a non-Hebrew woman. "And Miriam and Aaron spoke against Moses because of the Cushite woman whom he had married" (Num 12:1).[2] Moses's (first?) wife Zipporah is a Midianite, a group that the book of Numbers portrays as enemy of the Hebrews (Num 25:16–18; 31:1–24), although a genealogy in Genesis lists Midian as a descendant of Abraham (Gen 25:1, 4).

Moses lived for a hundred and twenty years, over three generations (Deut 34:7). He was a member of the Egyptian royal court, then he became a shepherd in Midian before he brought Israel out of Egypt, through Sinai, toward Canaan. We know little of his activities or education in the first period, but he would have been raised in the ways and wisdom of Egypt. Hints about his character could be deduced from three incidents: he killed an Egyptian in a fit of rage for abusing a Hebrew; he failed to stop one Hebrew slave from beating another; and he provided help to unknown

---

2. Unless otherwise noted, all biblical references draw from the NRSV.

Midianite sisters bullied by shepherds. All these incidents illustrate a common theme, a passionate concern for those who are abused and who suffer, which he would have learned from his Egyptian teachers and mentors. Exodus 2 indicates a commitment to the Hebrew people even though they rejected him as one of their own.

Fa'asinomaga: Birth of Moses (Exod 2:1–10)

The fa'asinomaga lens traces the different auala that point to the different discourses that make up Moses's identity. The foundational auala was established at birth. Moses was born in a time when the Hebrews were increasing in number and the Egyptian Pharaoh was worried that they might help Egypt's enemies. Moses was the son of Amram (Exod 6:20), a member of the Levite tribe, which descended from Jacob—so was Moses's mother, Jochebed. According to Gen 46:11, Amram's father Kehath immigrated to Egypt with seventy of Jacob's household, making Moses part of the second generation of Israelites born in Egypt. Moses's birth occurred at a time when an unnamed Egyptian Pharaoh had commanded that all male Hebrew children be killed by drowning in the river Nile. The narrative offers the first description of Moses's character by describing his physical appearance through his mother's eyes: "When she saw that he was a goodly child, she hid him for three months" (Exod 2:2, my translation). The narrator uses טוב (goodly) to describe Moses's physical features, which means that he was good, excellent of his kind, or pleasant to the eyes. This is the same adjective that describes the attractiveness of the fruit that lured the woman in the garden story (Gen 3:6). Something goodly is worth taking. It is also the adjective used to describe God's satisfaction with the creation (Gen 1). Something satisfying is worth keeping. Moses's goodly physical appearance, in my opinion, made it difficult for his mother to abandon him. Yet when she could no longer keep him hidden, she set him adrift on the Nile River in a small papyrus basket.

Moses's sister kept watch over the progress of the basket until it reached the place where Pharaoh's daughter was bathing with her handmaidens. Pharaoh's daughter spotted the baby in the basket and had her handmaiden fetch it for her. Moses's sister came forward and asked Pharaoh's daughter if she wanted a Hebrew woman to nurse the baby. Moses's mother was as a result employed as her child's nurse. He grew up and was brought to Pharaoh's daughter, and he became her son.

Moses's birth narrative weaves together the different auala that fa'asino the discourses that shape his character. He is a Hebrew, born in a land ruled by a dominant Egyptian discourse. Moses was born in the maga of the Hebrew (colonized) and Egyptian (imperial) discourses, a son of slaves and adopted son of Egyptian nobility. He is nursed by a slave mother and raised by a princess stepmother. The initial auala are fa'asino toward two extreme discourses as Moses begins his journey as an Egypt-born Hebrew. The narrative introduces two auala that fa'asino to the two discourses that make up Moses's identity. The first auala fa'asino to the Hebrew discourse through his birth mother. This is a discourse of oppression and slavery. The second auala fa'asino to the Egyptian discourse, which is the dominant imperial discourse.

Palagi: Moses the Hero, Murderer, and Fugitive (Exod 2:11–15)

Moses's character development pushes the boundaries of the discourses to which he is subject. He is the unconventional hero who becomes subject to several discourses. Moses is Hebrew but not Hebrew, Egyptian but not Egyptian, Midianite but not Midianite. He is exalted as the lawgiver and liberator of Israel, but the key to his success is his actions towards the Other. Liberation requires defiance on behalf of the oppressed and efforts to unify them. Other elements are essential too, such as a credible political purpose, a coherent strategy, and a legitimate status. Moses is a work in progress. His heroic acts of liberation begin in Egypt, where he killed an Egyptian slave driver for beating a Hebrew slave. The narrator states twice that the Hebrew slaves were from among Moses's people:

> One day, after Moses had grown up, he went out to where his own brothers were and watched them at their hard labor. He saw an Egyptian beating a Hebrew, one of his own brothers. (Exod 2:11, my translation)

The word אח (brother) can refer to a brother from the same parents (mother and father), to a brother with one common parent (father or mother)—as in the case of Joseph and his brothers (Exod 1:6)—and to a relative (in the extended family) or someone from the same community (like "bro" and "uso" for Samoans). Among Samoans, the latter are considered as if they are blood relations. The use of אח in the case of Moses and the Hebrew slaves conveys a family connection, a connection that makes sense of Moses's actions in Exod 2:12. Despite his heroic acts,

Moses does not gain any respect from his fellow Hebrews (Exod 2:14), who were brothers in the extended family sense. Since Moses buried the Egyptian secretly (2:12) and became afraid when he realized that others had discovered his act (2:14), the killing of the Egyptian stands as a private act rather than a public statement of his loyalties and commitments. He is committed to the Hebrews (qua Other). But he is also vulnerable to the Hebrews. The reader may assume that Moses would have continued living as an Egyptian if his act had not been discovered. Here we see the development of Moses's palagi character. He was born a Hebrew, raised as an Egyptian, showed solidarity for a Hebrew, and is afraid of being exposed by Hebrews. This scene is the first part in the narrative where an insight is given as to how the Other views Moses. This is important in Moses's identity construction, as it provides the relational powers that assign and assert, as well as expose and undermine, his identity. Through the murder of the Egyptian, the narrative displays Moses's clumsy assertion of his Hebrewness and his unartful expression of solidarity for who he thinks are his people.

Moses's concern for his Hebrew brothers is too undisciplined, and as yet he does not display an ability to lead his people. His attempt to help them is misunderstood. He does not have at that point sufficient polycultural capital and capability to act strategically on behalf of or to negotiate effectively with the Hebrews to gain credibility and their trust. Substantial power in determining meaning lies in the hands of the Others (Hebrews) who assign Moses as a murderer rather than a savior. He is a murderer in the eyes of the Hebrews and becomes a fugitive in the eyes of the Egyptians. Moses is pushed to the periphery to seek refuge in Midian.

Polycultural Capital

The development of Moses's character is evident through the polycultural capital that he acquires throughout his journey. The multiple cultural exposures are the experiences that build his polycultural capital in all discourses, allowing him to navigate strategically through the auala that fa'asino to the discourses of the colonizer and the colonized. Moses's passion for justice for the Other sets the trend for a new kind of leader for God's people. This is the key element that made Moses effective in God's liberation plan.

Moses's polycultural capital includes his early life as a prince, which provided him with knowledge of and access to the Egyptian authorities.

His later identity as a Midian shepherd made Israel more responsive. But the most pertinent polycultural capital is Moses's drive for transformation and his concern and passion for justice on behalf of the oppressed. Apart from these assets that Moses acquired during his journey, he is also equipped with polycultural capital and capability for his mission. God equips Moses with a Hebrew fa'alupega: his brother Aaron comes as a communication support agent to help promote Moses and build his credibility, to perform miracles which supersede the Egyptian magicians, and to cast plagues that oppress the Egyptian oppressor.

Moses's character development equips him with the necessary polycultural capital to push the boundaries of the Hebrew discourse (of slavery and oppression under the Egyptian rule) and negotiate an alternative discourse based on hope and promises. The main ingredient for Moses's transformation is his passion and concern for the Other (who is actually one of his own). This passion sent Moses on a journey that allows him to develop his palagi character and polycultural capital, which he eventually uses to maneuver in between different discourses to push boundaries and negotiate new meaning.

Conclusion

The application of the three categories of the Samoan Palagi reading lens brings out important themes that can inform the struggles of second-generation Samoan Christians born and raised in Aotearoa New Zealand and their struggle to assert themselves as Samoan Palagi Christians. The purpose of this exercise is not to encourage a replacement of the dominant discourses. Instead, the reading provides a model of empowerment whereby biblical characters who are positioned at the maga are championed through their ability to move back and forth between different discourses.

The Samoan Palagi reading of Exod 2–3 provides insights in addressing the current issues that face the Samoan church with its second- and third-generation members. There is value in taking a strength-based approach on the position of those who stand at the maga with several auala that fa'asino to different discourses. The initial step in the journey of identity in the Samoan church is to establish their fa'asinomaga in God as the basis for the promises and blessings of salvation. A second value occurs in having a renewed perspective of the palagi character as a dynamic position of fluid movement rather than a derogatory term that causes exclusiveness. A third benefit comes from acknowledging the polycultural capital that has already been acquired through the identity journey and using it strategically to navigate back and forth from different discourses.

The Samoan Palagi reading exercise enables boundaries to be pushed and meaning to be negotiated to ensure the Samoan church is flexible to cater to diverse members. The aim is to encourage Samoan Palagi readers to reconsider their position as second-generation Samoan Christians from a strength-based point of view. The Bible offers many narratives (e.g., Exod 2–3) that can empower these readers and other second- or third-generation ethnic groups who feel lost and/or marginalized in a foreign land.

This reading exercise, however, has limits. For one thing, I sidelined the theological capitals in and of Exod 2–3, which are preferred in traditional Samoan and Palagi churches. Second, I have ignored differences between Moses as Palagi and young Samoan Palagi in Samoa and abroad. Whereas Moses is favored in the biblical narrative, Aotearoa New Zealand-born Samoans, and other Polynesians, are the usual suspects under social and civil surveillance. Moses has theological and ecclesial capitals in Samoan and Palagi circles, whereas the majority of young Samoans are still watched but not heard. This Samoan Palagi reading of Exod 2–3 is thus an invitation, that through the Palagi Moses, the many Samoan Palangi in Samoa and in diaspora might also be seen, heard, and appreciated.

Works Cited

Anae, Melani. 1998. "Fofo-i-vao-'ese: The Identity Journeys of NZ-Born Samoans." PhD diss., University of Auckland.

Macpherson, Cluny. 1999. "Changing Contours of Kinship: The Impacts of Social and Economic Development on Kinship Organization in the South Pacific." *PS* 22.2:71–95.

Mila-Schaaf, Karlo. 2010. "Polycultural Capital and the Pasifika Second Generation: Negotiating Identity in Diasporic Spaces." PhD diss., Massey University Albany.

Tcherkēzoff, Serge. 1999. "Who Said the Seventeenth–Eighteenth Centuries Papālagi/'Europeans' Were 'Sky-Bursters'? A Eurocentric Projection onto Polynesia." *JPolyS* 108.4:417–25.

Tiatia, Jemaima. 1998. *Caught Between Cultures: A New Zealand-Born Pacific Island Perspective*. Auckland: Christian Research Association.

Sipora (Zipporah), Both Native and Foreigner: A *Marama iTaukei* Reading of Exodus 4:24–26

Inise Vakabua Foi'akau

I have wrestled for some time with the need to construct a *marama iTaukei*[1] (indigenous Fijian wo-man) reading, contemplating to use alternative lenses to reread what has been traditionally offered in my contexts (at once Fijian, Fiji-Australian, and Australian). This chapter is a step toward meeting that need, with a marama iTaukei reading of Exod 4:24–26. This is an uncommon text in the exodus narrative, for it shifts the focus to a new character—the unknown, unfamiliar, foreign, and silent wife of Moses, Sipora (Zipporah). It is a short text that invites readers to leave the dominating patriarch Moses to the side and for a while leave his character ambiguous (cf. Longman 2009, 104). The focus of this text, and of this essay, is on Sipora. In this reading, it is significant that Sipora is named in the midst of other references that leave her unnamed. I have chosen to use

---

1. A *marama* is a wo-man of eloquence, grace, maturity, respect, and dignity. Marama is feminine of *turaga* (man). Marama is more than a gender construct; it encompasses respect, admiration, esteem, wisdom, and equality. Marama can be used interchangeably with *yalewa* (young woman), but it is disrespectful to use yalewa to someone of status and/or maturity. *Vaka-yalewa* is a connotation for weakly, or without energy (Capell 1991, 136). Marama can be used across other ethnicities, such as *marama ni India* (Indian wo-man) or *marama ni Samoa* (Samoan wo-man). The phrase *marama iTaukei* refers to an indigenous Fijian wo-man of mature stature, regal and of social standing. The term *taukei* is an adjective meaning "the owner of," so *taukei ni vale* means owner of the house. The Fiji military-led government gazetted on June 30, 2010 that "The new law effectively replaces the word 'Fijian' or 'indigenous' or 'indigenous Fijian' with the word '*iTaukei*' with all written laws, and all official documentation when referring to the original and native settlers of Fiji" (https://en.wikipedia.org/wiki/Fijians; see also https://tinyurl.com/y7xa5bld).

her Fijianized name in honor of the many *yalewa bokala*[2] (wo-man commoner) and *yalewa tani* (foreign wo-man) who are nameless in *iTaukei* (indigenous Fijian) circles. In this way, Sipora becomes a naming of the nameless and a voicing of the voiceless.

Marama iTaukei

The marama iTaukei (indigenous Fijian wo-man) in her land could alienate those at the fringes, who are yalewa bokala (wo-man commoner), referring to any wo-man in a foreign land or in a village outside her traditional boundaries. Like Sipora, I find myself toggling between the two because I am both a marama iTaukei—a *kawa* (descendant) *I Nasagwalevu* of the *Yavusa* (tribal unit) *Tio*, in the chiefly village of Nailaga in Ba[3]—as well as yalewa bokala in my country of adoption (Australia). I write from the land of the Burramattagal people of the Darug nation. In this land, I am of no standing, I am a yalewa bokala. My indigenous heritage is known and understood when I am with my people in Fiji, but where I now live and write, I am yalewa bokala. I am a visitor from across the ocean. iTaukei protocol expects me to sit, head bowed and hands clasped, and to be silent.

My concern for the yalewa bokala is in response to questions raised that say marama iTaukei do not fully represent all indigenous Fijian wo-men. The dynamics within indigenous Fijian wo-men are complex, and those on the fringes of iTaukei community may not respond to marama iTaukei but to yalewa bokala. Though the latter is considered offensive and carries a negative historical connotation, those that regard themselves to be of lesser status could relate to the term. A metaphorical term, yalewa bokala is a slur in modern dialect—a wo-man of low social status, or whose patriarchal status is unknown within the inner circles.

---

2. *Bokala* is a prisoner(s) of war (in Rewa dialect); the bokala were brought to the chiefly village of Lomanikoro, strung on the poles in the village greens for display. That place is called *Naililili* ("to be strung"), and they later end up in the *lovo* (earthen oven) for the chief(s) and those in ranks who have traditional entitlements to the feast. In modern times, bokala is used in a slanderous manner to refer to people of lesser status, or commoners. Bokala can be used interchangeably with *kaisi*—a term for outcast, or stateless people.

3. Ba is one of the provinces in Fiji. As an iTaukei, and to be member of a landowning family or tribal unit, one registers in the *Vola ni Kawa Bula* (VKB), the Native Land Register.

Yalewa bokala can be uttered in the same breath as yalewa tani, a foreign wo-man. While the term yalewa tani can refer to a wo-man from a different ethnic background, in this context I look primarily at indigenous Fijian wo-man married or affiliated to the specific iTaukei community. In Unaisi Nabobo-Baba's study of her mother's village, a certain customary *meke* (traditional dance) is only performed by wo-men of Nadaro. Outsiders/foreigners or yalewa tani, including indigenous wo-men married into the village, cannot perform the meke unless granted by the *daunivucu* (dance teacher) (Baba et al. 2013, 109). In this village, a yalewa tani cannot dance the village dance. To a culture whose people's identity is traced through patrilineal lineage, an unknown lineage (a yalewa tani) is derogative to the iTaukei.

To acknowledge the layers of complexity and the differing dynamics within the iTaukei context, I also name and call attention to the yalewa bokala and yalewa tani. They are the ones expected to be silent and invisible in an iTaukei community. This chapter does not attempt to unify their voices but to hear and acknowledge them. This chapter is a building block for later development of marama reading to be inclusive of the many ethnic groups in Fiji, which is beyond the scope of this current work. In the next section, I reflect on how the marama iTaukei could use *solesolevaki* (communal gathering) to unsilence Sipora. In terms of methodology, discussed further in the following section, I propose a framework of solesolevaki, the gathering of indigenous people, with postcolonial twists in response to brief prompts in Musa W. Dube's (2000) *Postcolonial Feminist Interpretation of the Bible*. The remainder of the chapter offers a marama iTaukei reading of Sipora.

Though marama iTaukei, yalewa bokala, and yalewa tani are all subjected to patriarchal and (neo)colonial pressures, the marama iTaukei is a privileged subject, similar to the white Western middle-class wo-men who are privileged colonial subjects (Dube 2000, 112). A marama iTaukei's patrilineal line and her entitlement to her father's land, as well as her marital status and political, professional, and educational background, to name a few, privilege her and influence her perspectives. The yalewa bokala remains in the other spectrum, in society's fringes and in the kitchen *bure* (hut), and does not have the same experience and benefit as the marama iTaukei. The yalewa bokala experiences the doubly-colonized pressures encountered by Third World wo-men (Dube 2000, 112). These different life experiences entitle each wo-man to her own readings. The marama iTaukei reading offered in this chapter brings forward and lifts up Sipora from the shadows of the narrativized imperial and patriarchal worlds of the narrative in which she exists so that her silenced voice may be heard through the voices of the marama iTaukei. For unless we speak, Sipora in the iTaukei context remains in the literary shadows of her husband and her oppressors.

Toward Rereading

How might the marama iTaukei use solesolevaki to unsilence Sipora? Could the usually silent marama iTaukei, yalewa bokala, and yalewa tani become voices that tell Sipora's story? These questions invite one to look at the authority of the Bible in Fijian communities (both in Fiji and overseas).

The Bible has found its way into the social and administrative structures of the iTaukei society. The ceding of Fiji to Great Britain established a wave of colonization and brought big changes to the governance of the *vanua* (land, country, people).[4] The title of the book *A Shaking of the Land* (Thornley 2005) depicts the impact that this change made, as the governance of the vanua of Fiji was shaken and shifted to British administration. In 1874, Fiji was administered by a British-styled and British-led legislative council. The country's motto and emblem was *Rerevaka na Kalou ka doka na Tui* ("Fear God and Honor the King/Queen"), illustrating the power of colonization in governing the land.

How may the iTaukei (man and wo-man) reread the Bible? Do we continue to read this book as it was first read to us by the missionaries? Has anything changed since the fleet of "the light" first came ashore? Is the authority within the Bible itself or those who first read it to us? Now that the Bible is an integral thread intertwining the three pillars of iTaukei society—vanua (land), *lotu* (religion), and *matanitu* (state) (Tuwere 2011, 28)—can we question its authority? Is not the absolute authority given to the Bible and its traditional readings problematic? Can a new offering to the marama iTaukei be acceptable to those who now hold the authority of the Bible in Fiji (who are located in mainline churches)?

---

4. Ilaitia S. Tuwere (2002, 33) explains the vanua in two contexts. Literally, vanua is land. Symbolically, it represents earthly turf, flora and fauna, rivers and mountains, fishing ground and more. The term can be used to refer to one's country, district, village, or people.

Getting people to open their Bibles is not the challenge, for this holy book has been translated into Fijian, is accessible, and has made its way into iTaukei life. The challenge, rather, is how Fijian people may read it differently. Do the marama iTaukei have the courage to read it differently? How might we include the views of those who are disregarded in society or who identify themselves as yalewa bokala? And how do I, and sisters in my situation, read, no longer as marama iTaukei but as yalewa bokala and yalewa tani in a foreign land?

Solesolevaki

Solesolevaki (communal gathering) is a way of life in a traditional iTaukei setting that brings people together. It is a form of reciprocity involving the exchange of collective labor and the promotion of social cohesion and good relations within the community. It is an effective way of bringing people together for a common cause. I propose solesolevaki as a model for dialogue and for reading Sipora's story with the eyes of a marama iTaukei, both in a traditional setting and in a capitalistic and Western-influenced space. This chapter proposes solesolevaki to invite and give space for indigenous wo-men to read Sipora. The iTaukei are communal people, and this act of communal gathering is not new. Solesolevaki has been a practice in Fiji for centuries. A framework for solesolevaki involves the following:

(1) The call for solesolevaki is usually done by the village crier or herald, openly inviting all who hear to respond to the gathering. The herald walks from one side of the village green to the other, inviting and instructing. Those that respond know their responsibility and commitment to the task at hand, and with heads together, laborious tasks can be achieved successfully. Sipora can be embraced in such a setting not only by using a traditional reading but also in inviting and encouraging participants to marama iTaukei reading, where the traditional and postcolonial are not exclusive of each other.

(2) Solesolevaki fosters dialogue, and the Oceania way of dialogue is *talanoa* (story, storytelling, conversation). Solesolevaki in this essay is twofold: it offers an actual gathering of wo-men to discuss the text (a gathering of people), and it symbolically brings together their readings (a gathering of insights). Engaging in talanoa will enable both objectives. While an academic research would demand an ethical engagement for participants, a vanua engagement for talanoa is different. iTaukei protocols take precedence and make the solesolevaki more effective. For the purpose of

the solesolevaki to hear the voices of marama iTaukei as well as of yalewa bokala, talanoa may remain informal yet purpose driven.[5]

The task of inviting wo-men to engage a decolonizing method within an academic framework will be challenging. When a task is too difficult and challenging, an old Fijian dirge is repeatedly chanted, illustrated by a canoe manually drawn to sea: the carriers continuously chant *bibi na senico mamada na waqa oqo ooo-ooo*. This is translated as, "a dandelion flower is heavier than this ship." At *ooo-ooo*, everyone collectively pulls the canoe. The chanters coordinate themselves with the pulling of the boat and the chanting until the canoe is afloat. Solesolevaki makes the task lighter, easier, and enjoyable, whether the task is pulling a newly built canoe out to sea for her maiden voyage or reading a biblical text differently in a new light.

(3) Solesolevaki requires an offering of Fijian oral artifacts. As people of oral history, oral artifacts are encouraged. As observed by Alan R. Tippett (1980, 21), iTaukei have a colorful selection of oral artifacts used by the early missionaries in mission and worship. These artifacts were not introduced by the early missionaries but borrowed from iTaukei and used effectively in churches. The artifacts include epic chants and hymns, *polotu* (chants), proverbs, storytelling, riddling, proverbial legal sayings, and dirges. Most marama iTaukei are familiar with and users of these artifacts. These artifacts can be leveraged as mediums for hermeneutical interpretations of biblical texts and to tell our stories alongside Sipora's story.

(4) Solesolevaki opens the space for intricacies and gifting, encouraging iTaukei wo-men to offer their gifts and oral artefacts for the purpose of enabling the task at hand. What this approach offers is new lenses to the same Bible that has been around for almost two centuries. In response to the call, wo-men bring what they can offer.

(5) For an effective solesolevaki, divides are broken, and space is made more neutral. A marama iTaukei can work alongside a yalewa bokala and a yalewa tani. Though tasks may still be different, it is important that customary class divides are relaxed. The yalewa bokala does not have to keep her head lowered but can sing and chant, laugh and rise

---

5. Unaisi Nabobo-Baba (2006, 27) uses talanoa as a research method. In indigenous research among Fijians, talanoa (rather than formal interviews) is used to gather the knowledge that the researcher seeks. Talanoa embodies Fijian protocol in the sharing of information.

from her lowered status. In this space, she is given the opportunity to talk and share her story.

(6) Solesolevaki can be playful. An iTaukei gathering attracts different dynamics of relationships. Dancing (*meke* as oral artifact) is a gesture expressed by individual dancers or is mutually performed by two or more people to relate to one another, express emotion, and tell a story. Dancing can be playful and teasing or equally graceful and elegant. Dancing allows movement beyond areas of comfort and familiarity, across and beyond boundaries. In a village green, dancers can move freely beyond their common boundary, and it is done with fun and lightheartedness.

There are advantages in solesolevaki for reading biblical texts. For the development of marama iTaukei reading, the following characteristics are significant: solesolevaki makes reading a communal event (in the place of the traditional, scholarly picture of the reader sitting in a library on her or his own), an opportunity to exhibit and celebrate cultural oral artifacts (talanoa and meke), and a boundary-crossing occasion (allowing wo-men of different statuses to cooperate. Solesolevaki in the iTaukei context is similar to the *kautaha* (village cooperation) mode of reading in Pacific hermeneutics (see Havea 2012).

Dube's Postcolonial Space

I propose solesolevaki in talanoa with Dube's (2000) postcolonial feminist approach. Dube confronts her readers with a popular anonymous short story orally narrated and passed down by word of mouth. The popular anecdote is: "the white men came with the Bible. The white men prayed, and after the prayer the white man had the land while the native people had the Bible." This anecdote opens the mind up to the issues of race, patriarchy, colonization, the role of Christianity, and the problematic interpretation of biblical texts (Dube 2000, 1). Dube sees the Bible as a tool that facilitated European imperialism, and those who adopted Christianity have struggled with the paradoxes of this book along with the legacies of betrayal exercised by those in power to control them (Dube 2000, 2). Dube inserts her wisdom into reading in a postcolonial space. Even though biblical texts have been used to oppress, this reality has prompted Dube to draw from her lived context and to raise the question on how to read (Chang 2014, 4, 14). Dube's postcolonial struggle invites several questions (Dube 2000, 15) that have become relevant for marama iTaukei reading:

1. What is the postcolonial condition, and who are its subjects?
2. How can postcolonial subjects read without perpetuating one as superior to another?
3. How should we read cultural texts that were instrumental to its establishment?
4. What are the impacts of these on land, power, and people?

Postcolonial hermeneutics connects the past with the present, the colonizers with the colonized. From a Botswana-African context, Dube (2000, 15) argues that postcolonial subjects describe both the former colonizer and the formerly colonized to what is termed today as First World and Two-Thirds Worlds, developed and underdeveloped. Dube explains that she follows in the footsteps of Homi Bhabha, for whom the challenge is not to dwell in the past but to seek transformation for liberation (15). In the footsteps of Dube, the key challenge for iTaukei wo-men involved in solesolevaki is to recognize colonial and patriarchal signposts through literary devices in the Bible and to use those as platforms to decolonize mindsets and finally to transform views about biblical texts and ignored characters for liberation.

I bring marama iTaukei, yalewa bokala, and yalewa tani together with an invitation to solesolevaki for the task of reading Sipora. The call itself indicates the complexity and challenging nature of this task, but most importantly participation. Solesolevaki is part of the iTaukei way of life. The gem of solesolevaki is the reciprocity of exchange of collective labor with social interaction, network, and offering. This gathering makes the task easier and achievable. It can be serious to enable the task and be playful with different iTaukei dynamics to make it enjoyable and social. Bringing solesolevaki together with Dube to the reading allows all to be heard, to share stories and experiences, and to adopt the awareness to recognize literary devises that have stood tall over the ages and oppressed many, especially wo-men. This is the gift Dube brings to solesolevaki: the eyes to see the devices that subjugate wo-men from biblical to modern times.

Reading Sipora

The biblical text for this solesolevaki is Exod 4:24–26 (Lako Yani 4:24–26), which is rendered in *Ai Vola Tabu* ("authorized" Fijian translation by the Bible Society of Fiji) as follows:

24. Ia ni sa tiko e dua na bure ena gaunisala, sa veitata kaya ko Jiova, ka segata me vakamatea
25. A sa taura e dua na vatu gata ko Sipora, ka drutia laivi na vusona na luvena, *ka biuta ki yavana*, ka kaya, Na watiqu ni vakadavedra ko iko
26. Sa qai biuti koya me lako ko koya; a sa kaya na yalewa, Na watiqu ni vakadavedra, ena vuku ni veicilivi

For the sake of non-Fijian readers, I add a back translation of the Fijian into English, and the KJV for comparison:

Back translation:
24. And there was a hut by the road, YHWH encountered and sought to kill
25. Sipora took a sharp stone, and shred the young shoot of her child, and placed it at his feet and said "You are my husband that sheds blood"
26. The person was let go, the woman said "My husband who sheds blood for circumcision"

KJV:[6]
24. And it came to pass by the way in the inn, that the LORD met him, and sought to kill him.
25. Then Zipporah took a sharp stone, and cut off the foreskin of her son, and cast it at his feet, and said, Surely a bloody husband art thou to me.
26. So he let him go: then she said, A bloody husband thou art, because of the circumcision.

Exodus 4:24–26 is a misfit in the exodus story; it is often tucked away and not read. The backdrop of the text is the narrative of the exodus. Moses kills an Egyptian and then escapes Pharaoh. Moses flees Egypt and seeks refuge in Midian for forty years. He takes Sipora, the daughter of Jethro the priest, as a wife (Exod 2:21). Moses names their first son Gershom, which means "I have become a resident foreigner in a foreign land" (Exod 2:22 NRSV). Sipora is not frequently read in the story, and her name resonates with few readers of the Bible. For many Fijian readers, she is only recognized if associated with her husband Moses or her father Jethro (or Reuel). She is a Midianite by origin; her Hebrew name צפורה (Zipporah)

---

6. The KJV and the Good News Bible are the most popular English translations among contemporary Fijian readers. I have chosen the KJV for this exercise because that was the translation available to the early translators of the Bible into Fijian.

means a tiny female bird.[7] This brief story quickly switches to YHWH in verse 24. Like the KJV, it is unclear in the Fijian translation whom YHWH sets out to kill. In verse 25, Sipora responds by performing the ritual of circumcision on her son. The Fijian translation does not use the terminology of circumcision but puts it euphemistically: she shredded or peeled off his "young shoot." She placed the peeled skin on someone's feet, but the Fijian translation does not clarify if it was Moses's or her son's feet. However, her speech at the end of verses 25–26 is directed to her husband. In this encounter, Sipora is the main character whilst the agencies of Moses and her son are unclear. Only the NIV translation names Moses in the text. The Fijian Bible, NJB, KJV, and JPS use masculine adjectives, thus confusing the character being addressed, whether he was Moses, his son Gershom, or maybe a servant/slave who went along with them. Moses and Gershom literally disappear into one another, given that the Hebrew text (in contrast to the Fijian translation and KJV) is ambiguous both about who was being circumcised and about whose feet was touched with the foreskin.

Naming Sipora

Exodus 4:24–26 is that rare occurrence when Sipora is named. Prior to that, when she was unmarried and among her sisters, she is referenced but unnamed (Exod 2:16–20). Her name is first mentioned in Exod 2:21 when she is presented by her father Jethro[8] to Moses for marriage. As a potential wife, she is named and singled out from her sisters. In Exod 2:22 she gives birth to Gershom. She appears to earn the privilege of being named in the text because she serves as a good wife and a mother. Similar to the yalewa bokala and yalewa tani, and being a woman, Sipora was probably not recognized in her own homeland. In Exod 4:20 she is again unnamed; she is only referred to as "his wife" when Moses makes his journey back to Egypt. Exodus 18:1–6 is the last mention of Sipora, when Jethro takes her and her two sons to meet Moses in the wilderness. Jethro speaks with Moses while Sipora and her children fade out and are not mentioned. Her sons are also muted and forgotten. In Num 12:1 there is a reference to a

---

7. In consequence to the event narrated in Exod 4:24–26, at a later time, she and her two sons, Gershom and Eliezer, were sent back to her own kinsfolk, the Midianites, with whom they sojourned until they rejoined Moses (Exod 18:2–6).

8. The father-in-law of Moses was "priest of Midian," and sometimes called Reuel (Exod 2:18), Jethro (Exod 3:1), and Hobab (Judg 4:11) (Kirsch 1998, 108).

Cushite woman as Moses's wife, but it is debatable whether the wo-man is Sipora or another wife of Moses.

The naming of Sipora is important in the iTaukei context. Like most cultures, *vakatokayaca* (naming ceremony) is significant and is celebrated in the iTaukei culture. Depending on seniority in family settings, it is usually the role of a marama iTaukei to name newborns in her family. In some parts of Fiji, names are borrowed not only from ancestral lines but also from events or important people. Some children, for instance, are named after cyclones, floods, anniversaries, achievements, or misfortunes. In this regard, names remind villagers of historical events. To be unnamed equates to irrelevance in society, like the yalewa bokala, or to be unknown (especially when father's name is not known), like the yalewa tani. Their names are hardly mentioned, and their stories are hardly told. One of the customs of iTaukei is the adoption of family names from male lineage during marriage. The marama iTaukei loses her identity (which was tied to her father) and assumes the name of her husband. She is also referred to as the "wife of" her husband or labeled by her husband's title in society. This naming convention runs through the three pillars of Fiji: in vanua as *radini vanua* (chief's wife), lotu as *radini talatala* (minister's wife), and in matanitu as *radini minister* (minister's wife). Traditionally, to be known on your own merit, by paving your own identity in a patriarchal society, is a challenge. Unwed wo-men, wo-men without sons, or childless wo-men face an even bigger challenge. Too often their self-worth in society is diminished.

Moving Boundaries

The Fijian idiom *butuka tu* ("standing on my land, my ground") speaks volumes and allows one's voice to be heard. Transiting into or through someone else's land, space, or traditional boundary diminishes one's authority and value, whereas the authority and value of the landowner become greater. Clans or families inherit communal roles, and each one's authority and value relate to one's roles. For people allotted the kitchen, their voices are authoritative in the kitchen; when they move to other roles, such as mixing ceremonial *kava*, their voices diminish. Boundaries determine one's role and status and which action or voice is accepted. Likewise, a child's laughter in the village grounds, or a youth speaking in a village meeting, is validated by her or his status in the village. Elders would ask *na luvei cei ya* ("Whose child is that?") and seek to identify the child's father (instead of the mother) in order to determine if the child has "ground" to speak in the gathering.

Several translations (Fijian, NIV, NJB, KJV, JPS) agree that Sipora, her husband, and her son(s) were travelling. What they do not agree about was the location of the event, as well as who was circumcised. The Fijian translation states that they are in an inn on the roadside (so KJV, NIV, and JPS); NJB does not refer to a lodge but states that they were on a journey. Travelling from Midian toward Egypt after several years, it is not clear if Moses still regards Egypt as home. Outside of Egypt, Moses is stateless. He is a bokala. Similarly, out of Midian, Sipora moves away from her status as marama iTaukei. Her status in her land diminishes. She too is moving from being a marama iTaukei to becoming a yalewa bokala—a wo-man of the fringe, of the border, of no social standing in the land where she is and the land to which she goes. At the point of transition (whether in an inn or on the roadside), and in the land of Egypt where she will end, Sipora is also a yalewa tani, a wo-man of no or unknown heritage. Interestingly, at the point where she transits from being iTaukei to becoming bokala and tani, the narrative names her. She is Sipora, and she responds to an act of YHWH. She is an agent on the move.

Covenanting with YHWH

At the border, at the stateless land, in transit from Midian on the way to Egypt, YHWH comes to kill either Moses or Gershom (Exod 4:24). Sipora responds by taking either a knife or a sharp stone and performs the ordinary ritual of circumcision, on either Moses or Gershom. The text is not clear. But the text is clear that she, Sipora, is active, and her actions are accepted by YHWH. Circumcision is strictly men's business in the iTaukei community. Wo-men prepare special mats and food, but the actual ritual is men's secret business. The involvement of Sipora in the rite of circumcision is taboo in an iTaukei context. Is Sipora acting out her role as a priestess, or is she just strong and adamant in nature? Is she like any iTaukei mother who, though maybe silent and usually invisible in society, stands strong and courageous to save her son, or husband, when in danger?

The text is playful as well, as suggested by the NIV in Exod 4:25b. Sipora cuts off the foreskin of possibly her son and casts the skin on either Moses or her son's feet. Euphemism is at play, as the Hebrew reference for his feet (*le-rag-lav*) can be translated as man's genitals. The text allows one to imagine Sipora taking the bloody foreskin and smearing it on Moses's genitals to indicate that the circumcision is done, or similarly on Gershon. The Hebrew text tones down and disguises Sipora's bloody actions on Moses, and when explored, the narrative sounds insulting to the patriarchal figure.

Actions aside, iTaukei language can be playful and use literary devices to relate an event, person, or place. Kinships, family dynamics and relationships can be complex, and certain words or topics cannot be discussed in an open conversation, depending on the relationships between two or more parties. Among siblings (brother and sister), clans, villages, and provinces, such dynamics occur. In everyday conversations, it is perceived as vulgar to directly describe genitalia and sexual activities (see essay by Kolia in this collection). These are taboo topics that cannot be directly and openly discussed; an allegorical term would be used to disguise the real subject of the conversation.

In this reading, Sipora serves as the heroine by circumcising her son (or was it her husband?) and smearing blood on her husband's feet/genitals (or was it her son?). Is this part of the ritual of covering YHWH's people with blood to protect them from destruction or merely a playful heroic act of Sipora on her husband? The end of the text leaves us with the image of a blood-smeared Sipora with a sharp stone in her hand, proclaiming to YHWH that the blood of circumcision has been shed. The initiation of either Moses or Gershom is complete. They are now part of YHWH's covenant. Sipora, the yalewa bokala/tani, officiates the covenanting of the blood. She is named; she (is) bloodied; then she is silenced.

The Offering

Models for postcolonial feminist reading within Oceania are a challenge to find. An even greater challenge is to find one from Fiji. This marama iTaukei (incorporating yalewa bokala and yalewa tani) reading is offered with hope that it marks a path for others to come together in the weaving of marama hermeneutics. Solesolevaki is not an ideology. For centuries, it has been a practice in the iTaukei communities and across the oceans. It is practiced in Fiji today as well as beyond its shores. The oral culture surrounding these communities, while making solesolevaki workable, lacks documentation. This chapter documents solesolevaki as a model to unweave layers of imperialistic, colonial, and patriarchal biblical texts, in this case using a text from Exodus.

This reading makes the unknown Sipora known, the invisible Sipora visible, and the silent Sipora heard. In doing so, I encourage marama and yalewa readers of Fiji and of Oceania to recognize signposts of imperial, colonial, and patriarchal texts, wrestle with them, engage in solesolevaki, read texts anew, and with the richness of oral artifacts, have their voices heard.

Works Cited

Baba, Tupeni L., Emita L. Boladuadua, Tevita Ba, Wasevina V. Vatuloka, and Unaisi Nabobo-Baba. 2013. *Na vuku ni Vanua, Wisdom of the Land: Aspects of Fijian Knowledge, Culture, and History*. Suva: Native Academy Publishers, IISF.

Capell, A. 1991. *The Fijian Dictionary*. Suva: Government Printer.

Chang, Hee Won. 2014. "Just An/other Reading: Numbers 22:1–35." Bachelor of Theology Hon. thesis, Charles Sturt University.

Dube, Musa W. 2000. *Postcolonial Feminist Interpretation of the Bible*. St. Louis: Chalice.

Havea, Jione. 2012. "*Kautaha* in Island Hermeneutics, Governance, and Leadership." *PJT* 47:3–13.

Kirsch, Jonathan. 1998. *Moses: A Life*. New York: Ballantine.

Longman, Tremper, III. 2009. *How to Read Exodus*. Downers Grove: InterVarsity Press.

Nabobo-Baba, Unaisi. 2006. *Knowing Learning: An Indigenous Fijian Approach*. Suva: Institute of Pacific Studies, USP Press.

Thornley, Andrew. 2005. *A Shaking of the Land/Na Yavalati ni Vanua: William Cross and the Origins of Christianity in Fiji/Ko Wiliame Korosi kei na i Tekitekivu ni Lotu Vakarisito e Viti*. Translated by Tauga Vulaono. Suva: Institute of Pacific Studies, USP Press.

Tippett, Alan R. 1980. *Oral Tradition and Ethnohistory: The Transmission of Information and Social Values in Early Christian Fiji, 1835–1905*. Canberra: St Mark's Library.

Tuwere, Ilaitia S. 2002. *Vanua: Towards a Fijian Theology of Place*. Suva: Institute of Pacific Studies, USP Press.

———. 2011. "Na Vanua, Lotu kei na Matanitu. Then, Now, and Where?" Pages 28–39 in *Talanoa Rhythms: Voices from Oceania*. Edited by Nasili Vaka'uta. Auckland: Massey University Press.

Not Just a Bimbo:
A Reading of Esther by a Singaporean Immigrant in Aotearoa New Zealand

Angeline M. G. Song

Islands are the "ultimate exotic locations" that conjure up images of getaway escapism in the dreams of metropolitan dwellers, declares Steed Vernyl Davidson (2015, 37). But in the case of Singapore, the romantic, exotic island vividly portrayed by Kipling and Maugham has all but disappeared. The country's rapid physical transformation from rustic *kampongs* to bustling metropolis since independence in 1965 is a result of the postindependence leaders' decision to pursue practical solutions to problems facing the island. A series of redevelopment schemes were carried out at blitzkrieg pace, which saw Singapore's rivers cleaned up, historic buildings and old thoroughfares replaced by skyscrapers of glass and steel, and even public cemeteries exhumed to make way for public housing, roads, and car parks.

Singapore is well known for its land reclamation projects. Since independence, Singapore has expanded its territory by twenty-two percent, from 58,000 hectares to 71,000 hectares, through land reclamation. Singapore also has had to import sand, as it has run out of its own. Extended stretches of its beaches are artificially built.[1] In fact, more than 80 percent of Singaporeans live in high-rise apartments—tiny, expensive pieces of real estate "pie in the sky" on leasehold land—and have never owned landed property. So, in/from Singapore, it is possible to do island hermeneutics without getting sand between one's toes.[2]

---

1. See "Such Quantities of Sand: Asia's Mania for 'Reclaiming' Land from the Sea Spawns Mounting Problems" (*Economist* 2015).
2. Steed Vernyl Davidson (2015, 38), building on Kortright Davis, argues that

Hermeneutic of Pragmatism

Most Singaporeans (feel compelled to) agree with the pragmatic policies of the leaders. Under the strong and influential People's Action Party, which has ruled Singapore since independence, the collective national psyche assumed a stance of practicality, efficiency, and survival. Our leaders managed to convince Singaporeans—predominantly made up of Chinese migrants but also Indians, Malays, Eurasians, and other races—that each individual needed to work hard and to remain strong and competitive.

Generations of Singaporeans learned to imbibe a worldview that goes something along these lines: "Nobody owes you a living.... If you do not take care of your own self-interests, no one else will." Pragmatism, as a result, affected many Singaporeans' outlook on life, influencing our behaviors and shaping our values. In many ways, I (and many other Singaporeans in diaspora) still carry a large imprint of this pragmatic way of thinking and being; it has become part of my DNA and therefore shapes my reading of Esther.

My Singapore island hermeneutics can therefore be described as a hermeneutic of pragmatism and survival. Contrary to the exotic, romanticized view of islands and islanders, mine is a pragmatic lens shaped by the practical philosophy of postindependent Singapore.

My Story, in My Reading Lens

I am the only adopted child of a single, unmarried woman who raised me up in postindependent Singapore. Consistent with their business-like approach to politics and governing, the Singaporean government eschewed giving out welfare handouts; hence, my adoptive mother had to work full-time in order to support me. She was a single woman working as an English-speaking secretary for the local comptroller of a large government department *and* raising a child in a morally conservative, Confucian Asian society in the 1970s.

My mother would not have considered herself a feminist. Rather, she worked for pragmatic reasons: to provide me with good food and good

---

sand can form "the basis for theorizing about island biblical hermeneutics" and had asked rhetorically: "Can anyone move within island space and not get sand in their shoes?" (54).

education, and a roof over our heads.³ She gave me opportunities in life, and we negotiated our way in a postcolonial, patriarchal society that was outwardly rapidly modernizing, but inwardly conservative with deep Confucianist underpinnings. The prejudices and hardships we encountered contributed to my developing an acute sense of empathy with people from unprivileged backgrounds and/or at the margins of society.

Today, I am a tutor-lecturer at a tertiary institution, teaching a program that helps adult learners gain literacy, numeracy, digital, and employment-seeking skills. The key aims are to help our students find jobs in their adopted country so that they can support themselves and their families and to help them attain the basis of a good education, upon which they can pursue further studies if they wish.

My students are predominantly of Pasifika origins, with a few Māori and refugees from South and Southeast Asia. As an immigrant of a minority race myself, the first step I take toward connecting with each learner is to minimize the implicit power dynamics between lecturer and student. Sharing my own life story with them also helps inspire and empower them. It is here among my students of minority races and unprivileged backgrounds that I am learning to "embrace the margins."⁴ The reading lens that I use is thus tinted by my lived experiences as a minoritized Other, a Malay Chinese (*Peranakan*) woman living in the North Island of Aotearoa New Zealand, working with other minoritized immigrants. With those personal points of awareness, I now turn to interpret the character of Esther in the Hebrew Bible.

A Bimbo in a Colonizer's World?

The character of Esther is a complex and controversial one. Feminist biblical critics have not always viewed her favorably, with several significant

---

3. Elsewhere, I have described in detail the reasons for my being given up for adoption by my biological parents and also discussed the circumstances under which my adoption took place, including the fact that I narrowly escaped ending up in another woman's household as an unpaid servant or groomed to be a prostitute (see Song 2015, 8–11).

4. I am building on the concept of embracing the margins from the islands, regarding them as spaces which can creatively be converted into "a unique position of strength through their marginality: they are both inside and outside of the continental spaces" (Davidson, Aymer, and Havea 2015, 6).

scholars reading her as beautiful but brainless, a pawn in a man's world and a disgrace to the feminist cause. Alice L. Laffey (1988, 216) describes her as a "stereotypical woman in a man's world" who "wins favor by the physical beauty of her appearance, and then by her ability to satisfy sexually." In a similar vein, Esther Fuchs (1982, 153) suggests that Esther is more interested in her makeup than in saving her people, and Nicole Duran (2003, 78) states that "Esther is, in effect, the scab undermining the impact of the striking worker's sacrifice" and likens her story to that of the American reality TV series *Who Wants to Marry A Millionaire?* (72–74). More recently, Michael Matthew (2016, 127–28) described Esther thus: "Esther was involved in a sexual contest, married a pagan king, defiled herself with the excessive luxuries of the Persian court, and there is no recorded complaint about abstaining herself from the royal meals or banquet [*sic*]."

Esther thus looks like a bimbo in a colonizer's world—gorgeous, unintelligent, and oh so willing to be invaded and tamed in both body and mind, in this case by the Persian king. Such interpretations bring to mind the way that islands are often represented as "easily conquered, tamable and available" (Davidson, Aymer, and Havea 2015, 6). Utilizing a hermeneutic of empathic pragmatism, however, I argue that rather than being seen as a mindless bimbo who unthinkingly obeys and panders to the men in her life, Esther represents an approach that is outwardly pragmatic but subtly subversive, in order to survive and thrive in the hostile, colonized environment into which she had been forced.

As a vulnerable Other negotiating two worlds—her innate and internalized patriarchal Jewish paradigm and her day-to-day realities of living in a colonizer-Persian environment—Esther demonstrates the necessity of cultivating allies and consolidating her own position. As the narrative progresses, Esther's character evolves and grows so that she eventually saves her Jewish people from within the boundaries imposed on her. She is able to raise חסד (*ḥesed*, a significant word that denotes the noble sentiments of faithfulness, devotion, unselfish fidelity, and steadfast love; see also Song 2010) in the hearts of two important men, which hints at something remarkable about her character.

A Matter of Survival

Esther's character provokes strong reactions from some feminist critics such as Duran (2003, 78), who proclaims that Esther "comes in willingly to do what Vashti would not." By contrast, Duran offers, Vashti shows the king to be what he really was—"a hedonistic fool" (74)—by her refusal to appear in front of her husband's drunken guests. Duran concludes that "feminists have found it easier to admire Vashti, however briefly she may appear in the story" (75).

As a postcolonial, minoritized immigrant woman, I interpret Esther's actions as those of a shrewd and pragmatic individual who was vulnerable and powerless. I suggest that Esther is forced into the harem, based on the semantic clues in Esth 2:8: the many young women "had been taken," and Esther too "was taken." Esther is grammatically passive.

Once inside the Persian compound, Esther has two choices: either disobey orders and do as Vashti did, risking being prematurely dismissed from the narrative; or make the best of the situation, cultivating allies in powerful places in order to survive to see another day.

I discern analogous situations among my adult learners. For instance, a solo mother who is unable to pay her rent struggles to find the time or energy to analyze the ills of society and pursue actions against an unjust system. Rather, her main concern is to find employment; consequently, she may be forced to play by society's rules in order to ensure that she and her two young children continue to have a roof over their heads and food on the table.

Drawing from my past experiences, the help of allies from the dominant side of the colonizer's fence can, at times, make a difference in the lives of the weak and helpless. There are a few individuals who are sensitive to the far-reaching implications of the dynamics of power and privilege and who quietly "un-privilege" themselves in order to render help to the marginalized. It is therefore plausible for me to imagine that Hegai in the Esther story is like that. I read Esther's pursuit of Hegai's advice regarding what to take into the king's bedroom as Esther being shrewd enough to realize the importance of cultivating the right allies in a hostile environment. I read Esther as realizing that Hegai, a eunuch, would know best what pleases King Ahasuerus, and so she obeys his counsel in order to survive and thrive. Yet this pragmatic strategy does not simply await the benevolence of the privileged, but rather it carefully cultivates entry points and access to power in order to co-opt the resources of the powerful (see also Davidson 2009).

I interpret Esther's actions as part of a necessarily oblique strategy (Maggay 2002, 269). I submit that the strategy of surviving, doing well, and even excelling in a foreign system by outward assimilation and avoiding overt rebellion is a familiar tactic for many colonized people. I have described this strategy as a Pragmatism of the Powerless where the disenfranchised survive by appearing to please the people in power, making the best use of the opportunities offered by the system, cultivating the right allies, and remaining humble and flexible (see Song 2015, 167–70, 194, 202–3).

If critics from the First World view Esther's actions as thoughtless, circuitous, or deceptive, a postcolonial person like me reads it as a necessarily oblique and subversive strategy. I heed the postcolonial feminist critic Musa Dube's warning that Western feminist interests not be conflated with postcolonial issues (see Song 2015, 87–88; Dube 2000). Building on her wisdom, I suggest that an Asian version of postcolonial feminism can manifest itself in different ways; our form of feminism does not always have to be about publicly burning bras and making overt ideological statements. Such explicitness would not be appropriate in our cultural traditions and may have an opposite and alienating effect on the general public.

Given the sociocultural context of Asian countries where the Confucian tradition of respecting authorities is a fundamental tenet, a subtler but no less potentially potent approach of subverting *within* the boundaries, with gradual and careful persuasion, might be more appropriate and effective. A pragmatic strategy of the powerless would build selectively on the awareness created by the Western feminist tradition with regards to resisting patriarchal oppression but seek *its own way* in issuing a subtle subversive approach in problematizing patriarchal and postcolonial oppressions. This strategy includes being pragmatic in maximizing the opportunities offered by a foreign system even while guarding the distinctiveness of one's own culture and values; it could mean cultivating allies among enlightened individuals from the other side of the colonial fence and resisting within the boundaries when the time is appropriate. So, I borrow the words of the master playwright Honoré de Balzac (1876, 223) to dismantle the proverbial master's house: *Mes enfants, faut pas heurter la chose de front, vous êtes trop faibles, prenez-moi ça de biais! Faites les morts, les chiens couchants* ("My children, you mustn't attack the problem head on, you're too weak. Do what I say and approach your problem obliquely! Pretend to be dead, to be sleeping dogs!"). In the case of Esther, instead of overtly rebelling at the start, she chooses to bide her time, learning the inner workings, protocols, and culture of her masters, while creating and consolidating her unique space and voice. Her character evolves and grows in stature as the narrative progresses so that, eventually, she is able to work within the system to save her Jewish people from annihilation.

Filial and Shrewd

As an adoptee, I find Esther's obedience toward Mordecai in Esth 2:10 to be consistent with that of an individual who is immensely grateful to her adoptive guardian for rescuing her. Even though Mordecai is Esther's cousin, for all intents and purposes in the narrative, he is her guardian or adoptive parent, having raised and taken care of her. I personally attest that an adoptee would want to be obedient toward an adoptive guardian or parent out of an immense sense of love and loyalty.

Esther's obedience to Mordecai is analogous to the Asian-Confucian concept of filial piety, where respecting one's elders is of paramount importance. In the Chinese culture, older people—especially elders in the family—are generally deemed to be wiser, having eaten "more salt," or having accumulated wisdom through their experience of life. So, from my Asian point of view, a relative like Mordecai would warrant fidelity, respect, and filial piety from Esther.

As a child, Esther would have obeyed Mordecai many times, and her obedience would have brought good outcomes. Obeying Mordecai as an adult would therefore have come naturally to her, as implied in Esth 2:20b: "for Esther obeyed Mordecai *just as when she was brought up by him*" (NRSV, my emphasis).

Esther Raises חסד

While not denying that Esther's beauty played a part in her winning the favor of those in power, I argue that her character is more than skin-deep. For instance, Esther raises (or lifts up) חסד (*ḥesed*) in the king (Esth 2:17). Since *ḥesed* denotes devotion and steadfast love, it is an unexpected choice of word given that the relationship between Esther and the king had barely started. The term *ḥesed* usually denotes a quality produced *within* a relationship; it implies some kind of relational profundity, and often indicates the closest bonds within a family or clan (Zobel 1986, 46–48, 51–52; Harris 1980, 305). The word also characterizes the relation of God toward God's people and may even suggest mutuality (Zobel 1986, 51–52).

King Ahasuerus, on the other hand, has been portrayed from the start as fickle and egoistical and thus embodies the antithesis of *ḥesed*. The narrator's choice of words suggests a strong positive point about Esther's character: Esther is able to "raise up" the noble sentiment of *ḥesed* in an emotionally volatile king.

I disagree with Greifswald Zobel's attribution of the *ḥesed* in Esth 2:9 and Esth 2:17 to God (Zobel 1986, 49). Instead, the text points to Esther as the one who raises or elicits *ḥesed* on two occasions, first in relation to Hegai and then in relation to King Ahasuerus. Whereas the emphasis is normally laid on the *giver* of *ḥesed*, Esther is the only character in the Hebrew Bible to נשא (raise up) *ḥesed* (found only in Esth 2:9 and Esth 2:17). These verses show Esther arousing fidelity in the hearts of Hegai and King Ahasuerus. Zobel's proposal, I suggest, incongruously imports God into a text whose narrator is careful not to mention God's name.

Persuasive Discourse

During her encounter with the king, Esther employs the language of a subordinate to a superior: "If it pleases the king" (Esth 5:4 NRSV) and later "If I have won the king's favor, and if it pleases the king" (Esth 5:8 NRSV). Here we see the antithesis of Vashti's response to the king—"But Queen Vashti refused to come at the king's command conveyed by the eunuchs" (Esth 1:12 NRSV)—which humiliates King Ahasuerus publicly. We can conclude that Esther is aware of the androcentric context and culture in which she must operate. She also possibly knows the self-indulgent nature of her husband, and she is shrewd enough to pander to it in order to gain leverage later. From the perspective of the powerless or disenfranchised, this kind of behavior is a necessary strategy. As James C. Scott (1990, 136) aptly puts it in his theory of class relations and the hidden transcripts of the powerless:

> If subordinate groups have typically won a reputation for subtlety—a subtlety their superiors often regard as cunning and deception—this is surely because their vulnerability has rarely permitted them the luxury of direct confrontation. The self-control and indirection required of the powerless thus contrast sharply with the less inhibited directness of the powerful.

In my personal experiences, (post)colonized children are often brought up to adopt a subservient or deferential tone when addressing members of the colonizer race, in a continual strategy of surviving and thriving. Similarly,

I propose that addressing the king in a subservient manner would have come naturally to Esther and that it would reflect the normal practice of one who had grown up as an alien in Persia.

Esther's (Non)belonging

The sociopolitical landscape of Aotearoa New Zealand is complex: it is a settler-nation that is "colonial (with regard to the treatment of their indigenous populations) and (as former British colonies) simultaneously postcolonial. There are settler and immigrant societies, with a multicultural population from all parts of the globe" (Docker and Fischer 2000, 5).

Since the passage of the Treaty of Waitangi Act of 1975, the nation's public institutions and linguistic and symbolic repertoire have been profoundly transformed by an ideology of biculturalism, shaped around a formalization of Māori-Pākeha relationships (Ballantyne 2012, 50). Take for instance the passport, an important marker of national identity: it features English and Māori texts, as well as an imprint of the Pākeha (white New Zealanders) and Māori coat-of-arms, "under the unifying power of the Crown, [to] underscore both the difference and interdependence of Māori and Pākeha" (Ballantyne 2012, 50). The national anthem is in Māori as well as in English. In other words, this island nation is Aotearoa New Zealand.

This bicultural vision, however, sits uneasily with the country's demographic profile, which historically has been, and is now rapidly becoming, increasingly diverse and multicultural.[5] Tony Ballantyne (2012, 53) describes this bicultural paradigm as a "selective" welcome for Asians. Asian capital is welcomed for economic reasons, but "the reality is that within New Zealand a persistent emphasis on Asian difference and otherness remains.... In the bicultural context of New Zealand, discourses on Asian values can operate in opposition to both Pākeha values and Māori values." I often feel that I do not belong in my adopted home country, partly due to the state-endorsed bicultural polices and partly due to my own hybrid (sub)ethnicity. The words of Malaysian-born Peranakan author

---

5. New Zealand has had significant Asian populations since the 1860s, if not earlier. For information on the long history of Asian migration to Australasia, the tension between the demographic diversity of New Zealand communities, the authority of the Treaty in general, and the "writing out" of Asians from the country's dominant bicultural narratives in particular, see Ballantyne 2012, 51–61.

Shirley Geok-lin Lim (1996, 169), an immigrant in America, strongly resonate with me:

> As an alien resident, I feared I was already asking too much. Too much acceptance of my British colonial accent, my brown color and Asian features. Too much tolerance of my difference: not white, not Jewish, not black, not Puerto Rican, the four groups whose needs and words filled the columns of the *New York Times*. A non-American, I could only hope to fill the interstices, foreign to all and mutable, like a small, helpful glue.

With this mindset, I deeply empathize with Esther—a female Other, vulnerable, unable to reveal her true identity—attempting to negotiate, perhaps even imbibe, the protocols, rules, and culture of an alien palace court system while remaining Jewish within. I read her as a young woman with a Jewish heart forced to wear Persian makeup, a young woman aching to belong but finding herself filling the interstices "like a small, helpful glue." I interpret Esther's self-identity as unstable, mutable, and evolving as the narrative progresses (on "hermeneutic of empathy," see Song 2015, 37–64).

Esther's Displacement

I gain insights into Esther's sense of displacement from colleagues and learners. Many of my Samoan students are in their late teens, sent by their parents to live with their aunts and uncles in New Zealand in the hopes that they will find a good job and send money back home. For these young people, their displacement is particularly acute: they are separated from their immediate and extended families, and they leave behind closely-knitted village communities. Back in Samoa, each person has a place in the overlapping extended families, and they look out for one another.

I have heard stories of a similar way of living from my ninety-three-year-old aunt, Rosie Cheok Tee Song, with whom my mother raised me. She immigrated with me to Aotearoa New Zealand, and up until today she will talk about what it was like when she was growing up in a kampong where there was a spirit of *Gotong Royong*, an Indonesian-Malay phrase meaning the communal helping of one another and caring for each other like extended family. Such an approach, in the old days in Singapore, promoted a communal identity among the village residents.

From this minoritized contact zone, through the two island spaces of my two contexts, past (Singapore) and present (Aotearoa New Zealand), I ask slightly different questions this time around: Did a presumably young Esther leave behind a familiar, familial social space within which she felt secure, knowing exactly her *place* and role? If that particular space had been a significant marker for her personal sense of self, then how acute a dislocation and disorientation she must have felt when she was forced to live in the Persian palace with its imperial cultural norms and expectations! In Esth 4:16, at a time of crisis where she had to make an important decision, Esther asked for "all the Jews who are present in Shushan" to fast on her behalf, along with her and her maidens. This verse suggests to me that Esther had had strong ties with her Jewish community.

Esther's Evolving Self-Identity

As the narrative progresses, Esther's self-identity evolves. This evolution is analogous to the need among immigrants and those in diaspora to reinvent themselves in order to survive in a foreign sociopolitical construct. Fuchs (1982, 157) opines that despite their literary predominance, both Esther and Ruth "serve as agents rather than free actants … Both obey rather than initiate." But I submit that Esther is a complex character who starts out being passive but develops as the narrative progresses. There is a turning point in the middle of the narrative (Esth 4:15) when she makes a tough decision in the face of a monumental crisis and from then on transforms into a shrewd and sapient queen with much agency.

Critics such as Jeffrey M. Cohen have accused Esther of being cowardly and procrastinating when she seems to hesitate before agreeing to save her people in her first direct speech (Esth 4:11). Cohen (1996, 104) contends: "Esther was not naturally endowed with courage and determination to wage her people's battles. Quite the contrary. It was Mordecai who initiated the entire resistance. It was Mordecai who forced Esther to take up her people's cause. By nature, she would have buried her head in the sand, while Haman hatched and carried out his genocidal plans." However, I argue that Esther's initial hesitation indicates that she thinks before she (re)acts. I suggest that her initial unwillingness was both natural and wise rather than cowardly. Having earlier been instructed not to reveal her identity, she now refuses to change course merely at Mordecai's behest, especially since such a change could cost Esther her own life. Esther is honest enough to admit that the king has not summoned her for thirty days (Esth 4:11), giving the impression that the relationship between Esther and the king was not idyllic, and this could jeopardize Mordecai's plan.

I also suggest that Esther has an identity-in-flux at this point. Imagine having to suppress one's ethnicity, which is so intrinsically interwoven with one's identity (on the significance of ethnicity and race in Esther, see Bailey 2009, 228–33), for a period of years in a foreign culture so as not to provoke hostility. Coming out and revealing her true identity would be perilous for Esther (Beal 1997, 37, 53). Moreover, it is the obdurate Mordecai who has caused the potential national catastrophe in the first place. Now he is demanding that Esther put her own life on the line in an attempt to solve a problem that he has helped to create!

The text does not make clear which (if any) of Mordecai's arguments or threats persuade Esther to follow his plan and put her life at risk by violating court protocol. Here we have to deal with one of the most tantalizing gaps in the whole narrative.[6] However, Esther's subsequent reply to Mordecai in Esth 4:16 reveals several aspects of her character.

First, we see a humble heart that stands in contrast to the character of the arrogant Haman (see Esth 3:6). Esther does not assume she is going to achieve her mission *on her own* as evidenced in her request that the Jewish people hold a fast on her behalf along with her and her maidens. Second, once Esther makes her decision (Esth 4:15), she gives total commitment, risking her own political position and even her own life. Her words "If I perish, I perish" (Esth 4:16 NRSV) reflect her courage in the face of a crisis of national proportions; her identification with her people and willingness to sacrifice her own life for them reflect the valor of a great leader. Furthermore, her carefully fashioned plan and concise, clear instructions in Esth 4:16 reflect not only an independent, thinking woman but a shrewd and resolute queen who has come (or is coming) into her own. Carol M. Bechtel (2002, 50) notes that Esth 4:16 reads like a battle plan, with Esther clearly the general.

I am not surprised therefore that, at this point, it is Mordecai who rushes away to do her bidding: "Mordecai then went away and did everything as Esther had ordered him" (Esth 4:17 NRSV). An important reversal has taken place, and it marks a turning point in Esther's character. Significant elements of the language used in Esth 2 to describe Esther's obedience to Mordecai reappear, as a mathematician might say, on the other side of the x-axis. In Esth 2:10 (NRSV), Esther does not "reveal" her Jewish identity because Mordecai had "commanded" or "charged" her not to do so.

---

6. Filling in the gap lies beyond the scope of this essay.

Now in Esth 4:17, Mordecai "does" (same verb in another form) everything that Esther "had commanded him." From here on, Esther becomes the key player in the story, effecting significant role reversals. First, she plays a key role in reversing the royal edict; those who would suffer because of the royal edict shifted from the Jews to those whom the book regards as the enemies of the Jews. Second, as a consequence of her actions, Haman ends up on the stake instead of Mordecai. Third, Ahasuerus ends up listening to Esther as he never did with Vashti. Fourth, Mordecai ultimately obeys Esther's orders instead of giving orders to her.

Toward the end of the narrative, the doubly marginalized and initially submissive Esther transforms into a strong and sapient queen who ultimately makes good use of the "unique position of strength through her marginality" (Davidson, Aymer, and Havea 2015, 6). She self-confidently returns (ideologically) to her roots/people, cleverly tricks her people's enemy from within the colonial compound, and saves the Jewish nation. In doing so, I believe she shows that beauty and brains are not mutually exclusive and that she is *not* just a bimbo in a colonizer's world.

Enigmatic Esther

While I have come to regard Esther as my subversive role model, I am, however, disturbed by her behavior at the conclusion of the narrative, where she does nothing to stop the mass killing of the Jews' enemies (Esth 9:5–15) and, worse still, requests King Ahasuerus for another day so that more killings can take place (Esth 9:13). The images of killing and genocide are so abhorrent to me that I have, so far, attempted to sweep the offending passages under the carpet.

I struggle with the story's ending and Esth 9:13 in particular. Is Esther's request to the king motivated by a genuine fear that her life and those of her people would still be at great risk should she allow some of her enemies to remain alive? Or is her request made at a moment of impulsive desire for revenge, or under duress—real or perceived—from the Jewish community?

For the present, I am learning to allow this troubling passage to confront me as a reminder that life is often messy and disorderly and cannot be organized into neat boxes. Esther remains for me a character from whom I have discerned helpful lessons but who also remains enigmatic, with aspects of her complex character presently remaining out of my reach.

As I ponder Esther's enigmatic character, I ponder my place in my current unique island of choice, Aotearoa New Zealand, which is simultaneously postcolonial, settler, multicultural yet bicultural. How do I position myself within this intricate and constantly evolving colonial-minoritized contact zone? At the beginning of my essay, I suggest that it is possible to do island hermeneutics without getting sand between one's toes. Perhaps so, if I were to maintain that one angle in my vision which reflects mainly the pragmatic outlook of my "first island" context. However, I have moved to another island, and my reading lens is being tainted by my living in close proximity with other minoritized immigrants within this island space. And I find, not unhappily, that increasingly, the sand from *their* home islands is getting into my shoes.

Works Cited

Bailey, Randall C. 2009. "'That's Why They Didn't Call the Book Hadassah!': The Interse(ct)/(x)ionality of Race/Ethnicity, Gender, and Sexuality in the Book of Esther." Pages 227–50 in *They Were All Together in One Place? Toward Minority Biblical Criticism*. Edited by Randall C. Bailey, Tat-siong Benny Liew, and Fernando F. Segovia. SemeiaSt 57. Atlanta: SBL Press.

Ballantyne, Tony. 2012. *Webs of Empire: Locating New Zealand's Colonial Past*. Wellington: Bridget Williams.

Balzac, Honoré de. 1876. *Scènes de la vie de Campagne: Les Paysans*. New ed. Edited by Calmann Lévy. Paris: Ancienne Maison Michel Lévy Frères.

Beal, Timothy K. 1997. *The Book of Hiding: Gender, Ethnicity, Annihilation, and Esther*. BL. New York: Routledge.

Bechtel, Carol M. 2002. *Esther*. IBC. Louisville: Westminster John Knox.

Cohen, Jeffrey M. 1996. "Vashti—An Unsung Heroine." *JBQ* 24.2:103–6.

Davidson, Steed Vernyl. 2009. "Diversity, Difference, and Access to Power in Diaspora: The Case of the Book of Esther." *WW* 29.3: 280–87.

———. 2015. "Building on Sand: Shifting Readings of Genesis 38 and Daniel 8." Pages 37–56 in *Islands, Islanders, and the Bible: RumInations*. Edited by Jione Havea, Margaret Aymer, and Steed Vernyl Davidson. SemeiaSt 77. Atlanta: SBL Press.

Davidson, Steed Vernyl, Margaret Aymer, and Jione Havea. 2015. "RumInations." Pages 1–24 in *Islands, Islanders, and the Bible: RumInations*.

Edited by Jione Havea, Margaret Aymer, and Steed Vernyl Davidson. SemeiaSt 77. Atlanta: SBL Press.

Docker, John, and Gerhard Fischer. 2000. "Adventures of Identity." Pages 3–20 in *Race, Colour and Identity in Australia and New Zealand*. Edited by John Docker and Gerhard Fischer. Sydney: UNSW Press.

Dube, Musa W. 2000. *Postcolonial Feminist Interpretation of the Bible*. St. Louis: Chalice.

Duran, Nicole. 2003. "Who Wants to Marry a Persian King? Gender Games and Wars and the Book of Esther." Pages 71–84 in *Pregnant Passion: Gender, Sex, and Violence in the Bible*. Edited by Cheryl A. Kirk-Duggan. SemeiaSt 44. Atlanta: SBL Press.

Economist. 2015. "Such Quantities of Sand: Asia's Mania for 'Reclaiming' Land from the Sea Spawns Mounting Problems." February 26, 2015.

Fuchs, Esther. 1982. "Status and Role of Female Heroines in the Biblical Narrative." *MQ* 23:149–60.

Harris, R. Laird. 1980. "חסד." Pages 305–7 in vol. 1 of *Theological Wordbook of the Old Testament*. Edited by R. Laird Harris, Gleason L. Archer Jr., and Bruce K. Waltke. 2 vols. Chicago: Moody Press.

Laffey, Alice L. 1988. *An Introduction to the Old Testament: A Feminist Perspective*. Philadelphia: Fortress.

Lim, Shirley Geok-lin. 1996. *Among the White Moon Faces: An Asian-American Memoir of Homelands*. New York: Feminist.

Maggay, Melba Padilla. 2002. "Esther." Page 269 in *The IVP Women's Bible Commentary*. Edited by Catherine Clark Kroeger and Mary J. Evans. Downers Grove: InterVarsity.

Matthew, Michael. 2016. "Daniel at the Beauty Pageant and Esther in the Lion's Den: Literary Intertextuality and Shared Motifs between the Books of Daniel and Esther." *OTE* 29.1:116–32.

Scott, James C. 1990. *Domination and the Arts of Resistance: Hidden Transcripts*. New Haven: Yale University Press.

Song, Angeline M. G. 2010. "Heartless Bimbo or Subversive Role Model? A Narrative (Self) Critical Reading of the Character of Esther." *DiJT* 49.1:56–69.

———. 2015. *A Postcolonial Woman's Encounter with Moses and Miriam*. PostRel. New York: Macmillan.

Zobel, Greifswald. 1986. "חֶסֶד." *TDOT* 5:44–64.

The Priestly *Ger* (Alien) Meets the Samoan *Tagata Ese* (Outsider)

Makesi Neemia

This chapter addresses a particular biblical perspective on land tenure related to the *ger* (commonly translated as "alien," "immigrant," and "sojourner") in the Priestly writings (P and H), through the lens of the Samoan *tagata ese* (lit. "outside-person") and her or his opportunities to claim customary land (and *matai* titles) through *tautua* (service).[1] The orientation of tagata ese toward service is a signal that belonging to a community involves participation and performance. Unfortunately, not all services are recognized or appropriately rewarded, and this is especially painful for the Samoan tagata ese.

The term *ger* in the Priestly writings is an inclusive term with regard to a subject's status and involvement within the Israelite (social and cultic) community. This is especially evident in land claims, cultic participation, and expectations. I suggest that this inclusive and accommodating social vision of the *ger* in the Priestly writings may serve as a hermeneutical model for endorsing the rights of the tagata ese to customary land.

---

1. *Tautua* is simply service, but it also refers to the person performing the service. A Samoan proverb, "*O le ala i le pule o le tautua,*" expresses the importance of tautua or service. The proverb is generally translated as "The path to authority is service." That is, rendering tautua to the high chief, *matai*, extended family, village, and church is the highest priority for aspiring future Samoan leaders. In searching for a successor to a matai title, the extended family usually looks favourably upon those who have rendered appropriate tautua. In most cases, these people are rewarded with bestowments of matai titles. However, there are also exceptions, where some are overlooked regardless of their tautua, and this is one of the main issues addressed in this chapter.

In the Samoan Bible, tagata ese is used to translate three of the four Hebrew words that refer to aliens, foreigners, or strangers: *ger* (Gen 23:4), *zar* (Isa 1:7), and *nokri* (Deut 17:15).[2] The fourth word, *toshav*, has a different translation—*le aumau* ("one who resides"; Gen 23:4). The three words (*ger*, *zar*, and *nokri*) translated with tagata ese differ especially with regard to their legal and social status. Even though these words perhaps carry a sense of foreignness and otherness, their status within the Israelite community is totally different. The use of tagata ese to translate three Hebrew terms suggests, on the one hand, a lack in the Samoan language. We do not have three different Samoan words to correspond to the three Hebrew words. On the other hand, one could also argue that tagata ese is rich enough to convey the meanings of three Hebrew terms. I lean toward the second explanation.

The following discussion is in three parts. First, a discussion of tagata ese in the Samoan context in light of the importance of tautua (service). I suggest that tautua is the most important aspect for the tagata ese's chance of claiming family membership, land, and matai titles. Through tautua, the tagata ese become acceptable. The discussion of tagata ese and tautua provides the frame for the second part: an exploration of the *ger* in the Priestly writings, especially in relation to the development of its social and legal status. The final part of the discussion is a dialogue between the historical investigation of the Priestly *ger* and the tagata ese in the Samoan context. As indicated above, the inclusive and accommodating social vision of the *ger* in the Priestly writings may serve as a hermeneutical model, affirming the opportunities of the tagata ese to acquire customary land (and matai titles). In return, the disappointment of the tagata ese who perform tautua but are not rewarded provides reasons for reconsidering the openness toward the *ger* in the Priestly texts.

Tagata ese, Tautua, and Land Claims

Tagata ese may refer to a person from a different family and village, a person from another country (foreigner), or simply a person who does not have any social, legal, or kinship ties to a particular family. It is important to note here that a Samoan church minister is tagata ese within the

---

2. This chapter focuses on *ger* but discusses the other terms in comparison. The meaning of *ger* has undergone significant developments, especially within the Priestly writings (P and H), but this term is not rendered as "foreigner" in English translations.

village parish where he (mainline Samoan churches do not ordain women) is stationed (which is usually not his home village). The extra high regard that Samoans give to church ministers is indication that tagata ese could have status and glory in village settings. Tagata ese could have power and privileges, but not all tagata ese receive the same respect and treatment.

Generally, tagata ese do not have rights to Samoan customary land (land that belongs to the community, distributed according to customs). A village plot could be given to a descendant of a beloved member of the community but not to a tagata ese. However, the tagata ese could have access to ancestral land. Peniamina Leota (2003) highlights these possible avenues: (1) through marriage into a family, (2) through adoption, and (3) through tautua. The first two are hereditary avenues, and the third is from one's service.[3] Through service, the tagata ese could gain privilege to customary land as well. This raises the question about the value of tautua, especially in cases where a tagata ese renders appropriate tautua but does not get full membership through obtaining the family matai title.

Many unfortunate tagata ese render tautua to a high chief and the extended family but are overlooked (because of prejudice and corruption) when a successor to a matai title is chosen. Those circumstances raise several important questions. What is the value of tautua in the Samoan context? Does tautua still influence tagata ese's membership in a family? That is, does tagata ese through tautua have a chance in claiming matai titles (a matai title endows entitlement to land in the Samoan context; see Meleisea 1987, 7–10) and land?

In order to fully comprehend the impact of being denied and rejected, it helps to look at the alternative. The accepted tagata ese would have full recognition as heir of the family and would receive the rights to both ancestral and customary lands. They would no longer be tagata ese but adopted heirs (*suli tama fai*). They and their heirs would be the same as true heirs (*suli moni*) with regard to land claims and matai titles. In other words, their tautua have earned tagata ese full membership within a family. Once this membership is received, tagata ese would inherit all ancestral connections to a family's matai titles and land as well. The outsiders can thus work their way into the inside and become the same as true heirs (suli

---

3. One important part of tautua is sharing with family and with the community and giving to the church (Shadrake and van Diermen 1998, 3).

moni). But when this opportunity is denied, tautua is burdensome upon the tagata ese.

The situation is awkward because a family or village, out of their good will, grants the rights of suli moni to the tagata ese. The family or village is not obliged to do so, and there is no customary lore or legal code to assure that the tagata ese receive the privileges of suli moni. The tautua of the tagata ese could in the end be for naught.

When tagata ese are deprived of full family membership, what should they do? Do they slave on, knowing that their status will never change? Do they continue, knowing that they will never have any claim to ancestral land (although they have performed the tautua expected of them)? For what end do they tautua?

The *Ger(im)* in P

The situation for the *ger* is different. The idea of the ancestors as *gerim* has been argued by a number of scholars to be a P construction. According to Konrad Schmid (2010, 84), "it is exclusively the P texts of Genesis in which the ancestors are referred to as 'foreigners' (גרים)." He further adds, in non-P materials the ancestors of Israel (Abraham, Isaac, and Jacob) did not wander from their land. In other words, they were not "foreigners" but natives of Canaan (84). However, this claim can only be sustained when Gen 12:1–4 is seen as post-P, and Schmid, among others, has argued exactly this.

With regard to Gen 12:1–5 and Gen 50:22–26, Schmid proposes that these texts are late redactions, but he remains unclear about whether they belong to a particular source tradition such as P. The elements that are traditionally assigned to P are 12:4b and 5 (Schmid 2010, 94). His understanding dismisses the classical idea of Gen 12 as a J text, arguing instead that Gen 12:1–5 and 50:22–26 are the redactional "bookends" for the entire block of Gen 12–50 and may at best be editorial seams to stitch the sections together.

Jean L. Ska (2009, 46–66) shares this view of Gen 12:1–4a as a late text. Ska first assesses the connections of Gen 12:1–4a to the preceding and following material. He claims that Gen 12:1–4a is an editorial work based on old sources that create a story of Abraham's migration. That is, the Gen 12:1–4a text "has no firm attachments either with what precedes or what follows" (53). Ska, like John Van Seters (1975, 224), understands Gen 12:1–4a as an introduction to all the Abrahamic cycle. However, he adds, if this is the case, then the text is a secondary passage. Moreover, Ska (2009, 66) dismisses the early dating of Gen 12:1–4a, suggesting that "it is difficult to put Gen 12:1–4a back to the beginning of the monarchy." He identifies the word מולדת in Gen 12:1, which is a common H word (e.g., Lev 18:9, 11), as evidence of the late editing of this text (Ska 2009, 46–66).[4]

Ska (2009, 66) then concludes that Gen 12:1–4a is a postexilic text "close to a crossroads where the deuteronomistic and priestly traditions meet and which sees the act of Israel's foundation in the faith and obedience of Abraham." Moreover, "Gen 12:1–4a reflects rather the theological and human concerns of a post-exilic community in search for its roots" (66). Rainer Albertz (2003, 246–71) also agrees to a late dating of Gen 12:1–3 and claims that an editor(s) during the exilic period, other than P and D, is responsible for this text (Gen 12:1–3). He refers to this exilic editor as RPH, a Redactor of the Patriarchal History.

Regardless of the different views about the authors/editors/sources of Gen 12:1–4a (or part of it), the majority of European scholars seem to agree that this is a late redactional text. If we follow this line of argument, then the non-Priestly text of Genesis does not present an immigration into the land of Canaan. In other words, they were not "foreigners" in Canaan but "through them, Israel was settled in the land" (Schmid 2010, 84).

In light of the preceding discussion, the ancestors as *gerim* or sojourners in Canaan could be sustained as a P construction (see von Rad 1966, 62–63). The non-Priestly ancestor story in Genesis nowhere narrates the ancestors as sojourners, although the verb *gur* is sometimes used. Elizabeth Robertson Kennedy (2011, 8) disagrees with this conclusion, stating "that the frequency of sojourn is a literary feature shared between the different historical sources of the text of Genesis," and she therefore finds it unnecessary to argue for "sojourn as a distinctive literary phenomenon in any one source." However, her position is rather unconvincing considering that all of the non-P texts in Genesis where sojourning appears (in different forms) to refer to places other than Canaan. As Schmid (2010, 84) points out, "Only in Gen 26:3 does a non-Priestly text state, from the mouth of God, that 'Isaac sojourned as a foreigner' in Gerar; yet Gerar was a foreign territory in the monarchic period." Non-P material also tends to

---

4. See also Brett 2012, 49–59. Mark G. Brett argues that the use of מולדתך in Gen 12:1, in a command to abandon Abraham's kin, undermines the endogamous emphasis of Gen 24:4. For Brett, this reflects the final editor's response to the exclusive policies of Ezra/Nehemiah during the Persian period.

use the verbal forms (referring to short-term stays) rather than the noun form *ger* (a status belonging to persons).

One of the main P texts in Genesis that mentions *ger* especially in relation to land is Gen 23. In his request to the Hittites for a burial place, Abraham says "I am a(n) sojourner/alien (*ger*) and stranger (*toshav*) among you" (Gen 23:4, my translation). This claim highlights his relation to the land. He is an outsider, and he needs land to bury his dead. The general understanding with regard to land is that a *ger* (sojourner/alien), like tagata ese, does not have a claim to the land. In this case, the *ger* does not possess any part of the land. However, he could buy a piece of land for this purpose (Rendtorff 1996, 79). But what Abraham buys can be described as a right to use land (usufruct), not ownership of land (see Nihan 2007, 66; Bauks 2004; Köckert 1995; Guillaume 2009, 102–22; Schmid 2010, 244–45). The *ger* here differs from the tagata ese, who serve but do not always get the right to use (but not to own, because the land belongs to the family or village) the land. When a *ger* buys, she or he has a contractual right to the land; in Samoa, the family or village could give the right of use to someone from a different lineage.

In P passages, based on the evidence, the ancestors are presented as immigrants or aliens (*gerim*), even though there are hints that they were previously seen as people originating in the land. The latter claim resonates with the non-P presentation of the ancestors as natives of the land. Probably the Priestly writers in this case incorporated an existing tradition about the ancestors with their own vision of the ancestors as *gerim* (see Albertz 2011, 53–69; Nihan 2011, 111–34; Brett 2014, 89–104; van Hooten 1991). If this is correct, then this creates a tension on how to view the ancestors' claim to land. According to Ska's and Nihan's claims, this tension points to two Abraham traditions—one tradition which promotes an alien identity and the other tradition that affirms the ancestral ties to the land. Jakob Wöhrle (2010) and Philippe Guillaume (2009) explain how to understand this tension, or this combination of traditions, as found side by side in the final form of the P tradition. According to Wöhrle, this presentation of Abraham mirrors the returning exiles' claim to the land. Even though they are natives returning, they are like immigrants because the land that they are returning to is not an empty land. They have to live side by side with other people, who are not necessarily Judeans, on the same land (Wöhrle 2010, 190). Brett (2014, 97; building on Bloch-Smith 1992, 110–12) also points out this ambivalence in the P tradition: "since although the ancestors are characterized as *gerim*, they are also said to be 'gathered to their kin' in death, which implicitly establishes the kind of connection to land that could be understood as in some sense indigenous." Brett adds a possible explanation of this tension, developing Wöhrle's work to suggest that it may be caused by the later dominance of the Golah community. That is, the earlier ancestral traditions preserved and maintained by Judah's citizenry, the עם הארץ, "have apparently been overlaid with the representation of Abraham as the ideal Golah immigrant" (Brett 2014, 98; see also Schmid 2010, 107–10; Nihan 2007, 387).

The *Ger(im)* in the Legal Materials

The laws for the *ger* are mostly concentrated in the Deuteronomic and H legal texts. In considering the Priestly legal materials, Nihan (2007, 112) maintains "only in H and in H-related passages do we find an attempt to define a comprehensive set of laws for the גר." The original P document only mentions the ancestors as resident aliens (Gen 23:4 and Exod 6:3) but does not establish any laws to do with non-Israelites living in the land. Even though some scholars argue H as an independent tradition, the majority tend to accept the view that H is a supplement of the Priestly materials (Nihan 2007; Stackert 2007). Following this trend, this investigation treats P and H as parts of the Priestly writings.

Most scholars agree that the word *ger* within the Pentateuch developed different meanings (see Albertz 2011, 53–59; Nihan 2007, 111–34; Brett 2014, 89–104; van Houten 1991). This claim is based on the different presentations of the *ger* in the Covenant Code (CC), Deuteronomic Code (DC), and Holiness Code (HC). Unlike other terms, such as *nokri* (foreigner/stranger) and *sakir* (hired labor), their legal status seems to remain unchanged throughout. Kenton L. Sparks (1998, 240), in his analysis of *ger* in Deuteronomy, views the *ger* as a social classification within which one finds both Israelites and non-Israelites. But the situation is different for the "foreigner" (*nokri*): even though they possess certain ties to the community by participating in the community's economic life, they are rejected from participating in cultic matters (242–43). In this sense, the P treatment of the foreigner perhaps shares similar sentiments with D, especially with regard to their participation in the cult. In the P or H texts, Exod 12:43 and Lev 25, the "foreigner" (*nokri*) is not looked upon favorably. They are excluded from the Passover meal and can also be made slaves for life. The law codes address different historical contexts in the life of the people of Israel. The term *ger* in the earlier codes (CC and DC) emphasizes the social obligations to the *ger(im)* while the Holiness legislations promotes cultic and ritual integration. As Albertz (2011, 66) puts it, "The differences have to do not only with different theological concepts of the Deuteronomic and Priestly legislators but also with the very different social and political challenges that the legislators had to cope with."

In contrast to earlier views about the *ger*,[5] Albertz agrees with Nihan that the *ger* is a non-Israelite in P. However, the *ger* is no longer a dependent alien as in the CC and DC, but potentially a wealthy and independent individual (Albertz 2011, 58; Nihan 2011, 121; Joosten 1996, 72–73). The *ger* is not a client of an Israelite household but a household head. In this regard, the *ger* now has legal status which she or he did not obtain before. According to Nihan (2011, 110), this is why the *ger* "is now mentioned in a series of laws alongside the Israelite citizen, and it is occasionally stated that the same law applies to the resident alien and the 'native' (אזרח)." This does not imply that the *ger* and the native in H have equal status (Nihan 2011, 121–29; see also Joosten 1996, 63). In other words, the *ger* has now been integrated in some of the cultic and ritual practices but not all. As Jacob Milgrom (2000, 1417) expresses, the *gerim* were "obligated to observe only the negative commandments, the prohibitions, but not the positive commandments, the performative ones." This emphasis on prohibitions relates directly to the pollution of the sanctuary and land. That is, "Transgression of apodictic prohibitions, even at the hand of non-Israelite residents, profanes the land and the people among whom YHWH resides, and this must be avoided." Therefore, the *ger* "may seek integration into Israelite religion but does not automatically do so" (Joosten 1996, 64).

The law of slaughtered animals (Lev 17:3) also highlights this distinction as Milgrom claims. The Israelite is required to bring all their slaughtered animals to the sanctuary but not the *ger*. The *ger* only brings those animals for sacrificial and religious purposes (Lev 17:8–9). This law implies "that strangers were not free to worship other gods, but neither could they be constrained to worship Yahweh" (Brett 2008, 117, citing Milgrom 2004, 191). Brett drives the differentiation of Israelites from non-Israelites further (Brett 2014, 100–104). He claims, following Baruch J. Schwartz, that "the Holiness Code equalizes the general conditions of occupancy of the land, so that Israelites and even the prior occupants of Canaan are bound

---

5. These views suggest that the *ger(im)* refer to other Israelites/Judeans, such as the remainees, the Samaritans, or members of other tribes excluding Judah and Benjamin.

by essentially the same ethical code, lest the land 'vomit' them out" (Brett 2014, 100–101). In other words, a so-called Holiness school provides an inclusive setting that accommodates both the indigenous אזרח and the nonindigenous גר (Brett 2014, 101). If the אזרח are in some contexts to be seen as "children of the golah," and the גר refers to the "peoples of the land" who never went to exile, then what the Holiness school proposes is a reconciliation between these two groups. Moreover, this reconciliation may also include the "surrounding '*goyim*' who troubled Nehemiah" (Brett 2014, 101). This alternative inclusive construction stands in direct opposition to Ezra/Nehemiah's exclusive "holy seed" discourse. As Brett (2014, 103–104) reiterates, "the use of the term '*ezrach* in H turns out to be less 'nativist' than the discourse of the 'holy seed.' If nativism proposes an exclusively 'authentic' indigenous tradition, which characteristically excludes hybrid alternatives, then the Holiness school is providing a more complex social imagination."

To further highlight this distinction between the *ger* and *'ezrach*, Nihan (2011, 122–24) points to land ownership and holiness as examples (see also Rendtorff, 1996, 85). Ownership of land is specifically for the native Israelite. In discussing the Jubilee laws (Lev 25), Nihan (2011, 123) argues that the implication of the law affirms that "ancestral estate may never be acquired permanently by a fellow Israelite." The land can be mortgaged, but it will automatically be returned to the original Israelite owner at the Jubilee. In other words, whether the original owner can afford to pay back the mortgage or not, the law makes sure he recovers his ancestral land. However, this is not the case with the *ger*. The law in Lev 25 implies that the *ger* does not have total ownership of the land, for the law implicitly stated that "an ancestral estate may only be temporarily sold to another Israelite, but not a foreigner" (Nihan 2011, 123; see also Albertz 2011, 58 n.2).[6]

With regard to the concept of holiness, H expands the sanctity of the temple to include the whole land (Joosten 1996, 137–92). Therefore, all inhabitants, Israelites and aliens alike, are responsible for the purity of the land. Failure to keep this ethical obligation would result in expulsion from the land as experienced by the prior occupants of the land and the Israelites in exile (cf. Lev 18: 24–30). Moreover, Christiana van Houten (1991, 157), drawing on Mary Douglas (1970, 49–57), agrees that "by understanding

---

6. Rainer Albertz questions this claim that the *gerim* were not entitled to own land. He suggests that not only the Holiness Code does not prohibit it but that it is also very unlikely the Priestly legislators have the power to prevent aliens owning property.

the concept of holiness, we can also understand the rationale behind these laws."[7] Prohibiting Molech worship (Lev 20:2) and blaspheming Yahweh's name (Lev 24:16) are examples of the need to keep the land holy because the land belongs exclusively to Yahweh. Furthermore, this concept of holiness can explain the contents of laws mentioning the *ger* and the native together. For example, contact with a dead corpse is rendered impure and affects holiness (Lev 17:15, 16), prohibiting blemished animals (Lev 22:8) highlights the need to be perfect to achieve holiness, and so forth. The significance of attaining holiness by all inhabitants of the land is "consistent with the larger vision ... of a God who has promised his people his abiding presence in his holy land if they keep the land holy" (van Houten 1991, 157). However, the inclusion of the *ger* in sacral laws is restricted. This restriction relates to maintaining the purity of the land. Nihan (2007, 128) notes that the *ger* is "consistently omitted from the exhortation to achieve holiness. This exhortation, which occurs at various key passages of H, is always addressed to the sole Israelites; compare Lev 19:2; 20:7-8, 22-26, and 22:31-33." Therefore, holiness to the Israelite not only maintains the purity of the land but also achieves "the sort of proximity to the patron deity which, in H's language, is expressed by the category of 'holiness'" (128).

The discussion so far locates this development of the Priestly *ger* traditions in a later period. That is, the dating of P and especially H is argued to be at the postexilic period, particularly the Persian period (fifth century BCE).[8] As already mentioned, the development of the *ger(im)* in the legal codes highlights the changing environment throughout Israel's history.

Given these changing contexts and especially the postexilic period, different hypotheses invite themselves. The current view sees this P construction of the ancestors as *gerim*, as an attempt to meet some of the needs of the Babylonia *golah* (Schmid 2010, 112; see also Wöhrle 2010, 189–206).

---

7. In this early work, Mary Douglas investigates the laws in Deuteronomy and Leviticus to establish a meaning for holiness.

8. Jan Joosten and others still argue for a preexilic date of P and H. Others like Israel Knohl (2007) and Jacob Milgrom (1991) maintain a preexilic date for P but not H. They see H as a long development reflecting the exilic to the postexilic period. Christiana van Houten (1991) argues for an exilic/postexilic date. Brett (2014) also agrees for a late dating of H (or its final redactions) but acknowledges some of its early history. Schmid (2010), Nihan (2007), Albertz (2011), and others maintain P and H's Persian period context.

Van Houten (1991, 117) argues along the same lines, that "The laws pertaining to the alien [*ger*] as well as the bulk of the Priestly legislation are illuminated when they are understood as a creative response to the crisis brought about by the exile and the subsequent reuniting of the returnees with those who had remained in Judah." The Priestly tradition reformulated the laws regarding the *ger* to accommodate their own current situation in Babylon. That is, they have now become aliens themselves. This accommodation is clearly seen in the development of the legal status of aliens, which van Houten (1991, 155) argues: "They are not only the resident aliens who need aid, but they are also given the rights of members of the community. They are granted not only civil justice, but also privileges of the insider on certain conditions." So, in this, P's conception mirrors the return of the Israelites to their homeland as *gerim* (sojourners/aliens).

The Priestly *Ger* and a Samoan Biblical Hermeneutic

The historical investigation of the Priestly *ger* raises significant points. The Priestly writings (P and H) indicate a development in the legal and social status of the *ger*. The Holiness school laws are more inclusive toward the *ger*. The *ger* has become synonymous with the "native," especially with regard to land claims and community membership. This inclusive vision also helps to maintain unity and peace within the community. However, to maintain this status, *gerim* are expected to fulfill their obligations to Yahwistic worship. In terms of tautua, the Priestly *gerim* are required to continue their tautua within the cultic community. But according to H tradition, the rights of the *gerim* are secure as long as they render the required tautua. Also, these rights are acknowledged by God through the H laws set down regarding the *ger*, laws that treat the native Israelite and the *ger* as the same. This is unlike the tautua of the tagata ese, whose rights are not secure; they could even be expelled from the family land when the new successor to the family matai title settles in. The service or tautua rendered by a tagata ese, regardless of how much and excellent that is, does not guarantee her or him any rights to family membership. In this regard, tensions and disagreements will breed disunity within the family.

The Priestly representation of the *ger* helps to enlighten Samoan land issues regarding the tagata ese in a way that highlights some elements of a Samoan biblical hermeneutic. The inclusive and accommodating attitude of the Priestly writings toward the *ger* may serve as a hermeneutical model for Samoans to deal with the tagata ese, their tautua, and their right to claim customary land. Also, the Priestly openness to the *ger* could help maintain peace and unity within the extended family.

The meeting of the *ger* with the tagata ese in this study shows the *ger* receiving more favor than the tagata ese. In this meeting, one sees the difference between conceptualization (*ger*) and reality (tagata ese). On the one hand, the *ger* is privileged in favor of the exile-returnees, who had a hand in the canonizing processes; on the other hand, the tagata ese are unprivileged for the sake of village politics and authorities. The tagata ese are outsiders, but they are not poor or uneducated. Their parents or grandparents could have come from one of the outer islands, to seek education and employment in the capital island of Upolu. They become tagata ese due to inter-island migration. In many cases, the tagata ese received better education and own more wealth and resources (being merchants, lawyers, or doctors, for instance) than the people of the family or village (into which the tagata ese have moved). So, it is for the pride of the poorer "true member" of the family or village that the tagata ese are not given full membership with rights and privileges. They could build their wealth, educate their children, perform tautua for the new family and the new village, and donate money to the church and the community, but they remain tagata ese with no matai title or right to customary land. In the eyes of the Priestly *ger*, there is injustice in cases where the Samoan tagata ese are not given full membership of the family or village.

A Samoan biblical hermeneutic, in addition to seeking sympathy and justice for the tagata ese on the basis of the conceptualization of the *ger* presented above, has a second task: to give the Priestly presentation of the *ger* a "shot of reality," on the basis of the experiences of the tagata ese. In other words, the reality of the tagata ese invites one to take the openness of the Priestly conceptualization of the *ger* with a grain of (sea)salt. Whether in reference to indigenous ancestors or to returnees from the Babylonian exile, the Priestly conceptualization of the *ger* does not take into account the politics in lived societies. There are tensions between people of different races and colors, as well as between groups in the same ethnic groups, especially when it comes to deciding who is inside (suli moni) and who is on top (matai). In the eyes of the many tagata ese who are not paid the dues that they deserve, the Priestly favoring of the *ger* is unreal.

Favoritism (or election) continues to play out in, but is not limited to, Samoan families and villages. A Samoan biblical hermeneutic must take this into account also with respect to the biblical texts and views to privilege, realizing that there are cultural and ideological limits to biblical conceptualizations. There is something helpful for the Samoan tagata ese, for instance, in the Priestly *ger*—biblical grounds for claiming the rights to customary land and matai title—but there is also something unreal about the Priestly *ger* in the eyes of the Samoan tagata ese. In other words, there is something critical in the Samoan world to *try* (use, test, score) in the analysis of biblical and Priestly teachings.

Works Cited

Albertz, Rainer. 2003. *Israel in Exile: The History and Literature of the Sixth Century B.C.E.* StudBL 3. Translated by David Green. Atlanta: Society of Biblical Literature.

———. 2011. "From Aliens to Proselytes: Non-Priestly and Priestly Legislation Concerning Strangers." Pages 53–69 in *The Foreigner and the Law: Perspectives from the Hebrew Bible and the Ancient Near East*. Edited by Reinhard Achenbach, Rainer Albertz, and Jakob Wöhrle. BZABR 16. Wiesbaden: Harrassowitz.

Bauks, Michaela. 2004. "Die Begriffe השמור und אחזה in Pg. Überlegungen zur landkonzeption der Priestergrundschrift." *ZAW* 116:171–88.

Bloch-Smith, Elizabeth. 1992. *Judahite Burial Practices and Beliefs about the Dead*. JSOTSup. Sheffield: JSOT Press.

Brett, Mark G. 2008. *Decolonizing God: The Bible in the Tides of Empire*. Sheffield: Sheffield Phoenix.

———. 2012. "The Politics of Marriage in Genesis." Pages 49–59 in *Making a Difference: Essays on the Bible and Judaism in Honor of Tamara Cohn Eskenazi*. Edited by David J. A. Clines, Kent Harold Richards, and Jacob L. Wright. HBM 49. Sheffield: Sheffield Phoenix.

———. 2014. "Natives and Immigrants in the Social Imagination of the Holiness School." Pages 89–104 in *Imagining the Other and Constructing Israelite Identity in the Early Second Temple Period*. Edited by Ehud Ben Zvi and Diana V. Edelman. London: Bloomsbury.

Douglas, Mary. 1970. *Purity and Danger: An Analysis of Concepts of Pollution and Taboo*. London: Penguin Books.

Guillaume, Philippe. 2009. *Land and Calendar: The Priestly Document from Genesis 1 to Joshua 18*. LHBOTS. New York: T&T Clark.

Joosten, Jan. 1996. *People and Land in the Holiness Code: An Exegetical Study of the Ideational Framework of the Law in Leviticus 17–26*. SVT 67. Leiden: Brill.

Kennedy, Elizabeth Robertson. 2011. *Seeking a Homeland: Sojourn and Ethnic Identity in the Ancestral Narratives of Genesis.* BIS 106. Leiden: Brill.

Knohl, Israel. 2007. *The Sanctuary of Silence: The Priestly Torah and the Holiness School.* Winona Lake, IN: Eisenbrauns.

Köckert, Manfred. 1995. "Das Land in der priesterlichen Komposition des Pentateuch." Pages 47–162 in *Von Gott reden: Beiträge zur Theologie und Exegese des Alten Testaments.* Edited by D. Vieweger and E. J. Waschke. Neukirchen-Vluyn: Neukirchener Verlag.

Leota, Peniamina. 2003. "Ethnic Tensions in Persian Yehud: A Samoan Postcolonial Hermeneutic." PhD diss., MCD Melbourne.

Milgrom, Jacob. 1991. *Leviticus 1–16: A New Translation with Introduction and Commentary.* AB. New York: Doubleday.

———. 2000. *Leviticus 17–22: A New Translation with Introduction and Commentary.* AB. Vol. 3A. New York: Doubleday.

———. 2004. *Leviticus.* ConC. Minneapolis: Fortress.

Meleisea, Malama. 1987. *The Making of Modern Samoa: Traditional Authority and Colonial Administration in the History of Western Samoa.* Suva: Institute of Pacific Studies, University of the South Pacific.

Nihan, Christophe. 2007. *From Priestly Torah to Pentateuch: A Study in the Composition of the Book of Leviticus.* FAT 2. Tübingen: Mohr Siebeck.

———. 2011. "Resident Aliens and Natives in the Holiness Legislations." Pages 111–34 in *The Foreigner and the Law: Perspectives from the Hebrew Bible and the Ancient Near East.* Edited by Reinhard Achenbach, Rainer Albertz, and Jakob Wöhrle. BZABR 16. Wiesbaden: Harrassowitz.

Rad, Gerhard von. 1966. *The Problem of the Hexateuch.* Translated by T. Dicken. New York: McGraw-Hill.

Rendtorff, Rolf. 1996. "The *Gēr* in the Priestly Laws of the Pentateuch." Pages 77–88 in *Ethnicity and the Bible.* Edited by Mark G. Brett. BIS 19. Leiden: Brill.

Schmid, Konrad. 2010. *Genesis and the Moses Story: Israel's Dual Origins in the Hebrew Bible.* Translated by James Nogalski. Winona Lake, IN: Eisenbrauns.

Schwartz, Baruch J. 2004. "Reexamining the Fate of the 'Canaanites' in the Torah Traditions." Pages 151–70 in *Sefer Moshe: The Moshe Weinfeld Jubilee Volume: Studies in the Bible and the Ancient Near East, Qumran, and Post-Biblical Judaism.* Edited by Chaim Cohen, Avi Hurvitz, and Shalom M. Paul. Winona Lakes, IN: Eisenbrauns.

Shadrake, Andrew, and Peter van Diermen. 1998. *Influence of Culture and Gender Roles on Women in Small Businesses in Western Samoa*. Palmerston North: Institute of Development Studies, Massey University.

Ska, Jean L. 2009. "The Call of Abraham and Israel's Birth-certificate (Gen 12:1–4a)." Pages 46–66 in *The Exegesis of the Pentateuch*. FAT 66. Tübingen: Mohr Siebeck.

Sparks, Kenton L. 1998. *Ethnicity and Identity in Ancient Israel: Prolegomena to the Study Sentiments and Their Expression in the Hebrew Bible*. Winona Lakes, IN: Eisenbrauns.

Stackert, Jeffrey. 2007. *Rewriting the Torah: Literary Revision in Deuteronomy and the Holiness Legislation*. FAT 52. Tübingen: Mohr Siebeck.

Van Houten, Christiana. 1991. *The Alien in Israelite Law*. JSOTSup 107. Sheffield: JSOT Press.

Van Seters, John. 1975. *Abraham in History and Tradition*. New Haven: Yale University Press.

Wöhrle, Jakob. 2010. "The Un-Empty Land: The Concept of Exile and Land in P." Pages 189–206 in *The Concept of Exile in Ancient Israel and its Historical Contexts*. Edited by Ehud Ben Zvi and Christoph Levin. ZAW 404. Berlin: de Gruyter.

Jesus the *Fiaola* (Opportunity Seeker): A Postcolonial Samoan Reading of Matthew 7:24–8:22

Vaitusi Nofoaiga

This chapter responds to the call to "return to the Bible" in the *RumInations* volume, with warm affirmation of the proposition that "biblical texts are like islands, and readers are like islanders" (Davidson, Aymer, and Havea 2015, 1). This proposition reflects how I see islanders in Samoa. There are, of course, other islands, other islanders, and other Pasifika languages, but an islander in Samoan is *tagata o le motu* (person or people of the "motu," a Samoan word that means "island" as well as "broken" or "disconnected"). The tagata o le motu is not one who is cut off or disconnected from civilization but one who is at a special place (in Tongan, a *motu atu* place) in and because of its ways, cultures, and peoples.

The word for "crowd" in the Samoan Bible—*motu o tagata* (island of people)—comes from the phrase tagata o le motu. In this connection, I propose that a Samoan islander (tagata o le motu) reading draws attention to, as well as takes the side of, members of the crowd (motu o tagata). This chapter accordingly explores discipleship from the tagata o le motu worldview, emphasizing the significance of the local motu o tagata in Galilee, arguably a motu (island) in Jerusalem-oriented minds.

Discipleship in Samoan Churches

One of the contentious subjects in contemporary Christian communities in Samoa is the ministry of the churches in relation to traditional interpretations and practices of discipleship, such as the expectation that "a disciple should leave her or his family and follow Jesus." The implication of this traditional interpretation and practice is the belief that the church's needs are more important than family needs. Public criticism of this tradition is beginning to emerge among Samoans, in particular the new generation, who consider it to be one of the main causes of the increase in domestic problems such as poverty[1] and abuse, especially of women (see Ah Siu-Maliko 2015, 270–75; Ah Siu-Maliko 2016) and children. As a Samoan reader of the Bible, I consider the voicing of that concern important, both for the new generation and for members of the older generation who regard the traditional understanding of discipleship as an important part of who they are as Samoans. Thus, a tagata o le motu understanding of how Jesus dealt with the needs and rights of the local people in a local place needs attention, and as such, is the focus of this chapter.

The chapter offers a Samoan postcolonial reading of Matt 7:24–8:22. Within this unit, Matt 8:18–22 contains traditional characteristics of discipleship. In verse 22, one could see the characteristic of "leave the family and follow Jesus": Jesus said to one of his disciples, whose father had just passed away, "Follow me and let the dead bury their own" (NRSV). This chapter revisits these words of Jesus in the literary context of Matt 7:24–8:22 as a rhetorical and narrative unit. For a tagata o le motu (islander), Jesus's response is insensitive and insulting. A Samoan would not disregard her or his dead parent. But for the sake of the motu o tagata (crowd), Jesus's response makes sense. Because the exchange between Jesus and the disciple took place toward the end of the day, when it was getting dark, the help of the disciple in serving the crowd was needed. In the next morning, he could then go and pay his respects to his father and mourn together with his family. So, the issue was not lack of respect for the dead or the disciple's responsibility to his family. Rather, Jesus's response has to do with timing. Seeing that Jesus will go in the direction of the disciple's home the

---

1. A letter to the editor of *Samoa Observer Newspaper* (February 5, 2012) titled "Charity and the Church" provides an example. This letter speaks of the problem of poverty in Samoa in relation to church ministers' status in Samoan society. The author states: "the arguments of poverty and the church are more complex than we give them credit for [sic] but one thing is for sure, the church [in Samoa] has become an institution whose servants [church ministers] live less like Christ and more like Rock stars.… The membership of the more established churches are leaving because many of its servants [church ministers] do not inspire the true meaning of faith, hope and charity, because they themselves do not lead by example nor want to live it but wish to receive it."

following day (Matt 9:1), the disciple could safely go along with the crowd and Jesus.

Toward a Postcolonial Samoan Reading

My reading is informed by my experience of life in Samoan society and shaped by the concept of hybridity, one of the analytical tools of postcolonial thinking proposed by Homi K. Bhabha. This postcolonial approach is transcultural, allowing the marginalized or colonized situation of a reader to become a key to interpretation. This approach does not impose the hybrid situation on the text but provides a departure point for seeking in the text an understanding that would enable transformation. I take advantage of the room that the concept of hybridity gives for the Samoan situation to be a key to interpretation. My hermeneutic nonetheless goes beyond intercultural criticism as a reading strategy in that I recognize the complexities of the interdependence between the colonized and the colonizer (Bhabha 1994, 2).

The concept of hybridity has limitations.[2] It identifies and describes something or someone that is *not* pure, but conceiving subjects as (social, cultural, or religious) impure is impolite and inappropriate. However, the weaknesses of the concept of hybridity—its biased roots, impure offspring, over- and under-emphasis of distinctions in different times and spaces—makes attention to subjects who fit the hybridity profile (e.g., the marginalized and minoritized) more urgent. To give up on the concept because of its ideological blind spots does not help hybridized subjects. For the purpose of this essay, I offer the Samoan *fiaola* as a supplement to the postcolonial concept of hybridity. Fiaola is what Samoans call someone who does not give up but seeks opportunities to improve her or his situation. A fiaola does not depend on the charity of others but seeks meaningful survival in the Samoan society. Upon the concept of hybridity, I construct my fiaola reading of Matt 7:24–8:22, in which Jesus is a strong-willed person who seeks opportunities for himself and for his followers. In this reading, Jesus is neither passive nor naïve. Jesus is driven and strategic—two of the marks of a Samoan fiaola. Reading Jesus as fiaola means that Jesus wanted and was seeking life. This reading

---

2. For discussions of these limitations, see Young 1995, 6–19; Gilroy 2004, 105–06, 117, 250 51; Engler 2005, 357–78; Hutnyk 2005, 96–99.

problematizes the assumption that life (eternal, or otherwise) was always in Jesus as well as challenges readers in Samoa and beyond who imagine that Jesus was apolitical and otherworldly.

Fiaola

The motivation for this revisitation of Matt 7:24–8:22 is twofold. First, it is an opportunity to introduce fiaola—drawn from my life experience of seeking survival in the Samoan social, cultural, and political worlds—as a lens for reading. Second, it is an opportunity to complement sociorhetorical criticism with a Samoan lens—fiaola.

Fiaola

Fiaola is the combination of two words: *fia* meaning "wanting to" or "willing to" and *ola* meaning "life." Fiaola therefore means "wanting life" or "seeking life." Put another way, fiaola means "vying for survival." Fiaola expresses my experience in seeking ways and opportunities, such as selling Samoan hot cocoa drink and collecting bottles around the town area of Apia day and night to help my family survive on a leased piece of land near the town area of Apia in the 1980s.[3] Those experiences evoked characteristics of fiaola that I propose as elements in the fiaola lens that I use in my reading of Jesus's relationship to the local people (crowd) of Galilee portrayed in Matt 7:24–8:22. These elements include:

1. Fiaola considers family needs more important than anything else;
2. Fiaola sees life from position of hybridity—fluctuating in between moments, situations, spaces, and opportunities, fiaola chooses what would provide the best option in meeting the family's needs;
3. Fiaola is courageous, strong-willed, and strategic and is not afraid to enter unfamiliar spaces or relationships to seek help for the family;
4. Fiaola seeks help from a *faaola* (savior or disciple) when necessary;
5. Fiaola who is able to provide for her or his family is considered a *faaola*.

---

3. I have explained my experiences in relation to educational opportunities and church responsibilities in Nofoaiga 2014.

Fiaola Reading

In life, fiaola is linked to *lotoifale* (household, local context). Concerning texts, the lotoifale I call *lotoitusiga* (literary world of the text). From fiaola's point of view a lotoitusiga has *tuaoi faatusiga* (literary boundaries) in relation to time, space, people, and culture shown in the *gagana* (language, rhetoric) of the *tusiga* (text). These tuaoi faatusiga form a *siomiaga fiaola faa-le-tusiga* (fiaola rhetorical and narrative unit).

The first task of fiaola reading is to identify a siomiaga fiaola faa-le-tusiga by identifying its *anofale* (the local world that is encoded in the unit). This is indicated by signs (e.g., opening and closing signs). Finding the anofale involves identifying how the language of the text shows the relationship of fiaola and faaola; how the fiaola and faaola are linked to specific households (families); and how the movements of fiaola and faaola relate to time and space (such as time of day and movement in between spaces).

Fiaola reading involves analyzing the *mamanu* (textures) of the anofale. This reading includes analyzing the *faasologa* (progression), *tagata-auai* (characters), and the *mamanuina o faaupuga* (word patterns). Part of the analysis explores how *upusii* (a recitation) is used in the anofale of the siomiaga fiaola faa-le-tusiga. The questions that guide the analysis include: Who is fiaola in the text? Who is faaola in the text? What needs does the fiaola seek from the faaola? How is fiaola and faaola each linked to local households in the text? How does the fiaola seek help in the text? How does faaola respond to fiaola?

A Fiaola Reading of Matt 7:24–8:22

Analyzing Matt 7:24–8:22 as a siomiaga fiaola faa-le-tusiga (fiaola narrative unit) involves exploring how Jesus's ministry to the local place of Galilee reveals Jesus's attention to the needs and rights of local people. Galilee is the anofale (local place) encoded in the text.[4] Jesus's ministry brings hope to the local people of Galilee and to Jesus as well in relation to his "kingdom of heavens" ministry.

---

4. The importance of Galilee for Jesus's ministry has recently received some attention, mainly in the quest for the historical Jesus (see Freyne 2004; Moxnes 2003, 23).

Our consideration of Matt 7:24–8:22 as a *siomiaga faa-le-tusiga* (narrative unit) focuses on the links between Jesus and the crowd to the local place of Galilee, emphasizing Jesus's relationship to different households in that unit. Jesus's use of the imagery of building a house in the parable of the wise and fool in Matt 7:24–27 anticipates his healing of sick people from different households in Matt 8:1–17. We also see in the *faasologa* (progression) of the unit Jesus's movement toward entering local households, which culminates in a transition of movement from one side of the sea to the other, as anticipated in Matt 8:18–22. The relations with local households and the movement over the land across the sea are presented within the frames of discipleship. Elaboration on that interpretation is based on the following structure:

1. *Amataga* (Beginning) Matt 7:24–29 — Discipleship as rebuilding of local households
2. *Ogatotonu* (Middle) Matt 8:1–17 — Discipleship as healing of the crowd
3. *Faaiuga* (End) Matt 8:18–22 — Jesus commands continuation of discipleship

The analysis is twofold. First, because Jesus teaches the crowd how to listen through the imagery of house building, we see every member of the crowd as belonging to a household in the local place of Galilee. We identify those local households as familiar, local dwelling spaces to which certain members of the crowd belong, and as their roles within their families. Second, we explore how the *gagana* (language), *faasologa* (progression), and *faamatalaina* (narration) of the text show how those spaces, relationships, and roles motivate certain characters to enter unfamiliar spaces in order to meet their needs. In this reading, fiaola is part of the motivation for entering unfamiliar spaces.

Amataga (Matt 7:24–29)

The words "will be like a wise man who built his house on the rock" (NRSV) are at the background of the setting in which Jesus undertakes his healing ministry. The parable is narrated with the images of building houses as metaphors for those who hear and act upon Jesus's teachings. These different households exhibit the familiar relationships with which various members of the crowd are linked and which determine their roles in particular relationships. This reflects how Jesus's ministry, in this part of the story, considers the needs of different local people in relation to their households. Thus, the imagery of house building foreshadows the locality of Jesus's ministry in the following parts of the unit.

Ogatotonu (Matt 8:1–17)

The narrator's presentation of Jesus's relationship to the crowd is carried into the middle part of the unit. This time, the narrator refers to different members of the crowd, suggesting different types of households in Galilee.

Leper as a Fiaola (Matt 8:1–4)

The healing of the leper reveals the first local household that Jesus deals with in the unit. This subunit expresses the locality of the leper's need. Jesus's moving down from the mountain with the crowd forms a transition from his proclamation of the kingdom of the heavens with words to his establishment of it with deeds. This transition also shows the setting of Jesus's healing activities as a public area within the background of local households. Those healing activities demonstrate the time of healing, reflected by his call to the crowd to listen in the first part of the unit: that time is now. More importantly, the healing of the leper begins with Jesus's demonstration of the type of listening about which he preached.

The local space to which the leper belongs is the Jewish religious household, according to which he is unclean, and thus he is an outcast. The leper fits the hybridity profile. But being a member of the Jewish religious community means that the leper has a role, namely, to seek cleansing for his leprosy. In seeking his own cleansing, he exhibits the signs of fiaola.

The hybridized unnamed leper is the first member of the crowd who responds in action to Jesus's appeal (7:24–27). The interaction between Jesus and the leper shows the movement of the leper from familiar to unfamiliar spaces and relationships. The leper is a sick person, uncertain how to make himself clean. The text suggests that he is a marginal character seeking help from Jesus, reflected in the use of the subjunctive "if you are willing" in his appeal to Jesus. These words do not show that the leper doubts Jesus's healing power but rather that he sees Jesus's teaching with authority as a means of help for his condition. As a result, the leper is cleansed.

The eradication of the leprosy does not mark the end of the healing event. Jesus wants the leper to go and show himself to the priest. "See that you say nothing to anyone; but go, show yourself" (Matt 8:4 NRSV). This command exemplifies how a local person should deal with her or his role as a member of a household. First, "not to say a word to anyone" reminds the audience of what Jesus says in his teaching of a good listener in Matt 7:24. Words are not enough to show that one has listened. Actions are also required, and actions speak louder than words. Second, part of this service to the Jewish household requires giving material gifts as determined by the purity laws. Thus, acceptance into his own religious household depends on the leper's own actions. He himself has to fulfill his duties.

The leper is a disciple sent by Jesus to return to his Jewish religious household and to continue being a Jew according to the Jewish custom. Jesus sends the leper, as the first healed of the crowd, to return to the household to which he belongs, and in and through him, Jesus's proclamation of the kingdom of the heavens reaches the Jewish household. The leper, in the end, is a fiaola who becomes faaola. He seeks opportunity for himself, and he becomes an opportunity for others in his household.

The Centurion as Fiaola (Matt 8:5–13)

The healing of the centurion's servant concerns a gentile household (Matt 8:1–13). The place of belonging for the centurion and his servants was the Roman imperial household. This healing story introduces a different familial relationship in the local world of Galilee, namely, the centurion as the master and his relationship to his slaves, his servants.

The centurion as a man of authority leaves the familiar space of his imperial household to enter the unfamiliar space of the crowd, a space containing people with different purposes and goals in following Jesus. The centurion is an example of a local person who seeks help from Jesus's ministry to fulfill his role as a leader of his imperial household.

The main purpose of this unexpected approach from a Roman leader (unusual because it is made to a Jew) is to save a servant. The unnamed centurion goes beyond the boundaries of being a Roman leader for the sake of his hybridized servant. As a person with recognized status, the centurion could send one of his servants to bring Jesus into the house. Rather, the centurion deals with the situation himself in a new space, in the eyes of the crowd. He enters unfamiliar spaces for the well-being of his servant.

The narrator tells of Jesus's amazement at the centurion. But it is not the end of the event. Like the healing of the leper, the healing of the centurion's servant finishes with Jesus saying to the centurion, "Go; let it be done for you according to your faith" (Matt 8:13 NRSV). The centurion who enters the unfamiliar spaces of the crowd and of Jesus's vision of the kingdom of the heavens returns to his imperial household. His positive response is an example of a member of the crowd who listens to and acts on Jesus's teachings. Jesus's command to him to "go" could be read as the sending of the centurion as a disciple back into his own household. Thus, the centurion's return to his household is a return not only to witness the healing of his servant but to rebuild his household.

Compared to the leper, the centurion seeks an opportunity for someone else (his subject). But similar to the leper, the centurion is a fiaola who becomes a faaola for his household.

Peter's Mother-in-Law as Fiaola (Matt 8:14–15)

The healings of Peter's mother-in-law (8:14–15) and of the sick and those possessed with demons (8:16–17) show other local households and relationships that Jesus engages in the story. First, we look at the local social and cultural household to which Peter and his mother-in-law belong. Second are the households of the sick and those possessed with demons. Including the healing of these characters shows the diversity and richness of the members of the crowd in Galilee and suggests that Jesus deals with each one of them.

There is one slight difference between these healing stories. The healing of Peter's mother-in-law is different because, this time, Jesus takes the initiative by approaching the sick. Jesus takes his ministry into the homes of local people. This demonstrates Jesus's ministry as a place-based ministry in relation to the situations encountered by local people linked to the households to which they belong.

The woman's response shows how she deals with her own situation. She is an example of a person in need who deals with her situation from her local place, where she is recognized in her society. The verb διηκόνει (began to serve) in the imperfect shows not only the beginning of her serving Jesus but also its continuation, which will take her beyond the boundaries of the patriarchal system that held her in her own home. She is a disciple not to the world but to her household. She, too, is a fiaola who becomes faaola.

Jesus as Fiaola (Matt 8:16–17)

The healings of those possessed by demons in verses 16–17 are climaxed with Matthew's use of Isaiah's prophecy in verse 17, where an assertion is made that the authority of Jesus the healer comes from his being a servant of God who "took our infirmities and bore our diseases" (NRSV) In this reading, Matt 8:17 uses Isa 53:4a as a upusii (recitation):

> LXX (Isa 53:4a): οὗτος τὰς ἁμαρτίας ἡμῶν φέρει καὶ περὶ ἡμῶν ὀδυνᾶται
> He bears our sins and is pained for us
>
> Matt 8:17: Αὐτὸς τὰς ἀσθενείας ἡμῶν ἔλαβεν καὶ τὰς νόσους ἐβάστασεν
> He took our infirmities and bore our diseases

Matthew recites traces of Isaiah's reference to Israel's return from exile in Babylon, the time when the Persian Empire led by Cyrus displaced the Assyrian Empire (see Brueggemann 1998, 9). With that background, some scholars identify the servant as Israel, Cyrus, or a prophet himself. It is not certain who the servant was, but it is important to note that the thought world of Isaiah the servant has already arrived. This aspect is reflected in the Matthean use of the verbs ἔλαβεν ("took") and ἐβάστασεν ("bore"). In the aorist tense, these verbs express completed actions. The narrative placement of the recitation, after the healing actions of Jesus, suggests that the taking of infirmities and diseases (to which the recitation refers) are those undertaken by Jesus in Matt 7:24–8:16. Thus, the Matthean recitation of Isa 53:4a endorses Jesus's actions in line with the understanding in Isaiah of a servant (in the present) who has achieved the tasks in question.

The Matthean use of the verbs ἔλαβεν ("took") and ἐβάστασεν ("bore") differs, however, from what the LXX suggests. The Matthean use of these words is about taking away suffering (see Nolland 2005, 361–62; Schweizer 1975, 217) in the form of ἀσθενείας ("sickness") (Nolland 2005, 362), which means physical sickness. The Matthean use of ἐβάστασεν in the second part of the recitation affirms the narrator's link to the immediate context of Jesus's preaching, teaching, and healing ministry. This is different from the LXX, which speaks of the servant's bearing other people's sins as part of the vicarious suffering mentioned in the first part of the sentence (he bears our sins).[5]

---

5. According to Martin Hengel (2004, 119), the LXX's rendering of Isa 53 strengthens the vicarious suffering emphasis, but such is lacking from the Jewish sources.

In Matthew, ἐβάστασεν relates not to Jesus's carrying of diseases upon himself but to his endurance of the long day of work. The first Matthean utilization of this verb is βαστάσαι ("to carry or bear") in 3:11, which is in the aorist infinitive active and describes John the Baptist's admission that he is not fit to carry Jesus's sandals. The context in which John the Baptist proclaims the kingdom of the heavens is in the wilderness of Judea (3:1), where he wears clothing of camel's hair and eats locusts and wild honey (3:4). That type of environment presents a picture of the kind of work John encounters. It is not easy work, and the Matthean narrator's use of βαστάσαι links John's words (he is not fit enough to carry Jesus's sandals) and John's long days of work in the heat of the wilderness (3:1–4). Thus, John the Baptist's words (3:11) are not about unworthiness as humility but unworthiness as not having physical strength to carry on the proclamation of the kingdom of the heavens. John was exhausted. He has been working long days, and he is too tired to carry even the sandals of Jesus.

Another use of βαστάζω ("I carry or bear") is its aorist participle active (βαστάσασι), which describes the actions of the laborer who have worked all day long in the heat in the parable of the laborers in the vineyard in Matt 20:11. This use of βαστάζω is linked to "evening," the time of the day in which the owner of the vineyard gives the laborers their pay (20:8). The Matthean recitation of Isa 53:4a also links "carrying" to a "long day of work" in the use of ἐβάστασεν in 8:17. The function of βαστάζω in the Matthean recitation is linked to "evening" in verse 16, the end of a long day of preaching (7:24–29) and healings (8:1–16).[6] This link is important for my fiaola reading. The connection expresses the kind of suffering Matthew speaks about in this part of the story.

The Matthean use of Isa 53:4a also appeals to the burden of carrying another person's suffering, but not in the sense of vicarious suffering. The use of Isa 53:4 points to the long day of work (since Matt 5:1) that Jesus endures in order to help those in need.[7] Carrying away other people's suffering in and through a long day of work is significant in the whole unit (7:24–8:22). The comment closes the middle section of the unit, antici-

---

6. France (2007, 321) claims that "evening" in verse 16 has little significance to the meaning of the sentence. For France, the focus of verse 16 was mainly to anticipate the uttering of fulfillment in verse 17, whose central emphasis is the authority of Jesus as healer.

7. I agree with Schweizer's (1975, 217) consideration of the day that ends in the evening (Matt 8:16) to have begun from Matt 5:1. So, it was a long day!

pating the reasons for Jesus's responses to the scribe and another of his disciples at the end of the unit (8:18–22).

Faaiuga (Matt 8:18–22)

At the end of the unit, Jesus gives orders to the crowd to go over to the other side of the water. A scribe approaches him and says, "I will follow you wherever you go" (Matt 8:19 NRSV). Jesus replies, "Foxes have holes, and birds of the air have nests; but the Son of Man has nowhere to lay his head" (8:20 NRSV). Here, the Son of Man fits the hybridity profile. Applied to himself, and in light of the story of the centurion, Jesus would benefit from the aid of a faaola.

One of the traditional interpretations of these words suggests that Jesus intends to be homeless in his ministry. With the fiaola lens, on the other hand, I see Jesus's response as an explanation that discipleship is a restless mission. This is evident in the phrase οὐκ ἔχει ποῦ τὴν κεφαλὴν κλίνῃ ("has nowhere he might lay the head"), in which the word κλίνῃ ("to cause something to incline or bend" or "to sleep") plays an important part. κλίνῃ is the word used to describe Jesus bowing his head before he died in John 19:30. "Lay the head" carries the sense of voluntary death.[8] Jesus's response to the scribe could thus be looked at as Jesus voluntarily helping the local people in need despite the danger that his ministry brings and that Jesus attends to the demands of his ministry without rest. Jesus is exhausted.

After the scribe's request, another disciple approaches Jesus. He wants to go and bury his father. This disciple is a family person who knows his role as a son. But Jesus's response shows the opposite. Interpreters see this dialogue as calling attention to the cost of discipleship, where the family is to be abandoned when one becomes a disciple. In such interpretations, Jesus places more value on the disciple following him than on the disciple's commitment to his family. Would a son leave his dead father behind without saying goodbye? Such a son should not consider himself part of the family that he has left behind. Is this what Jesus wants from and for this disciple?

The disciple speaks to Jesus in the evening; it was not an appropriate time of the day to bury a family member. Later in the story (9:1), Jesus gets into a boat and returns to Capernaum. The disciple would be a part

---

8. Cf. BDAG, s.v. "κλίνῃ."

of Jesus's return to Capernaum, and that would be a better time for the disciple to fulfill his family responsibilities. Thus, Jesus's response to the disciple is not a command to abandon his obligation to his family but to make use of his time as a disciple to help the local people in need. Jesus wants the disciple to remain faaola, rather than to go away as fiaola.

In this reading, Jesus's response to the scribe is not about Jesus not having a home or house to rest. Rather, it is an indication that the mission of carrying away the suffering of local people is not easy. Dealing with suffering people is a restless mission, requiring much time and energy. Because the story continues on to the other side of the sea, Matt 8:18–22 is both an end (to this unit) and a point of transition (going across to the other side). In this way, 8:18–22 is not only the conclusion of Jesus's ministry to local households on this side of the sea, but it also anticipates his proclamation of the kingdom of God to the other side. Our consideration of 8:18–22 as the ending part of the unit is related to the word "evening" in verse 16. The time of the day that Jesus's ministry in this part of the story has reached is near darkness.

Conclusion

The analysis of Matt 7:24–8:22 with a postcolonial Samoan fiaola lens shows how Jesus deals with the needs and rights of the local people in a local place, Galilee. I have looked at Galilee as if it was an island (motu). Jesus's relationship with the crowd (motu o tagata) requires that he deals with the needs that are pertinent to the local place of Galilee. The reading proposed shows that Galilee is not broken (motu) from the other side of the sea. Similarly, the events narrated in Matt 7:24–8:22 are not isolated from those in the surrounding stories.

The fiaola reading shows that Matt 7:24–8:22 as a siomiaga faa-le-tusiga (rhetorical and narrative unit) reveals important characteristics of becoming Jesus's disciple. First, Jesus summons fiaola members of the crowd to listen, and those who listen are sent back as faaola to their households. In this regard, there are other disciples apart from the twelve who are favored in the Matthean presentation of Jesus's ministry. Second, local discipleship is not easy. It requires endurance and patience because it is a "long day" of work. Discipleship involves *tautuatoa* (courageous serving; see Nofoaiga 2017).

Jesus attends to the fiaola in the crowd and sends them back as faaola. Local households and families are important to Jesus, contrary to the way that some Samoan local households and families are marginalized because of the discipleship models that churches favor. Finally, this chapter is both an introduction to fiaola as a frame for reading biblical texts and an invitation for Samoan and like-minded churches to reconsider their discipleship models.

In finding Jesus to have had a moment of fiaola himself, this reading challenges the popular assumption that Jesus was always faaola. Like John the Baptist, Jesus was physically and emotionally exhausted, and like the leper, the centurion, Peter's mother-in-law, and members of the crowd who were possessed by demons, the status of Jesus as fiaola does not mean that he was hopeless. Fiaola is not just about being weak and vulnerable but also about having the capacity to seek a way out of one's struggle. In other words, fiaola is not a position of despair. Rather, fiaola is a position of strength, and in Matthew 7:24–8:22, this applies to Jesus as well as to the Jewish leper, the Roman centurion, the local mother-in-law, and the ones possessed by demons. Finally, the invitation for fiaola reading issued in this essay comes with a plea that hybridized subjects (whether on basis of race, gender, class, color, sexuality, or citizenship) in texts and contexts be engaged as characters of strength in a motu o tagata that includes the leper, centurion, mother-in-law, demon-possessed, Jesus, and John the Baptist.

Works Cited

Ah Siu-Maliko, Mercy. 2015. "Public Theology, Core Values and Domestic Violence in Samoan Society." PhD diss., University of Otago.

———. 2016. "A Public Theology Response to Domestic Violence in Samoa." *IJPT* 10.1:54–67.

Bhabha, Homi K. 1994. *The Location of Culture*. London: Routledge.

Brueggemann, Walter. 1998. *Isaiah 40–66*. NICOT. Louisville: Westminster John Knox.

"Charity and the Church." Letter to the editor, *Samoa Observer Newspaper*. February 5, 2012.

Engler, Steven. 2005. "Tradition's Legacy." Pages 357–78 in *Historicizing "Tradition" in the Study of Religion*. Edited by Steven Engler and Gregory P. Grieve. RS 43. New York: de Gruyter.

France, R. T. 2007. *The Gospel of Matthew*. NICNT. Grand Rapids: Eerdmans.

Freyne, Sean. 2004. *Jesus, a Jewish Galilean: A New Reading of the Jesus-Story*. London: T&T Clark.

Gilroy, Paul. 2004. *Between Camps: Nations, Cultures and the Allure of Race*. London: Routledge.
Davidson, Steed Vernyl, Margaret Aymer, and Jione Havea. 2015. "RumInations." Pages 1–24 in *Islands, Islanders, and the Bible: RumInations*. Edited by Jione Havea, Margaret Aymer, and Steed Vernyl Davidson. SemeiaSt 77. Atlanta: SBL Press.
Hengel, Martin. 2004. "The Effective History of Isaiah 53 in the Pre-Christian Period." Pages 75–146 in *The Suffering Servant: Isaiah 53 in Jewish and Christian Sources*. Edited by Bernd Janowski and Peter Stuhlmacher. Grand Rapids: Eerdmans.
Hutnyk, John. 2005. "Hybridity." *ERS* 28.1:79–102.
Moxnes, Halvor. 2003. *Putting Jesus in His Place: A Radical Vision of Household and Kingdom*. Louisville: Westminster John Knox.
Nofoaiga, Vaitusi. 2014. "Towards a Samoan Postcolonial Reading of Discipleship in the Matthean Gospel." PhD diss., University of Auckland.
———. 2017. *A Samoan Reading of Discipleship in Matthew*. IVBS 8. Atlanta: SBL Press.
Nolland, John. 2005. *The Gospel of Matthew: A Commentary on the Greek Text*. NIGTC. Grand Rapids: Eerdmans.
Schweizer, Eduard. 1975. *The Good News according to Matthew*. Translated by David E. Green. Atlanta: John Knox.
Young, Robert. 1995. *Colonial Desire: Hybridity in Theory, Culture and Race*. London: Routledge.

ACROSS THE SEA

Is My Island Your Island?
A Response in Three Keys

Fiona C. Black

Where do we belong? This is the question foremost in my mind as I read these rich, thought-provoking essays in *Sea of Readings*. In what follows, I trace this thread of belonging through a few of the essays, paying attention to some of its accompanying features (e.g., migration/emigration, colonialism, and storytelling). Where we belong is, of course, a question about identity, which is at the core of islander criticism. In fact, the movement (if we might call it that) is, like any new current in biblical studies, also presently engaged in the process of self-definition, internally prompted but also externally encouraged. As an important part of this process, in his opening chapter, Jione Havea sketches out a definition of islander identities and criticisms. I also offer some thoughts on this as a means of keeping this critical conversation moving. Three keys suggest themselves to me as I read: vibing, moving, and belonging. I offer these in this guise partially in echo of Havea, who, it seems, wishes to encourage the fluid, nonlinear path. And for good reasons.

Vibing

Havea's request to the respondents of this volume—begin from a place you cannot see or hear, Tangikefataua Koloamatangi's essay—is unorthodox, but I like it. In Havea's presentation, Koloamatangi's essay is transposed for us and played in a nonoral, academic key:

> Koloamatangi's contribution written in Tongan for an oral presentation at the meeting of the Oceania Biblical Studies Association at Tonga in 2012 ... is offered here in Tongan out of respect to the limits of translation and the untamability of orality. May it herein encourage biblical

scholars to learn and respect the vibes and workings of native tongues and to learn the speak of the subaltern (local, common, native).

For me, this framing of Koloamatangi's essay puts the politics of definition squarely on the table. Who is an islander? Who speaks as part of islander criticism? How does that speaking take place? Is it necessarily mediated, and by whom?

As instructed—and curious and willing—I begin with what I cannot see and hear, relying therefore on representations and vibes. In many ways, this is the reality of islandedness and of the problem of definition. It is instructive that so much of what Koloamatangi seems to be putting on the table for our consideration (via Havea) is not reducible to monochromatic, definitional features but exists in movement, in the performative, the unrepresentable, and the oral. Even if I could read Tongan, therefore, and if I did not have Havea's representations, I wonder at how "translatable" this work could be. Indeed, can islandedness in this mode be represented, repackaged, and formulated for the academic microscope? And is islandedness ever anything but movement, performance, and the like? One has to be careful not to exoticize the island—or the island-in-us—by writing such a thing, as if it were an elusive creature. At the same time, it might be that attempting to define or encapsulate the island is important, given some of the risks for islanders that are present when islands are left wide open to encroaching elements and explorers (see below).

What, then, are the vibes in this first essay? Havea-Koloamatangi indicates rich and cross-fertilizing opportunities for reading the Bible, especially as it comes in nonwritten forms. There is hopefulness and promise here, but at the same time, the reading is potentially radical. This is what I take from their insistence that all sides of Scripture merit our serious consideration (Koloamatangi). They indicate that Scripture's backsides require just as much of our attention as the frontsides; moreover, they suggest that the backsides are a resource for the subaltern. Would Koloamatangi have been comfortable with pushing things this far? (I know Havea would be.) Yet I find myself uncomfortable. Is it because I cannot fully access what has been written? Or because I wonder about the connection being made between "filthy backsides" (of Scripture?) and the subaltern (Koloamatangi)? I see evidence here of the weighty line navigated by much of minoritized criticism in biblical studies: the risks to the marginalized incurred by reading differently are ideological, methodological, and sometimes literal.

Nevertheless, this position is provocative and promising. It suggests pushing the limits, reading in the wrong direction, willfully looking somewhere else, asking difficult questions. It also suggests a willingness to upend Scripture's comfortability and its hegemonic past. It seems to me that islanders, by virtue of their historical position as the colonized, often find themselves engaged in or preparing for such work. As a matter of being—of belonging—they must address prior claims, "fight against the isms and schisms," and negotiate future demands. Are islanders, then, people who *push things*? Koloamatangi's article indicates an upending of the structures of biblical studies, though I am uncertain if he gets there fully. Others also indicate a willingness to modulate and modify.

Mosese Ma'ilo and Brian Fiu Kolia seem to want to *push it*, too. Ma'ilo sees the importance of risking that islanders "air their dirty laundry," in his reading of the novel, *Sons for the Return Home*, against the Prodigal Son story, the payoff being that it allows room for *talalasi*, telling and retelling stories. This, he sees, is a crucial practice for islanders, who do not find in the Bible an accurate representation of themselves or their stories. The risks, though, are ones of exposure, which should not be underestimated. Ma'ilo's critics may point to these in their objections and embarrassment, but for Ma'ilo, talalasi is worth the pursuit, for it gestures toward the promise that honesty and self-reflection are essential parts in moving forward. But moving forward toward what? Kolia writes of reconciliation with the Bible, indicating that something is at odds. He, then, also *pushes it* by engaging with the messier, off-limits material of the Bible (would this—the Song of Songs—be an example of Koloamatangi's backsides?). In contrast to Ma'ilo, who advocates retelling, Kolia wants to read from a different direction, to read with *tapu* (taboo) in mind, to read by making apologies and from the ground up (*tulou*).

From where do such desires in Ma'ilo and Kolia to upend and reorient come? Is the work of being/belonging one of continual navigation, a necessity that comes both from the evolutionary realities of being born on the sea and the historical markers of colonial heritage? I wish I could read more of this. Is there, moreover, much distance between the retelling (talalasi), the redirected reading (tulou), and the backsided reading of these three readers? Methodologically speaking, in all three approaches, there is the intention to work beside, across, or despite a series of biblical texts and stories in an effort to bring out what it is that is not said or that cannot address island (Samoan, Tongan) identity and context. This work is necessarily contextual (for Ma'ilo, Samoa of the 1970s; for Koloamatangi,

Tonga of the present day), but I still find myself wanting greater articulation of Pasifika identities, colonial histories, and biblical conflicts. Put another way, where both Ma'ilo and Kolia advance a new strategy of reading (talalasi and tulou, respectively) and where Havea has elsewhere articulated his own (*talanoa*; Havea 2016), the fuller potential for these as radical decenterings of colonial biblical studies is as of yet unrealized. These are early days. A future dialogue on a theoretical-critical level about such approaches would be enriching for Pasifika contextual studies. How, for instance, would talanoa and talalasi work together? Is tulou a form of retelling itself, or is it attempting to work with the master's tools?

As I ponder these kinds of questions, I return to vibes/vibing as a methodological tool. For Koloamatangi, it is an essential pillar of present and future compositional work. For me, it is a reminder of the politics of saying and not-saying: some things might be intimated (they might need to be); others are inferred. It is a reminder that communication goes on in so many ways, not only in minoritized or contextual biblical studies, but all the time as we read texts. I find myself continually looking for more ways to explore these themes (which are also pertinent to texts where I work, such as as the Song of Songs, incidentally). But vibing also suggests a means of communication when one is able to speak bluntly or not given the opportunity to speak at all. So, as Koloamatangi may have made clearer in his exposition, it is the case that the backside or the underbelly of culture and life experience develops its own alternative discourse. This way of speaking means opportunity, but it also brings risk of exposure to what is tapu and also to being misunderstood.

Vibing is also suggestive of the unspoken aspects of interpretation when it is attuned to oral roots, for instance, its "cultural elements such as embodiment, opticality, aurality, tactility, vocality, and tacit cultural codes as interrelated and necessary accessories in holistic communication" (Spencer Miller 2013, 47). These are overt (I believe) in Koloamatangi, and they are present, though much less commentated, in Ma'ilo and Kolia. For instance, the positional changes and permutations of tapu and tulou assist Kolia to frame his proposed reading; they remain an excellent source for the metaphorical positional change in perspective. As such, they are a backdrop, but could they be the center? What might an embodied, moving reading look like? I find myself wondering what Pasifika/islander criticism could be with more of these movements and senses brought to the fore. In his calls for dance and protest, Havea might too (in the opening chapter to this collection). It is not just that these bodily inflections may be a central part of oral-preferring cultures and so should be recorded, but that they might have decolonizing power and identity-building potentiality in their alternative ways of meaning-making.

Moving

Other kinds of positions or movements call for our attention in these readings, such as the physical emplacements and displacements of islander readers. Part of the reality of islander identity is surely where one calls home. Home, moreover, indicates other questions, too: What is our past? Is it a singular or collective past? How do we interact with other island subjects (and are all such subjects of the same standing)? And suppose we have emigrated, or are displaced? What is the status of the new land? How does the new home—the "away home"—relate to the one that has been left behind? When so much of islandedness seems rooted to a certain place and a family's place in that space, the experience of many, either in constant movement and relocation or in permanent exile, is surely of enormous significance for how one thinks about islandedness and reading with islander eyes.

Ma'ilo gestures toward such matters in his exploration of the prodigal son. But I want to ask him: have the global movements of islanders, perhaps the result of economics, crime, or the pursuit of work or a better life, created generations of island prodigals whose past reality is an essential part of the present? Indeed, we might wonder why people decide to leave islands, to find themselves always on the move. And are those who have gone always prodigal? It has been suggested that the Caribbean (the place of my own heritage) has experienced the largest sustained movement of people in the globe, not only because of the obvious—the historical influx of slaves and indentured workers—but also because of the current, constant movement of people through relocation due to economic hardship, environmental disaster, and tourism. I suspect Pasifika has a similar legacy of migrations, theirs also caused by current environmental threat (Havea). How, then, do we come to talk about identity, about belonging, when the islands and the people in them with whom we are in relation are always a moving target?

Indeed, migrations are complex in their effects on island subjectivities. The islander who lives away—as argued, for example, by Angeline M. G. Song—must view her former home through a pragmatic, not a romantic, lens. Song points out that the exotic island, in her case Singapore, has all but disappeared, leaving in its stead an island that has, for the sake of "modernity," all but excised its historical and cultural past. So it is that Song finds, contra Steed Vernyl Davidson, that her only choice is to do islander criticism *without* sand between her toes. It is important not to obscure the loss Song seems to exhibit, and yet, her essay brings an important issue to the fore that is not yet fully explored by the essays in this volume. The island that has been left behind is always the subject of memorialization, of nostalgia. But the island that exists for present-day commentary—the "modern island"—is also constructed. We must therefore take seriously that, as much as it is the place of lived reality, the island is also a space of the imagination. Indeed, with the psychic demands placed on them by those who have left and the losses and expectations of those who remain, islands become a contested, messy space. And when these constructions of place are as active in the constitution of islands as the projections placed on them by (neo)colonizers and tourists alike, then defining *island* and *islandedness* is a complex and weighty business indeed.

Song's discussion also makes focused use of her own story. For the greater project of islander criticism, particular life events and features indicate the complexity of migration and islander subjectivity and constitute essential contextualizations. In Song's particular case, the socioeconomic conditions both of her birth and adoptive families, the risks of troubling "alternative futures" for her when she was a child, and the political discourse of 1970s Singapore assemble a multilayered picture that not only helps to track the disappearance of the original island, as she would construct it, but also to indicate future inheritances for those who now call Singapore home. In my own case, race, class, crime, and political independence play critical roles in the constitution of the islands, and necessarily of my own construction of them. These particularities bear spelling out because they impact and sometimes impede one's ability to track island identities. But, I also wonder if, like the bodily interventions mentioned above, they may be a useful means of interrupting the colonial story and of helpfully reconceiving the island, especially the island that has been left behind. Put another way, if everyone's story is not the colonizer's *everystory*, there is surely room to explore the complexity of individual island identities as they navigate both colonial complacency and decolonial practice.

There is, thus, a vital subconversation already at work among some of the articles, which I am hopeful can be pursued as island criticism develops further. This has to do with how islanders identify themselves in relation to the land(s) in which they find themselves. There is not only the matter of what has been lost, but of the constant, often painful navigations one must make in the adopted land, which are of course complicated by the particular subjectivities and situations of those who experience them.

Song and Ma'ilo are both concerned with diaspora identity, asking, in different ways, how islandedness persists in subjects who have left the islands. But they are also asking (are they not?): what is the island, and where do I belong? Inspired by their work, I see opportunity for more applied theoretical engagement in islander criticism with the politics of memory, history, law, and citizenship, which surely have many component parts that are peculiar to island histories. For even those who are not living in diaspora must negotiate their effects. For instance, Makesi Neemia's contribution complicates our understanding of how we are emplaced via the complexities of land tenure and inherited land, and it invites the question of who more properly belongs. Further, Vaitusi Nofoaiga urges the importance of considering the local and the contextual in the face of colonization by missionaries (and its legacy, one infers), urging that we acknowledge that there is not only one island in an island. In the future of (Pasifika) islander studies, one looks forward to greater analysis and commentary of these pieces of land and the emplacement of their subjects.

Belonging

Is my island your island? These last two observations about method and context bring me back to the matter of definitions. As the introduction to this volume elaborates, the politics of definition are troubled. Yet Havea feels compelled to try, in part because of some responses to the prior volume *Islands, Islanders, and the Bible: RumInations*[1] that particularly sought this. He offers definitions in two modes. The first is the expected range (islanders and islanders encompass x and y); it is not his preferred means, since it opens up the possibility for too many problematic results. The second mode, as he says, "foregoes the bathwater and jumps straight into the sea." It is a sketching out of island territory along three themes: waters, ways, and worries.

---

1. These took place at a book panel discussion at the 2016 Annual Meeting of the Society of Biblical Literature (Islands, Islanders, and Scriptures Section). Havea references this in his introduction.

Definitions are always political: who defines; who is excluded; who is included; and who belongs. Historically, islanders know that definitions, especially those imposed upon them, have had important and sometimes grave ramifications for their freedom. In the present, too, definitions concerning citizenship, birth, and connections to place have real implications for an individual's access to food and fresh water, to safety and protections under the law, and to the ability to thrive.[2] I understand Havea's reluctance about definitions and also appreciate his candor, but as he notes, not all islanders will see themselves in these categories (from mode 1 especially). Unlike Havea, then, I do not think that the best response to the many permutations of island identity is to open up all possibilities and allow the practice of definition to remain fluid. Fluidity, I propose, is maybe even more damaging than rigid definition. Havea's practice is based on the impulse to be welcoming, which he sees as innate for islander cultures; but surely this quality may just as easily be imposed as innate. That is, there is a particular poignancy in the idea that as colonized peoples, islanders had to become accustomed to receiving, to being open for colonization, to welcoming. Today they continue this practice in the form of tourism. Where this is a nice idea, the realities of such welcome are different for outsiders than for those who must always welcome, sometimes to the extent that they suffer loss. Indeed, where does such welcome stop?

Relatedly, the idea that anyone who *wants* to belong may do so troubles me. Does this impulse not endlessly repeat the opportunity for cooption and colonization? I think of my own country of origin (Bahamas), engaged as it is by selling off its land to offshore buyers, allowing the environmental encroachment of its waters, and repackaging its cultural product for visitors. This is what happens when a historical quality becomes a means of survival. Environmentally, ethically, and ideologically, the risks are too great to propose that anyone who wants to be an islander may be. Tourism, or neocolonization, is surely the proving ground for such definition. To this end, if belonging remains as open-ended as Havea envisages it could, I wonder how emerging, postcolonial nations might navigate their

---

2. One specific example from the Bahamas sees the children of Haitian immigrants caught between two citizenship laws: *jus sanguinis* in the Bahamas, which grants citizenship to a child born in the Bahamas to a Bahamian citizen and *jus solis* in Haiti, which determines citizenship by place of birth. As a result, they cannot have citizenship in either land and so have become part of a stateless generation, who are discriminated against under the law and in society generally.

identities. Indeed, my impulse is to *push back*, to insist that the definitions that truly matter be negotiated with fairness and justice, so that those who always find themselves disadvantaged and excluded be allowed to flourish. This is not work to accommodate island wannabes and lovers, then, but the insider-outsiders—the poor, the terminally incarcerated, and the migrants who support the economy with few rights. This means, among other things, sustained engagement with the causes and effects of colonial legacies. It also means worrying less about insiders and outsiders and maybe working to unlatch the connections between defining/belonging and the necessities of material existence. Our focus, then, becomes the lived realities of islanders, not the ideological formation of the islands by others.

The introduction's interlude ("Diversion"), in fact, takes me to this observation. Can those who represent and engage in a form of minoritized criticism actively "grease the pump of protest" (Havea) if they find themselves constantly facing in the other direction, anticipating welcomes, with painted-on island smiles? This surely overstates Havea's position, but overstatement might help to elucidate some of the difficulties. I fear that we cannot have it both ways: open, fluid, inviting island identities that nevertheless have enough self-awareness and opportunity for self-reflection that they might become a critical base from which to speak on behalf of those who cannot, even in their midst, speak for themselves. To put this another way, it is true that my own country has been engaged in a forty-year exploration of who the Bahamas is, post-independence. This work is fraught, contentious, troubled, energizing, enlivening, rich, and dynamic. But it is ongoing. Do we yet know who we are? Do we agree? (Is there even a "we"?) If the same can be said of many postcolonial islander nations, I wonder at the relative instability of the place from which we need to speak. This does not mean that we refrain from protest until we have our own ducks in a row, but on the contrary, that we continue the meaningful work of self-definition in earnest, recognizing its urgency in a turbulent world.

As noted, though, the above form of definition was not Havea's preferred mode, and the waters, ways, and worries suit his intentions better. I also find them more comfortable conceptually (though of course, different modes will appeal to different readers) because they give the physical and cultural realities of island existences a place in the conversation. This is enlivening. It seems, further, that what Havea is exploring is really that the how or what of island criticism is more useful in the elaboration of islander criticism than the who. As we saw above, certain methods or hows have been proposed by Kolia, Koloamatangi, and Maʻilo; a fourth is mentioned by Havea but explicated elsewhere (Havea 2016). These would fit into two of the "ways" Havea explicates, orality and relationality. As I indicated above, these ways in the future will have an opportunity to reflect on each other, to borrow and cross-fertilize. But more than this, as a reader of these Pasifika readings—especially one who is used to looking at islander issues from a Caribbean frame—I want to understand better how to situate what I read with respect to the particular geographical, environmental, cultural, and political contexts from whence they have developed. I also want to encourage the broadening of this methodological work, cross-regionally. It is especially important that these identifying, contextualizing features are offered up if this form of minoritized criticism is *not* going to be able to contribute in the typical, expected ways of text-critical and bibliographic work. But, *pace* Havea, this does not mean they do not have to accept that they probably will not be read but rather that they have to proselytize. What they are able to contribute speaks, thinks, and means differently. These differences are, I believe, deeply meaningful for the future of the discipline. And for the rest of the guild? We must open up a space to hear the vibes and appreciate the grooves of islander work.

Works Cited

Havea, Jione. 2016. "The End-or Medium." Pages 81–98 in *Psychoanalytic Mediations between Marxist and Postcolonial Readings of the Bible*. Edited by Tat-siong Benny Liew and Erin Runions. SemeiaSt 84. Atlanta: SBL Press.

Spencer Miller, Althea. 2013. "Rethinking Orality for Biblical Studies." Pages 35–67 in *Postcolonialism and the Hebrew Bible: The Next Step*. Edited by Roland Boer. SemeiaSt 70. Atlanta: Society of Biblical Literature.

Not @ Sea: Finding and Foraging among Family Resemblances across the Oceans

Gerald O. West

I was not as "at sea" as I thought I might be when reading these essays. When I heard that one of the essays I should respond to is in Tongan, I was particularly excited, precisely because I would not be able to understand it! Particularity rules, or ought to, in contextual forms of biblical scholarship. Therefore, I wondered whether all the essays, including the other three I was asked to respond to, would be so particular that I would struggle to translate them. Working as I do with local communities in South Africa always in their own languages, languages that I do not always understand, I am content not to understand. That others make their own meanings that are particular to them in their struggles with the God of life against the idols of death is what is important, whether I understand or not.

However, I was grateful for the editor's introduction to the Tongan language essay because I do want to understand what I can, eager as I am to glean from others working with the Bible engaged in familial struggles with the God of life against the idols of death. This phrase, which I have repeated, harks back to Latin American liberation theology (Hinkelammert 1986), voicing the contested nature of theology and also of the Bible that is common to my context, and it would seem, the contexts of these essays. Like Ruth, I am fortunate to have been invited to "glean among the sheaves" (2:7, 15). What I focus on from among these essays are those family resemblances that resonate with African biblical interpretation, for this is my context, the one to which I offer *tautua*. Already I am borrowing, using Makesi Neemia's suggestive phrase (which I only partially understand). For in the struggle for survival, liberation, and abundant life, we must find and forge what resources we can.

My response therefore participates in two movements. The first movement is to bring African contextual biblical interpretive categories to the essays in order to identify kindred categories of analysis. The second movement is to discern what I can of what is different and discordant, probing and prodding African biblical scholarship in other directions—toward the sea, which brought us our colonizers (including my own intermediate ancestors) but which also offers us allies from Oceania.

From African to Oceanic Biblical Scholarship

I take courage, in approaching the islands from Africa, noting Inise Vakabua Foi'akau's alliance with Musa W. Dube's African postcolonial feminist engagements with the Bible. If Dube's work is recognizably familiar and so potentially useful, I am encouraged to explore (to use a European metaphor) or track (to use an African metaphor) other family resonances. So, I drift with Dube toward Oceanic shores, wondering what resonances I will find and mindful of my imposition, *mlungu* that I am (although the etymology of one of the isiZulu terms for whites in South Africa, *mlungu*, is not clear—one of the common accounts of this term associates Europeans with the white foam or scum that collects along the tide-line on the beach).

In a recent publication, I argued that African biblical scholarship has always been both post-colonial (I prefer to use the hyphen, for it allows for a pause between terms and historical moments) and tri-polar (West 2016a). In an even more recent publication (West 2018), I will develop each of these claims and add a third, that African biblical scholarship should be overt about the Bible as a site-of-struggle. These three claims offer a useful way of locating African biblical scholarship within its global and local contexts. However, while the first two claims are descriptive of what African biblical scholarship is and has always been, the third claim is more prescriptive, recognizing that while some African biblical scholarship works with a contested Bible, all African biblical scholarship ought to. Biblical interpretation has always been a site-of-struggle for African biblical scholarship, but African biblical scholars have not been as clear about the Bible itself as a site-of-struggle.

Post-colonial

African biblical scholarship is intrinsically post-colonial, both because the Bible was brought to Africa as part of the missionary-colonial enterprise

(1415–1787 and 1787–1919) (West 2016b, 14–18) and because biblical studies as an academic discipline is itself an import into Africa from Euro-American contexts (from the 1930s) (Ukpong 2000, 12; Mbuvi 2017, 153) and therefore a post-colonial or, perhaps more accurately, a neo-colonial reality. African biblical scholarship is historically post-colonial and ideologically postcolonial (without a hyphen, postcolonial refers to a mode of thinking), adopting a default ideological postcolonial attitude toward the Bible and biblical scholarship.

I hasten to add that though I use the hyphen in post-colonial, I mean something more local and particular than what Euro-American commodified forms of postcolonial studies have come to connote. Before postcolonial studies arrived at its center in the metropoles of Europe and the United States, African biblical scholarship (and related analytical discourses) were post-colonial. The language used at the time was "inculturation," but the import was "post-colonial" (e.g., Ukpong 2000). The culture and/as religion of Africans that was denigrated by the colonial-missionary enterprise was "revitalized" (Sanneh 1989, 53) by African biblical interpretation. So, I hark back to a homegrown term ("inculturation"), while using the more familiar notion ("postcolonial").

Would the essays in *Sea of Readings*, I wondered, be post-colonial in the local senses that are familiar to African notions of inculturation? Would they manifest local, particular senses of being post-colonial? The editor's introduction to the essay by Tangikefataua Koloamatangi invokes, in the final sentence, the speaking subaltern—for as "we," "southerners," "Third Worlders," Islanders, and Africans know, the subaltern always speaks. This clear reference to what is the precursor ("the subaltern") of what would become the post-colonial indicates a post-colonial orientation, perhaps, to Koloamatangi's contribution. There are other signs too, albeit in the English words of the editor. For example, in asserting that, "without claiming that scriptural texts shape the works by these Tongan composers, Koloamatangi celebrates their creative wisdom," the Bible is put in its proper post-colonial/inculturated place. Furthermore, indigenous, local resources are used to provide a post-colonial rereading of the Bible, so that "A singer or performer of Tongan poems and songs is thus invited to tune in to the *toumui* of the compositions, and in a similar way, so should readers of biblical texts tune into the (filthy and infested) backsides of scriptural texts." And finally, Koloamatangi's contribution is celebrated for being "written in Tongan for an oral presentation." Notwithstanding the scholarly tradition that recognizes oral precursor forms of most biblical texts, the Bible that has been brought to African and Oceanic shores has been a book.

In his essay on (yet again) Jonah, Jione Havea takes up this recognition of oral presences when he asks, "Could the book of Jonah have been the product of a process similar to su'ifefiloi?" This is a clear postcolonial move, using an indigenous/local concept and using it to reread a missionary-colonial brought text. "What if," Havea continues, "the prose consists of several stories from different times and places, so that there were separate stories that a narrator wove together" in a su'ifefiloi-type (story-weaving) way? Though Havea argues that "the opportunity provided by su'ifefiloi is the possibility that this biblical narrative is the weaving of multiple stories, and this would not be a controversial suggestion in the ears of source and tradition critics," his emphasis in this essay is not (as it would be for typical source and redaction critics) to identify the component parts (or sources) of this weaving and their "origins" but to put each of these constituent stories to use. What su'ifefiloi *does* is provide "an opportunity to read the same narrative in the interests of different, including minoritized, characters." Havea makes this clear in his concluding invitation, stating that he "offer[s] this reading with an invitation: let us seek and engage the wisdom of the native writers of Pasifika, and let us cooperate in the stor(y)ing of scriptures." Following the inculturation/post-colonial logic of the Nigerian biblical scholar Justin Ukpong (2002, 22), for whom African contexts are always "the *subject* of interpretation of the Bible," Havea makes Pasifika contexts the subject of biblical interpretation.

Neemia's essay too bears post-colonial marks. As with the other two essays, this essay makes a particular, local context the subject of biblical interpretation, bringing the Bible into dialogue with Samoan claims to customary land. In a fairly typical inculturation-subaltern move, Neemia uses what he considers to be the "inclusive and accommodating social vision of the *ger* in the Priestly writings" to recognize (and so revitalize) "traditional" or indigenous notions of land "ownership." In the words of the author: "the inclusive and accommodating social vision of the *ger* in the Priestly writings may serve as a hermeneutical model for Samoans to deal with the tagata ese, their tautua, and their right to claim customary land." Samoans are challenged to see local matters differently from how missionary-colonial forces might have presented them.

But, significantly, Neemia goes boldly further, using P's "inclusive and accommodating social vision" to address the situation of the "many unfortunate tagata ese [who] render tautua to a high chief and the extended family, but are overlooked (because of prejudice and corruption) when a successor to a matai title is chosen." Though this move in the essay is not as developed as the more traditionally post-colonial move to reclaim religion and/as culture, it resonates with similar work by Makhosazana Nzimande (2008), whose intersecting of the post-colonial with class over against traditional/indigenous cultural dynastic and hierarchical tendencies daringly inaugurates, I have argued, a fourth phase in South African Black Theology (West 2016b, 346).

Levesi Laumau Afutiti's essay is implicitly post-colonial, emphasizing how "Samoans regard their language, with reference to its wisdom sayings, as a repository that contains their cultural and traditional values." Against an implied imperialism, "the Samoan language has served as an *oo* (receptacle) for storing Samoan values." Language is the "basket that holds her nature, life, and identity," within which "Samoan cultures and traditions are embedded in proverbial and wisdom sayings," constituting a "Samoan text." Here, then, is a Samoan "text," another sacred text to read alongside the missionary-colonial brought Bible. This "text," Afutiti argues, stores the past, the pre-colonial past, the "worldview(s) inherited from past generations."

Tri-polar

There are three intersecting poles in my analysis in this section: the African context, the biblical text, and the ideo-theological forms of dialogue between African context and biblical text. While most characterizations of African biblical hermeneutics tend to portray a bipolar approach—referring for example to "the comparative method" (Anum 2000, 468; Ukpong 2000, 12; Holter 2002, 88–89), in which African context and biblical text interpret each other—it would be more accurate to describe African biblical hermeneutics as tri-polar. The essays by Havea, Afutiti, and Neemia show signs that the tri-polar elements in African biblical hermeneutics work in the case of Pasifika as well.

Implicit in bipolar-like formulations are aspects of a third pole mediating the engagement between the African context and the biblical text—the pole of appropriation. Ukpong (2000, 24), a key commentator on the comparative method, refers overtly to the goal of comparative interpretation as "the actualization of the theological meaning of the text in today's context so as to forge integration between faith and life, and engender commitment to personal and societal transformation." What connects or entangles text and context, then, is a form of dialogical appropriation that has a theological and a praxiological dimension (Draper 2015). This ideo-theological third pole can take various forms, resulting in at least six intersecting yet different theoretical emphases in African biblical interpretation: inculturation (with an emphasis on culture and religion), liberation (with an emphasis on politics and economics), feminist (with an emphasis on gender and patriarchy), psychological (with an emphasis on individual and communal well-being), post-colonial (with an emphasis on missionary-colonialism), and queer (with an emphasis on gender and sexuality) biblical hermeneutics (West 2016a). Andrew Mbuvi (2017, 163) offers a partially overlapping set of ideo-theological orientations but includes an emphasis on reconstruction and democratization hermeneutics.

Neemia's essay is properly tri-polar, evident in three parts of the essay: on *tagata ese* in Samoa, on ger in the Priestly writings, and on a dialogue between the historical investigation of the Priestly *ger* and the tagata ese in the Samoan context. The ideo-theological theory enabling and directing the dialogue between text and context has elements of both inculturation (culture) and liberation (class) forms of appropriation, though the latter is not as developed as the former.

Havea similarly employs a tri-polar approach, bringing the concept of su'ifefiloi (story-weaving) into dialogue with the stories of Jonah, using cultural, class, gender, and queer theoretical resources, "in the interests of different, including minoritized, characters." Though Koloamatangi is less easy for me to track, there is the characteristic "back-and-forth" movement (Draper 1991, 243) between biblical text and Tongan "text," each constituting the other through conversation (or even contestation).

Afutiti too works overtly within a tri-polar frame. Making the Samoan context the subject of biblical interpretation, he constructs an inculturation hermeneutical mediation in which the *alagaupu* and *muagagana* "have teachings for ordinary people." Afutiti is eclectic in his choice of methods, both demonstrating a literary rhetorical sensitivity to the way in which wisdom literature functions and using sociohistorical methods to make an argument, for example, for Paul's use of Greek wisdom in introducing the gospel in Acts 17:28. For Afutiti, the tri-polar logic is clear: "In the light of the book of Proverbs and Paul, why should there be a problem with using Samoan proverbial and wisdom sayings? It is biblically sound to posit that traditional sayings are in the framework of God's acts through preaching to nurture life. In this sense, our Samoan proverbial and wisdom sayings have authority, for they too are God's gifts to nurture God's people."

African biblical scholars too tend to be eclectic when it comes to which methods they use to analyze biblical text (and local context) within the tri-polar approach. The essays in this volume demonstrate a similar disregard for methodological purity, with authors using an array of methods to do the necessary work of bringing context and text into conversation. Havea uses literary methods while Neemia and Afutiti use historical-critical methods.

Site-of-Struggle

In Africa's long and deeply ambiguous engagement with the missionary-colonial brought Bible (West 2016b), the predominant tendency among African biblical scholars has been to work with the Bible with a hermeneutic of trust, using inculturation theory to reappropriate the Bible over against missionary-colonial deprecations of African religion and/as culture. However, Itumeleng J. Mosala (1989, 185) is adamant that "the texts of the Bible are sites of struggle" and that any appropriation must foreground this reality of struggle. Unless the Bible is recognized and reread as itself, intrinsically, a site of struggle, there is always the risk that the oppressor's form of the text, the final form, will have the final word (Mosala 1989, 28; West 2017).

Significantly, though both Havea (using literary tools) and Neemia (using sociohistorical tools) recognize the layeredness of the biblical text and therefore (implicitly at least) the different social sectors that produced the biblical text, there is no strong sense of contestation inherent to the text. Havea does recognize some level of contestation, deliberately using a su'ifefiloi mode of reading because it "provides an opportunity to read the same narrative in the interests of different, including minoritized, characters." He privileges reading in the interests of the sailors, the sea, and the people of Nineveh, arguing that "spirit of su'ifefiloi encourages readers to story/hear/fakaongo the characters and stories that have been silenced/fakalongo/stored because of the interests of Jonah, Israel, and God." Havea argues that the "opportunity provided by su'ifefiloi is the possibility that this biblical narrative is the weaving of multiple stories," and while recognizing that "this would not be a controversial suggestion in the ears of source and tradition critics," he does not go on to make the Mosala-like claim that source and redactional criticism require the recognition of contending ideological forces at work. Neemia's methodology is more familiar to Mosala than Havea's, so Mosala would be puzzled as to why Neemia does not do more careful ideological work with his different redactions. Mosala would affirm Afutiti's critique that Samoan pastors, like African pastors (and theologians), are so fixated "to safeguard the Bible as the word of God" that they cannot see the value of the Samoan oral sacred texts.

Perhaps Havea and Neemia, like so many of the authors in this volume, identify with their local Bible "re-membering" communities in ways that Mosala finds problematic? Havea and Neemia (and Koloamatangi) include, if not directly in their essays, communities of Christian faith in which the Bible is a sacred text. Both Havea and Neemia yearn for this sacred text to be read more inclusively and so are reluctant to use forms of scholarship that might alienate these faithful communities, preferring to offer them additional resources with which to interpret more inclusively. Afutiti too remains connected to communities of faith, overtly, but is insistent that "Samoan proverbial and wisdom sayings, like other traditional sayings, are God's gift" to Samoa, and that there is plenty of precedent in the Bible itself for the use of local resource. But Afutiti stops short of a Mosala-like move, using the struggle around Samoan proverbial and wisdom sayings that he analyzes so clearly as a hermeneutical entry point to engage the contested realities of biblical wisdom literature and the Bible in general.

As in these essays, in African biblical scholarship communities of African Christian faith, though just outside (or in Afutiti's case, inside) the margins of our scholarly essays, are always present.

From Oceanic to African Biblical Scholarship

Looking at these essays from an African biblical scholarship perspective recognizes significant family resemblances. I felt comfortable among these essays, each and all of them. They felt familiar, even the one I could not understand. Indeed, I feel much more at home among these essays than I do in the midst of Euro-American biblical scholarship. Unfortunately, I think, "we" have allowed various factors to separate us in sites where we could forge interoceanic collaboration. What began as an attempt within the Society of Biblical Literature to forge intercontinental collaboration, "the Bible in Africa, Asia, and Latin America," and expanded to include some of the islands, "the Bible in Africa, Asia, Latin America, and the Caribbean," has fractured. I applaud the turn to particularity but mourn the potential collaboration. This collection of essays makes it clear to me why I mourn, for so much resonates, echoing across the oceans that both divide and link us.

What, then, do I take from this Pasifika particularity? I take away the commitment of this volume to its own accent. When Dube and I put together a volume of *Semeia Studies* (then a journal) on African biblical interpretation similar to this volume (West and Dube 1996), we received considerable opposition from some on the Semeia Studies board who argued that they could not understand our accent. Fortunately, the general editor, Daniel Patte (one of the respondents to this Oceanic volume) resisted the board and affirmed the African editors. How good it is to hear an unfamiliar accent!

I take away the many local concepts reluctantly translated into English. Havea stops translating su'ifefiloi early on in his essay, allowing each use of the term to encrust the concept with other elements beyond his translation of story-weaving and his description of "the art of weaving a mixture of different flowers and leaves to form a long *ula* or necklace." Similarly, Neemia allows his use of the concepts tautua and tagata ese to open up their array of (contending?) meanings, meanings beyond what he offers by way of translation. Afutiti too saturates the reader with Samoan sayings and invokes the reader to hear Samoan wisdom from the past, offering just enough translation to enable the reader to follow his flow but just not enough to summon the hearer to listen more carefully. That Havea, Neemia, and Afutiti embody within their own lived realities more than the English translations of the concepts they use is important to note. For those of us who speak more than one language in contexts with multiple languages, translation is always a feature of our land- and seascape. Both Havea and Neemia know that these concepts are only partially translatable, yet they persist with the vernacular, refusing to bow the knee to the neocolonial pressures of Euro-American biblical studies. The "we" of Havea's essay includes those, should they have been present at Koloamatangi's performance of his contribution, who could and would have asked the person sitting next to them to share something of their understanding of what was being said. We always turn to those more native than we are to help us understand, and there is always translation, offered as a gift. By translating for us, they offer a remarkable tautua, including us in that embodied moment a place among the tagata ese.

This, again, is why I mourn less collaboration than I hope for, because to be in-corporated among the tagata ese requires being together, as bodies. But the invitation from these essays is clear: you are welcome among us when we meet as the Oceania Biblical Studies Association. Perhaps this kind of embodied meeting place is not possible in sites like the Society of Biblical Literature meetings, which is why when the Society of Biblical Literature met in Seoul, South Korea (2016), the Society for Asian Biblical Studies met among themselves prior to that meeting, having invited all Society of Biblical Literature members to join them. And though Society for Asian Biblical Studies occupied a track within the Society of Biblical Literature meeting, the atmosphere was not quite the same as it had been when "we" met on our own terms.

The vernacular conceptual contribution of essays like these is, I would argue, immense. Like African biblical scholarship, itself a "nascent discipline," "the nature and content" of which "are very much in flux" (Mbuvi 2017, 149), Oceanic and Pasifika biblical scholarship is still charting its terrain (on both land and sea) and terminology. As we would say in South Africa, raising our fists in defiance against neo-colonial forces, "Long live the vernacular, long live." Allow me to illustrate. In the essay by Vaitusi Nofoaiga, there is a recognition of the limitations of the terminology, the conceptual apparatus, we have inherited from Euro-American forms of post-colonial theory:

> The concept of hybridity has limitations. It identifies and describes something or someone that is *not* pure, but conceiving subjects as (social, cultural, or religious) impure is impolite and inappropriate. However, the weaknesses of the concept of hybridity—its biased roots, impure offspring, over- and under-emphasis of distinctions in different times and spaces—makes attention to subjects who fit the hybridity profile (e.g., the marginalized and minoritized) more urgent. To give up on the concept because of its ideological blind spots does not help hybridized subjects.

Well said, I would say. This essay, as well as the essays by Brian Fiu Kolia, Martin Wilson Mariota, Foi'akau, Angeline M. G. Song, and Neemia, engages with aspects of hybridity, but in each case, other terms and concepts are used, in most cases the untranslated use of vernacular terms.

Conclusion

This is the stuff of feasts, so sated, I allow myself to drift back to African shores. But before I go, I reiterate that I think there is much here that we can collaborate around, should we meet in collaborative contexts. For example, as already indicated, the essay by Afutiti takes up, recovering, "Samoan proverbial (*alagaupu*) and wisdom sayings (*muagagana*)," wondering how such might "be utilized in biblical exegesis?" The recovery of local, indigenous wisdom is an enduring strand of African biblical scholarship, recently given new impetus by the increasingly nuanced work of African scholars like Madipoane Masenya (2013). And the nuance is needed because, as Masenya argues, proverbs embody the patriarchal "world" that generated them. Furthermore, as the South African liberation biblical scholar Gunther Wittenberg (1991) has argued, proverbs also embody the economic systems that generated them. How do we "use" our scholarship to serve our communities, many of which are communities of faith, while recognizing that our sacred texts (both local and colonial) are embedded within intersecting social systems that tend to bring death rather than life? With this question, inviting further meetings, I take my leave, drifting back on the ocean currents and tides to end up once again the mlungu, on southern African shores, reflective and much the wiser.

Works Cited

Anum, Eric. 2000. "Comparative Readings of the Bible in Africa: Some Concerns." Pages 457–73 in *The Bible in Africa: Transactions, Trajectories, and Trends*. Edited by Gerald O. West and Musa W. Dube. Leiden: Brill.

Draper, Jonathan A. 1991. "'For the Kingdom Is Inside of You and It Is Outside of You': Contextual Exegesis in South Africa (Lk. 13:6–9)." Pages 235–57 in *Text and Interpretation: New Approaches in the Criticism of the New Testament*. Edited by Patrick J. Hartin and Jacobus H. Petzer. NTTS 15. Leiden: Brill.

———. 2015. "African Contextual Hermeneutics: Readers, Reading Communities, and Their Options between Text and Context." *RT* 22:3–22.

Hinkelammert, Franz J. 1986. *The Ideological Weapons of Death: A Theological Critique of Capitalism*. Maryknoll, NY: Orbis Books.

Holter, Knut. 2002. *Old Testament Research for Africa: A Critical Analysis and Annotated Bibliography of African Old Testament Dissertations, 1967–2000*. BTA 3. New York: Lang.

Masenya (ngwan'a Mphahlele), Madipoane. 2013. "Engaging with the Book of Ruth as Single, African Christian Women: One African Woman's Reflection." *VE* 34.1: art. A771. doi: 10.4102/ve.v34i1.771.

Mbuvi, Andrew M. 2017. "African Biblical Studies: An Introduction to an Emerging Discipline." *CBR* 15.2:149–78.

Mosala, Itumeleng J. 1989. *Biblical Hermeneutics and Black Theology in South Africa*. Grand Rapids: Eerdmans.

Nzimande, Makhosazana K. 2008. "Reconfiguring Jezebel: A Postcolonial *imbokodo* Reading of the Story of Naboth's Vineyard (1 Kings 21:1–16)." Pages 223–58 in *African and European Readers of the Bible in Dialogue: In Quest of a Shared Meaning*. Edited by Hans de Wit and Gerald O. West. SRA 32. Leiden: Brill.

Sanneh, Lamin. 1989. *Translating the Message: The Missionary Impact on Culture*. ASMS 13. Maryknoll, NY: Orbis Books.

Ukpong, Justin S. 2000. "Developments in Biblical Interpretation in Africa: Historical and Hermeneutical Directions." Pages 11–28 in *The Bible in Africa: Transactions, Trajectories, and Trends*. Edited by Gerald O. West and Musa W. Dube. Leiden: Brill.

———. 2002. "Reading the Bible in a Global Village: Issues and Challenges from African Readings." Pages 9–39 in *Reading the Bible in the Global Village: Cape Town*. Edited by Justin S. Ukpong. GPBS 3. Atlanta: Society of Biblical Literature.

West, Gerald O. 2016a. "Accountable African Biblical Scholarship: Postcolonial and Tri-polar." *CanCul* 20:35–67.

———. 2016b. *The Stolen Bible: From Tool of Imperialism to African Icon*. BIS 144. Leiden: Brill.

———. 2017. "The Co-optation of the Bible by 'Church Theology' in Post-liberation South Africa: Returning to the Bible as a 'Site of Struggle.'" *JTSA* 157:185–98.

———. 2018. "African Biblical Scholarship as Tri-polar, Post-colonial, and a Site-of-Struggle." Pages 240–73 in *Present and Future of Biblical Studies: Celebrating Twenty-Five Years of Brill's* Biblical Interpretation. Edited by Benny Tat-siong Liew. Leiden: Brill.

West, Gerald O., and Musa W. Dube, eds. 1996. *"Reading with": An Exploration of the Interface between Critical and Ordinary Readings of the Bible; African Overtures*. SemeiaSt 73. Atlanta: Scholars Press.

Wittenberg, Gunther H. 1991. "Job the Farmer: the Judean *am ha-aretz* and the Wisdom Movement." *OTE* 4.2:151–70.

Going with the Flow

Daniel Patte

I chose the title "Going with the Flow" not only because it is fitting for a volume entitled *Sea of Readings: The Bible in the South Pacific*, but also and primarily because it expresses what all of us readers of the Bible—including Western exegetes—need to acknowledge, following islanders. First, this volume exemplifies that we *necessarily* "go with the flow" of the text; whatever we might be reading, we identify among its many waves one that seems most promising, catching it and surfing it, even as we let the other waves pass by. "Going with the flow" of the text necessarily involves choosing one of its dimensions as most significant. Second, this volume exemplifies that whenever we read a text *as Scripture*, we *necessarily* "go with the flow" of the biblical stories, by interweaving them with the stories that hold together our lives in our cultures and contextual situations (whatever they might be). This interweaving of stories is necessary because when one reads a text as Scripture, one reads it for a Word-to-live-by, in the concrete reality of our unfolding lives (not in the abstract!). Therefore, the biblical stories and the stories of our lives necessarily become intertwined and need to be intertwined. Third, this volume exemplifies that, by reading the Bible as Scripture/Word-to-live-by, we *necessarily* "go with the flow" of the ideology(ies) that frame our cultures and social conditions, even as we "go with the flow" of the biblical text's ideology—understanding ideology in the neutral sense of Louis Althusser's (1984, 36) definition: "ideology is a representation of the imaginary relationship of individuals to their real conditions of existence." Therefore, for us who are far away from the islands of the South Pacific, this volume is in no way exotic (presenting outlandish and colorful, dreamlike views beyond the concrete solidity of real life as we know it). Rather, this volume makes explicit how all of us actually read Scripture—something that we must acknowledge, even though many of us, especially in the West, pretend that our readings are solidly *grounded* into the scriptural text. We, readers in the West, should do well to remember what hermeneutics (e.g., Gadamer, Ricoeur) as well as linguistics and semiotics (e.g., de Saussure, Greimas, Eco) have long taught us. There is no reading without a "fusion of horizons" exemplified by the "history of reception" (*Wirkungsgeschichte*, Gadamer 2004). Therefore, mixing metaphors, I can say that there is no reading without: (1) "going with the flow" of the text by choosing and catching one of its waves, the wave that we deeply feel fuses with our horizon (while we let the other textual wave go by); (2) "going with the flow" of its stories by interweaving it (fusing it) with our own stories; and (3) "going with the flow" of our cultural situations, fusing our ideological horizon with that of the text.

But how do we learn to do that? We are reluctant to let go; we hold on for dear life to whatever is at hand, rather than "going with the flow." For me, personally, it took many encounters with readers of the Bible whom I could not help but respect, even though they were so different from me that I could not understand them at all. This is my experience with reading the essay by Tangikefataua Koloamatangi, "Ko e Punake mo 'e ne Ta'anga, pea mo e Folofola" (ch. 5). Since I do not know the Tongan language, I have to admit that I did not understand anything about this essay; the characters on the page were simply dead letters, not translated in order to preserve the "untamability of orality." What irony! Looking at the page, I could not hear anything. Yet the editor whispered in my ear that Koloamatangi emphasizes that the Bible/Scripture has a *toumui*—a backside, necessary to hold the structure of the home together—even though it is often filthy and infested. This was enough to evoke for me the worship service of the Church of the Eleven Apostles (and African Initiated Church) I attended in 1999 in Kasane, Botswana. I did not understand a single word, since everything was in the Setswana language. At first, I strove to understand what was said with the help of the few words that a kind translator whispered in my ear, but I soon realized I was missing the essential: by simply "going with the flow" of the untamable orality and awkwardly participating in the body-language of the congregation, I shared in the Spirit that moved it. Thus forming, Koloamatangi's essay in the Tongan language is similarly an invitation to "go with the flow" of this sea of readings.

– 1 –

Reading necessarily involves going with the *flow of the text* because a text is not a static object with a meaning content—it is an organism in suspended animation until readers intervene. "Going with the flow" of the text means selectively bringing back to life certain parts of this organism by latching onto particular textual features that are perceived to be pregnant with meaning from the reader's particular cultural perspective. This is what Vaitusi Nofoaiga illustrates with the essay "Jesus the *Fiaola* (Opportunity Seeker): A Postcolonial Samoan Reading of Matthew 7:24–8:22."

Reading Matthew through a fiaola hermeneutic while "seeking for survival in the Samoan social, cultural, and political worlds" expresses in the Samoan language something similar to what I expressed by the phrase "Word-to-live-by," since "Fiaola … means 'wanting life' or 'seeking life.'" Thus, generally speaking, fiaola hermeneutic is reading the biblical text as Scripture. But soon Nofoaiga becomes more specific: since his fiaola reading contributes to "seeking survival in the Samoan social, cultural, and political world," he envisions fiaola as an approach for sociorhetorical criticism. This means that he chooses to latch on sociorhetorical textual features as the features perceived as most pregnant with meaning for him and his community. The designation of his method as sociorhetorical criticism signals that he made a choice among the dozens of critical exegetical methods found in methodological textbooks (see McKenzie and Haynes 1993; Gooder 2008; Moyise 2013). Or, I could say from a semiotic theory perspective, that he chose to "textualize" (to make a meaningful text out of) the string of words that we call "the Gospel of Matthew" by privileging *one* of its many types of textual features[1]—leaving out as less significant other textual features. This is what anyone does when reading any text. But the way in which these textual features are defined always is highly cultural-specific.[2] This is what Nofoaiga exemplifies by his essay. While his fiaola reading is a sociorhetorical analysis of Matt 7:24–8:22, the fact of reading it as "a *siomiaga fiaola faa-le-tusiga* (*fiaola* rhetorical and narrative unit)" shifts the focus so as to include paying close attention to the way in which "Jesus's ministry to the *local place* of Galilee reveals Jesus's attention to the *needs and rights of local people*" (emphases added). The narrative units and the narrative progression in Matthew—"going with the flow" of

---

1. The list of all these textual features is so long that presenting it requires a long dictionary such as Greimas and Courtés 1982.

2. Thus, there are several, distinct semiotic theories. Greimas and Courtés's French semiotics is quite different, for example, from North American, Russian, and Indian semiotics, each with its specificity.

the text—are perceived through Samoan lenses, "going with the flow" of the Samoan sociocultural experiences and needs.[3]

– 2 –

Alternative to identifying those textual features that are particularly meaning*ful* for us in our particular cultural settings (Nofoaiga's essay), "going with the flow" of the text can also involve interweaving the stories of the scriptural text together with our own stories, as is strikingly illustrated by Mosese Ma'ilo's essay, "Island Prodigals: Encircling the Void in Luke 15:11-32 with Albert Wendt."

In *Sons for the Return Home*, a fascinating and powerful novel,[4] Wendt retells the parable of the prodigal son in two interwoven ways: the prodigal leaving for a distant land being, on the one hand, the Samoan family and the British family leaving their homes to move to New Zealand ("both immigrant prodigals in Aotearoa New Zealand"), but also, on the other hand, the immigrant children (the son of the Samoan family and the daughter of a British *pakeha/palagi* family) who are prodigals as members of the immigrant families—although, since they barely remember their countries of origin, they also become prodigals at the end of the story by going "back to their respective roots (London and Samoa) at the end of the story." In addition to these changes, as Ma'ilo points out, the presentation and conceptions of "the distant land" (Luke 15:13), of the "pigs" (15:15), of the "return" (15:20-24), and of "home" (15:20-32) are totally different in the novel and in Luke, although in both each of these themes plays an important role. As Ma'ilo clarifies, in so doing Wendt practices *"talalasi* ("big telling" or "telling big") … a Samoan device for telling and retelling stories and histories" and a term that expresses "the legitimacy of many tellings and their standing on equal platform of authority during exchange of oratorical speeches."

Should not such extravagant telling and retelling of biblical stories be rejected and dismissed as misuses of biblical stories, twisting the biblical texts beyond recognition? This is just a novel! Entertaining! But without legitimacy. Granted, one might want to retell a biblical story (e.g., in preaching), but if one does so, one must respect its narrative flow. Otherwise, the

---

3. Happily with minimal references to Western critical commentaries, otherwise the Samoan insights would not have been brought to the surface.

4. I was happy to discover it: I could not put it down after beginning to read it!

story does not convey the same faith-vision, does it? With talalasi, the Bible is "no longer the *absolute story*" (emphasis original) in the framework of which we should inscribe our lives. Such were the puzzled responses of my students when they read Jione Havea's (2004) (extraordinary) commentary on Numbers using what he simply calls (in the limited space of the *Global Bible Commentary*) an "Island-story-telling," telling and retelling a series of stories found in Numbers. Before doing so, he warns the readers that while reading a biblical book of Scripture—as Word-to-live-by—might mean for many appropriating it for one's context (using the biblical story as corrective lenses to correct the story of one's life), he does not do so because there is nothing "corrective in a story [Numbers] that endorses the proscriptions of people like mine" (45). By practicing an "Island-story-telling," Havea "contextualize[s] it in order to allow the foreign and strange to be different" (45) and concludes: "Island-story-telling is not so much about forming conclusions as about responding, redirecting, transgressing, engaging, disagreeing, teasing, angering, crossing, challenging, and letting go" (50). This is exactly what Wendt did, as Ma'ilo makes explicit, by emphasizing that when the Bible is viewed as the *absolute* or as "'the *only* story' [it] leaves us [islanders] with a void, a silent incompleteness in understanding who we are as islanders." The islanders' experience is denied. "Distant land," "pigs," "return," and "home" in Luke 15 do not reflect anything in the islanders' experience, which is silenced (an important theme in the novel). Conversely, these are totally silent and void; they can make sense for islanders only if these themes are transgressed, crossed, challenged, redirected. This is contextualizing the biblical story, but not in the sense of forcing the foreign to fit into it and leaving out in the silent void what does not fit. Rather, this is contextualizing the biblical story, in the sense of "allow[ing] the foreign and strange to be different" (Havea 2004, 45) in that story, so as "to encircle the void created by reading the Bible as the absolute story." Yes, Wendt's *Sons for the Return Home* is a legitimate and truly inspired retelling of the parable, prolonging it in the islanders' lives as scriptural stories are supposed to do.

Is this a sacrilegious use of the Bible, which should be viewed as the *absolute story* to which all other stories should be conformed to have any value and legitimacy? This is indeed what "missionaries wanted our forebears to think" both in the islands and in their Western homes. But, this is a hypocritical claim. It would not demand much investigation to show that the sermons of such missionaries are/were far from respecting the historical reconstruction of "distant land," "pigs," "return," and "home" (to which

Ma'ilo appropriately refers in passing) and therefore far from respecting the story in Luke 15, despite their claim that it is to be taken as absolute. Actually, such sermons retell the parable of the prodigal son *as a Western (British or American) story*—making it a decidedly individual-centered story (removing all its original community-centered frame) so as "to encircle the void created by reading the Bible as the absolute story" in their own cultural settings. While I do not have at hand concrete examples of the history of the receptions of the parable of the prodigal son, which would demonstrate this point, I have many such examples in the case of the history of receptions of Romans (see the volumes in Trinity Press and Bloomsbury T&T Clark's series, Romans throughout History and Cultures). No one has read or reads a text of Scripture such as Romans without inscribing in it the stories of one's life and therefore without retelling the story of Paul's interaction with the Romans (as expressed in his letter) in the stories of one's culture. And this is true in the case of *all* (Western) scholars who claim to follow the story of Romans as the absolute story by presenting a *critical historical* study of it that they claim is the only one legitimate and plausible.[5] This is what Fatima Tofighi (2017) has demonstrated by showing how, in all such studies, Paul's main categories are Europeanized and have contributed to establish European categories, "encircling the void of who [they] are"—a void that would not exist if Paul's story of his interactions with believers in Rome remained in the Greco-Roman world.[6]

– 3 –

Finally, reading a biblical text as Scripture always and necessarily means reading it with (or even within) a community. Such a community is ever present in the readers' lives, and therefore its ideology (in Althusser's [1984] neutral definition) necessarily frames their interpretations. This is what Angeline M. G. Song strikingly demonstrates in her essay, "Not Just a Bimbo: A Reading of Esther by a Singaporean Immigrant in Aotearoa New Zealand," by illustrating how her Malay-Chinese immigrant reading

---

5. Of course, as historians they would "humbly" say, following the "principle of criticism," that their interpretation has only "a greater degree of probability" to be legitimate than all other interpretations!

6. See Tofighi 2017. While the Europeanization of Paul and his letters is commonly invisible to Western Christians, it is quite visible from the Muslim Iranian perspective of Fatima Tofighi.

of Esther is radically different from that of Nicole Duran (2003), who reads Esther from her Western feminist perspective.

From my Western, progressive perspective, I readily agreed with Duran's (2003, 74) interpretation, that "feminists have found it easier to admire Vashti, however briefly she may appear in the story": by refusing to appear in front of the king's drunken guests (Esth 1:9–12), Vashti showed the king to be what he really was—"a hedonistic fool" (Duran 2003, 75). By contrast, Esther "comes in willingly to do what Vashti would not" (78). Song encapsulates Duran's interpretation in a stinging way by saying that this is reading Esther as if she was "a bimbo in a colonizer's world—gorgeous, unintelligent, and oh so willing to be invaded and tamed in both body and mind, in this case by the Persian king." Is it not obvious that one should object to Esther's behavior, especially when it reflects so much of the way in which colonialists envision the islands, often representing them as "easily conquered, tamable, and available"? Of course, islanders, and even more so a Malay-Chinese immigrant in Aotearoa New Zealand, should join Duran in fighting sexism/patriarchalism and colonialism as embodied by Queen Esther. As is well known, we Westerners know what is best for islanders! Including what it means to be freed from colonialism! Right?

Song brilliantly unmasks our Western ideological preunderstandings by proposing a reading of Esther solidly framed by her multidimensional cultural perspective. She is from Singapore where "it is possible to do island hermeneutics without getting sand between one's toes"—a first surprise. In their way of life and interpretations, Singaporeans practice what Song calls "a hermeneutic of pragmatism and survival."

This pragmatic ideological perspective[7] was reinforced for Song by her adoptive mother's sacrifices to provide her with the best possible opportunities in life and by her experience as a Malay-Chinese immigrant to Aotearoa New Zealand, where as a tutor-lecturer she is in turn supporting adult learners, mostly new immigrants of minority races. It is in such context(s) that she learned to "embrace the margins" by creatively converting one's marginalized site into a place of strength through that very marginality. This is a matter of survival both for oneself and for others. For this Esther becomes a model: throughout the story, Esther is marginalized, but she

---

7. From the perspective of Althusser's (1984) analysis of ideology as neutral, I would debate Song's hesitation to call this perspective ideological.

converts her "marginalized site" into a place of strength where she can help other marginalized subjects. Esther's "outward assimilation and avoiding overt rebellion is a familiar tactic for many colonized people" and more generally "for colonized people"—as James C. Scott (whom she quotes) has shown. This is a way of reading biblical texts as a scripturalizing of daily life, transforming the practice of everyday life so that marginalized sites become places of strength (see Certeau 1984; Wimbush 2013). This is what Song's essay does, along with the essays by Nofoaiga and by Ma'ilo. Going with the flow of the text even as they go with the flow of everyday life in the "Sea of Islands," in the process transforming the practice of everyday life so that marginalized sites become places of strength, they empower us, their grateful readers, to transform our practice of everyday life so that marginalized sites become places of strength. Yet, at the heart logic of this going with the flow of the text as well as of the story and ideology of our contexts, it is essential to affirm that, when its Western character is acknowledged, the reading of Esther by Duran is itself, for women in the West, part of a necessary process for transforming the practice of everyday life so that the marginalized sites (in which women are reduced to "gorgeous, unintelligent, and oh so willing to be invaded and tamed in both body and mind," ready to enter the TV contest of *Who Wants to Marry a Millionaire*) might become places of strength. "Going with the flow" is an ongoing process, following the back and forth of the waves.

Works Cited

Althusser, Louis. 1984. *Essays on Ideology.* London: Verso.

Certeau, Michel de. 1984. *The Practice of Everyday Life.* Translated by Steven Rendall. Berkeley: University of California Press.

Duran, Nicole. 2003. "Who Wants to Marry a Persian King? Gender Games and Wars and the Book of Esther." Pages 71–84 in *Pregnant Passion: Gender, Sex, and Violence in the Bible.* Edited by Cheryl A. Kirk-Duggan. SemeiaSt 44. Atlanta: SBL Press.

Gadamer, Hans-Georg. 2004. *Truth and Method.* 2nd ed. Translated by Joel Weinsheimer and Donald Marshall. London: Continuum.

Gooder, Paula. 2008. *Searching for Meaning: An Introduction to Interpreting the New Testament.* Louisville: Westminster John Knox.

Greimas, Algirdas Julien, and Joseph Courtés. 1982. *Semiotics and Language: An Analytical Dictionary.* Translated by Larry Crist, Daniel

Patte, James Lee, Edward McMahon II, Gary Phillips, and Michael Rengstorf. AS. Bloomington: Indiana University Press.

Havea, Jione. 2004. "Numbers." Pages 43–51 in *Global Bible Commentary*. Edited by Daniel Patte. Nashville: Abingdon.

McKenzie, Steven L., and Stephen R. Haynes, eds. 1993. *To Each Its Own Meaning: An Introduction to Biblical Criticisms*. Louisville: Westminster John Knox.

Moyise, Steve. 2013. *Introduction to Biblical Studies*. 3rd ed. TTCABS. London: T&T Clark.

Tofighi, Fatima. 2017. *Paul's Letters and the Construction of the European Self*. STCPRIB 10; LNTS 572. New York: Bloomsbury.

Wimbush, Vincent L. 2013. *MisReading America: Scriptures and Difference*. With the assistance of Lalruatkima and Melissa Renee Reid. Oxford: Oxford University Press.

Ancient Roots of the Islander Narrative of Inferiority

Camilla Raymond

One of the liabilities of subaltern identity, of being a minority in spaces where power and privilege matter, is the perpetual awareness of difference. What results from this climate is the tendency to renegotiate special cultural tastes and sensibilities for the sake of assimilating. Drawing attention to failures not correlative with normative practices and ideas from the dominant culture, it is easy for subalterns to assume a narrative of inferiority.

Borrowing from Levinas and Hegel, Judith Butler (2001, 24) explains that the "normative horizon" within which one understands self is narrated recursively both by the gaze of the Other and by the subject's affirmation of that gaze. A narrative of inferiority is only possible because the subaltern consents to the judgements of the Other, whether true or not. For the subaltern biblical critic, what are implications of this pattern (25)? Are we immune to the colonializing gaze? I think not. For even the most enlightened subaltern, cultural narratives are unwittingly adopted, reinforcing the colonializing mindsets that we are the subjects and they are the object. We are incomplete without frequenting their gaze for validation. And even I, by adopting the nomenclature *subaltern*, which means "inferior in rank or status," have fallen victim to this gaze in the absence of a more elevating, more affirming alternative. Because of this pattern, the residual effect is a perpetuation of the habit of incessant self-critique. With these preoccupations, I respond to the location and situation of island biblical criticisms presented by Jione Havea, Martin Wilson Mariota, and Inise Vakabua Foi'akau.

In Mariota and Foi'akau's chapters, each author raises important questions regarding subaltern identity and the matter of who is on the periphery and who is on the margins of the normative horizon between biblical spouses, Moses and Zipporah. Do our conclusions have historical precedent outside of the postcolonial critique? I offer my critique as one who is a product of British colonialism and migrations from the Caribbean islands, one whose view of Moses and Zipporah is also colored by a mindset of inferiority. But this complex is not only the islander's bondage. Zipporah is the resident clergy daughter steeped in the codes of religious life her father purveys, a system that unconsciously imposes an optic that persists during the post-Sinaitic (after-Sinai, as place of theophany and covenanting) and Second Temple Jewish period. Moses is clearly the homeless migrant, yet privileging descendants of the patriarchs—Abraham, Isaac, and Jacob—this system treats Moses as the powerful protagonist. All genealogies outside the Abrahamic lineage function as support roles in the grand narrative of the Hebrew male, though he be a diasporic one. The Second Temple storytellers are the divine narrators who, using indigenous language, choose for us the texts, and creatively weave the *talanoa*, dictating to the *fakaongo* all that we are supposed to know.

In keeping with my post-Sinaitic/precolonial interests, I first summarize Mariota's and Foi'akau's postcolonial readings, then offer a critique of Jewish, then Hellenistic, storytelling, in dialogue with the historical roots of the postcolonial readings. I conclude with where postcolonial biblical critique can find liberty (e.g., in the case of Zipporah).

Postcolonial Readings of Moses and Zipporah

Mariota's and Foi'akau's lived experiences of internal and external migrations compel explorations of the biblical couple in a fusion of ideological concerns from a Pacific islander worldview. Mariota studies Moses from a male perspective (Exod 2–3). Succumbing to forced migration from his inherited Egypt on pains of capital punishment, Moses finds asylum with a Midianite priest and marries his daughter, Zipporah. Eventually, a "burning bush" encounter lances his returned migration to Egypt, where Moses liberates the Hebrews from bondage. It is because Moses has polycultural capital, Mariota argues, that he can arguably move seamlessly between these three cultural discourses—Hebrew, Midian, and Egyptian.

Moses's cultural dexterity serves as the basis for Mariota's contemplations about the opportunity costs for second-generation Samoans living in Aotearoa (New Zealand) who still speak their native language. For the dominant "white" (*palagi*) New Zealander culture, a loss of indigenous language makes little difference; within the Samoan church, whether by mimicry or authenticity, cultural literacy is a sacred mandate. Mariota calls this advantage, "moving between discourses." A polycultural can traverse "boundaries of structure that are deemed to be stable" to meet larger social priorities, whether navigating Samoan or Māori space. To be at home in both worlds is possible through the *faʻasinomaga* lens that polycultural palagi wear. Palagi possess a generative capacity to interact recursively with time—pasts, presents, and futures—and space. They have the capacity to choose rightly for themselves while traversing a variety of life paths (*auala*). That is how Mariota conceives of Moses, and ultimately this has to do with how he sees himself.

Foi'akau reminisces on Exod 4 from a female Fijian perspective. In verses 24–26, Zipporah forestalls divine judgment that threatened death upon her family. Her heroism is possible because of her cleric knowledge of a ritual mandate and the neglect of her husband's orderly performance of it. Taking matters into her own hands, she administers circumcision and assumes the image of an independent, powerful story-mover. Within their exogamous marriage, Zipporah is a fascinating composition of social status, maturity, and power, a *marama iTaukei*. However, because there is only a passing mention of her in Exod 18:2–3, she is marooned to the periphery of our consciousness after chapter 4. Foi'akau argues that at the end of the tale, Zipporah remains a *yalewa bokala* (a common woman, with no status, who holds her head down). She is converted in our minds to a *tani* (foreigner) in the *solesolevaki talanoa* (storytelling within the communal gathering).

These readings provoke ruminations concerning the subject-object relationship between the reader and biblical characters. When we intend to read backwards, to understand Moses and Zipporah's late bronze age mass-migration context, the more pressing preoccupations of island existence and identification seduces *faaSamoa* (in the Samoan way) and *iTaukei* (in the Fijian way) rereadings. But Foi'akau's questioning of this rereading inspires another question. Did not the colonial gaze begin long before the British flags arrive on the Pacific Isles? Did not ancient biographers rereadings of these post-Siniatic stories emerge from identity preoccupations experienced among Second Temple Hellenistic Jews? A few select Jewish and Hellenistic examples will help with these questions.

Ancient Biographies of Moses and Zipporah

Jewish Sources

What I explore in the Jewish talanoa of Moses and Zipporah is what is left out and what is included, the language used and the narrative goal of retelling the same story in the first place. Racialization does not overtly come from the Hebrew Bible account. The traditional Western perspectives lure readers into promoting Moses as the heroic central character. This is, however, not how Moses understood himself. He named his offspring Gershom, rationalizing the name's meaning with, "because I am a resident alien in a land with political and economic jurisdiction that is distinct from the one from which I am native" (Exod 2:22, my translation).[1]

Not until Exod 3 is the unnamed priest identified as Jethro, which means "abundance" or "excess." The Septuagint (LXX), in contrast, is more forthright, repeating his name with ownership of the flock and the sheep's water reservoirs (2:16). Rooting the Midianite priest within a wisdom tradition, Jethro later taps Moses with a supply of necessary administrative advice to rescue Moses from imminent leadership burnout (Exod 18). By Num 12, Moses's siblings, outspoken in their jealousy toward Zipporah, call her a Cushite. This generic nickname throws the gaze of readers upon her skin pigmentation rather than any accurate description of her actual geography of origin (cf. Mo'ed Qat. 16b). However, Zipporah, if indeed the unnamed woman in Num 12 refers to her, is not from northern Africa. She is more rightly from the northeast corner of the Arabian desert region. Miriam and Aaron ultimately heap divine punishment upon themselves by questioning Moses's competence because of this kind of bride. But the Yahwist swiftly rescues Moses, punishing Miriam and Aaron's brazenness with leprosy and elevating Moses as servant of God.

Such grounds for Moses's alien status, multiethnic preference, and dependency on the Midianites and God must first be recognized if we are to make sociological comparisons to his wife's status. Moses recognizes his own marginality, self-identifying as a foreigner. In my opinion, what sublimates this assertion in our reading is the post-Sinai visage through which

---

1. In the MT, כי אמר גר הייתי בארץ נכריה (ὅτι πάροικός εἰμι ἐν γῇ ἀλλοτρίᾳ in the LXX). For the subtle differences between *gēr* and *nokhrî* (both terms are used in Exod 2:22) that I have captured in my translation, see Achenbach 2011. On *gēr*, see also the essay by Neemia in this collection.

we retroactively evaluate the couple. The Sinai legal code ultimately is the durable standard through which we unconsciously sieve characters with supporting roles to the central metanarrative of the Judeans.

This bias is axiomatic in pseudepigraphal works and later rabbinic texts. Jubilees begins abruptly at Sinai, leaving out Zipporah's story altogether. The writer has God filling in Moses on the pertinent Judean history Moses missed due to his own story of displacement and foreign upbringing in Egypt (Jub. 1:1–5). Straight away, the Maccabean priestly author's political agenda is evident. He writes following the historic defeat of the Seleucid occupation of Judea and a new Jewish-Maccabean establishment. His oversight of the preceding stories of bondage, slavery, and traumas from migration in Exod 1–18 is an intentional creative appropriation. The preoccupation with authoring a plum Judean priestly identity that matures apart from the influence of any colonialisms or outside cultural inspirations is of consequence to his own postcolonial inferiority complex (Charles 1968, 8). Similarly, later rabbinic texts do not esteem these Midianites. Midianites are written off as idolaters. Any liaison between them and Moses is sanitized. Pious post-Sinaitic emendations in the midrashic material celebrate Moses's heroism as rescuer of the seven helpless Midianite daughters. Without Moses, for that matter, they would otherwise have been textually violated by the shepherds (Exod. Rab. 1:32–33).

Hellenistic Sources

The prior samples of Judean storytelling present an unsentimental, marginalizing view of Jethro's household. Hellenistic biographers, culturally distant from the world of Judean identity anxieties, not only offer their story but also embellish it in Greek dramatic form. They write before Jews resettle the land, during a time of Greek Ptolemaic and Seleucid occupation. Yet their midrashic and haggadic tendencies reveal that these diaspora Greek writers are Jewish palagi. They are polycultural narrators, telling their story in a language we are compelled to hear.

Relying on the Greek Pentateuch to re-suture links between Hellenistic Judaism and Abrahamic lineage, Demetrius's third-century BCE Egypt chronography narrates a point of view that asserts the conviction, "Hellenistic Jews are veritable Jews too, mind you." Moses's status is elevated not through Jethro. Moses is of proper Levitical descent and upbringing. Correspondingly, Zipporah descends from Keturah, one of Abraham's wives. While such storytelling decisions do not marginalize the Midianites, they insist upon an identity that centers Judeans within a genealogy that affirms and normalizes only certain identities. Demetrius wants to assert that Moses and Zipporah are both tied to the Abrahamic plumb (Dem. 2.16–19, 3.1, *OTP* 2:851–53).

The Persian Jew Artapanus writes around 350–250 BCE and quite possibly is referring to the Jewish temple at Leontopolis in Lower Egypt. His romantic history emerges from a tradition that is not threatened by pagan influence but proudly uses native language in authentic talanoa. The protagonist has the Greek name Mousaios (Moses). Among many civic initiatives, he divides the states into thirty-six towns and assigns local gods to each sector. Moses's surrogate mother, Merris, is betrothed to Chenephres, who is jealous of Moses. Chenephres conscripts a band of farmers to assassinate Moses. Moses's army wins every battle, which lasts ten years. He founds the city of Hermes, where he enjoys peace with the Ethiopians and teaches them the practice of circumcision. When Merris dies, Chenephres seizes the opportunity for the ambush of her funerary procession to assassinate Moses (who was expected to lead it). Hearing of the plot, Aaron alerts Moses to flee to Arabia, where he takes up asylum with Raguel and marries his daughter (Holladay 1983).

In these Hellenistic readings, Moses is dependent on the constancy and resourcefulness of the Midianite platform provided by Jethro and Zipporah. However, feminist concerns are neglected, as Zipporah's heroic circumcision is absent from both accounts. Yet, it turns out that the modern subaltern does not suffer alone from cultural inferiority. It is the Judeans, writing in the shadows of a history of subjugation, who are awkwardly obsessed with building foundations and affirmations from the center-object superstructure. But reaching for a plumb identity is a historical impossibility. As the Hellenistic writers would concede, the symbol of the *maga* (see Kolia's essay), which bifurcates and unites two historical paths of identity, reminds us that both now belong to the same *palagi lou*.

Returning to the South Pacific

Like the Judeans, modern subalterns acknowledge cultural roots. Yet, those roots are often limited and sustained by grand discourses that authorize them (see the section on water in Havea's "Islander Criticism: Waters, Ways, Worries" in this volume; see also Winslow 2005, 21). Even gifted writers who reconstruct postcolonial identity and gender difference can fall under the same formatting that concedes valuation to the "normative horizon" over the subaltern. While we critique the system, we are subdued by its gaze. We are subdued by a colonial mindset that overlooks evidential states of familiarity with native space and place if we perceive them as powerless within the larger superstructure.

Recognizing the limits of this cultural *moana* (deep sea), Havea defines the normative horizons, expresses the subaltern's narrative of inferiority, then threatens these boundaries by crossing them though language, text selections, and talanoa (Havea, section on Ways). As my patrilineal cousin Louise Bennett (2011) articulates in a London poetic performance, indigenous languages are the means through which the texts and stories of our culture are propagated; only subalterns have the dexterity of narrating them. Our power lies in the language we know and must proudly use. Tangikefataua Koloamatangi's untranslated composition exemplifies this empowerment with Tongan language, text, and story. It does what subalterns must demand. It re-sutures our dependence on the indigenous talanoa. It calls the festive solesolevaki, where the feminine and masculine are present both corporeally and in the symbolic tastes and sensibilities of the islander imagination, and compels the Other to listen.

Works Cited

Achenbach, Reinhard. 2011. "Gêr Nåkhrî Tôshav Zâr." Pages 29–51 in *The Foreigner and the Law: Perspectives from the Hebrew Bible and the Ancient Near East*. Edited by Reinhard Achenbach, Rainer Albertz, and Jakob Wöhrle. BZABR 16. Wiesbaden: Harrassowitz.

Bennett, Louise. 2011. "Fi Wi Language." Recorded 1983 in London. Miss Lou audio. https://www.youtube.com/watch?v=W58MtDzanqA.

Butler, Judith. 2001. "Giving an Account of Oneself." *Dia* 31.4:22–40.

Charles, Robert Henry, ed. 1968. *The Apocrypha and Pseudepigrapha of the Old Testament in English: With Introductions and Critical and Explanatory Notes to the Several Books*. Repr., Oxford: Clarendon.

Holladay, Carl R. 1983. "Artapanus," Pages 189–243 in *Historians*. Vol. 1 of *Fragments from Hellenistic Jewish Authors*. TT 20; Pseu 10. Chico, CA: Scholars Press.

Winslow, Karen Strand. 2005. *Early Jewish and Christian Memories of Moses' Wives: Exogamist Marriage and Ethnic Identity*. SBEC 66. Lewiston, NY: Mellen.

Contributors

Levesi Laumau Afutiti was a minister of the Christian Congregational Church of Samoa. He received his theological education at Malua Theological College (Samoa) and the Pacific Theological College (Fiji). He was a person of good humor with passion for indigenous knowledge and for finding alternative ways (to the Western historical critical school in which he was trained) of reading.

Fiona C. Black is Associate Professor at Mount Allison University in Sackville, NB, Canada. She is currently dividing her time between work on the reception history of the Song of Songs and the senses and affect of the Bible on Caribbean postcolonial identity, specifically as it is explored in Bahamian life and culture.

Inise Vakabua Foi'akau is a research student in biblical studies at the School of Theology, Charles Sturt University (Parramatta campus: United Theological College). Foi'akau moved with her family to Australia in 2000, and she recently graduated with a Master of Theology from CSU. Her primary research work is on developing *marama iTaukei* (indigenous Fijian wo-man) reading.

Jione Havea is a native Methodist pastor from Tonga, a research fellow in religious studies at Trinity Methodist Theological College (Aotearoa/New Zealand), and an honorary research fellow with the Public and Contextual Theology Research Centre, Charles Sturt University (Australia) and with the University of Divinity (Australia). Havea (co-)edited, among others, *Islands, Islanders, and the Bible: RumInations* (SBL Press, 2015) and *Postcolonial Voices from DownUnder: Indigenous Matters, Confronting Readings* (Pickwick, 2017).

Brian Fiu Kolia is from the Samoan islands of Savaii (main village of Sili) and Upolu (main village of Satapuala) and is currently a Lecturer in Old Testament Studies and Languages at Malua Theological College, Samoa. Kolia holds a Master of Theology (Old Testament) from Pacific Theological College (Fiji), Bachelor of Divinity from Malua Theological College, and a Master of Commerce (Accounting) from Western Sydney University (Australia). He recently published "O se Faitauga Faa-Tulou o le Pese a Solomona 8" ["A Tulou Reading of Song of Songs 8"] with *Malua Journal* (2016) and has "O le Atua na to'ai faa I'a a Po: Esoto 12:12" ["The God who Arrived like the Fish in the Night: Exodus 12:12"] forthcoming in *Malua Journal*.

Tangikefataua Koloamatangi was a sportsman in his younger days, and a poet, composer, and cultural instructor in later years. His compositions continue to be sung by kava groups throughout Tonga, especially the Huolanga club at Kolomotu'a, and his choreography lives on in the performances of Queen Salote College and several local dancers. He had a deep, full-bodied voice, a joyful and engaging mind, and a lively and welcoming presence.

Mosese Ma'ilo is the Principal of Piula Theological College (Samoa), where he resides and lectures in biblical studies (New Testament and postcolonial biblical hermeneutics). He holds a PhD in Postcolonial Bible Translation from the University of Birmingham, UK. He is also an ordained minister of the Methodist Church in Samoa and a past president of the Oceania Biblical Studies Association. He recently published *Bible-ing My Samoan: Polynesian Languages and the Politics of Bible Translation* (Piula, 2016).

Martin Wilson Mariota is currently a senior advisor at the Ministry of Education working for the ECE Regulations and Planning team at National Office Wellington. Mariota holds a Master of Theology with First Class Distinction from the University of Auckland, a Bachelor of Divinity from Malua Theological College, and Bachelor of Business studies in Accountancy from Massey University. He has over seven years of experience in the public sector as a Tax Investigator at the Inland Revenue Department as well as several roles at the Ministry of Education, such as the Pasifika Unit and the Early Learning Taskforce.

Makesi Neemia is a Samoan ordained minister of the Congregational Christian Church of Samoa. He is currently a lecturer in Old Testament Studies, Language, and Literature at Malua Theological College, Samoa. His areas of interest include island hermeneutics and postcolonial reading of the Old Testament.

Vaitusi Nofoaiga is an ordained minister of the Congregational Christian Church of Samoa with a PhD from the University of Auckland. Nofoaiga is a Lecturer of New Testament Studies at Malua Theological College (Samoa) and has published "Exploring Discipleship in Matthew 4:12–25 from tautua i le va [service/servant/serve in between]," *Pacific Journal of Theology* (2014) and "Avea Ma Soo I le Lotoifale: O ia lava na na aveina o tatou vaivai, ma na tauave o tatou ma'i (Matt 8:17)," *Malua Journal* 4.1 (2016). His *A Samoan Reading of Discipleship in Matthew* was recently published (SBL Press, 2017).

Daniel Patte, Professor Emeritus, Vanderbilt University, was general editor of *Semeia* (1992–1998). His concern for moral responsibility (*Ethics of Biblical Interpretation* [Westminster John Knox, 1995]) led him to a practice of "Scriptural Criticism" (formulated with ninety-three colleagues of the Society of Biblical Literature seminar Romans through History and Cultures [also a ten-volume book series]) that accounts for the exegetical, hermeneutical, and contextual choices that any interpretation of the Bible necessarily involves. With colleagues from around the world, he edited the *Global Bible Commentary* and *The Cambridge Dictionary of Christianity* (clarifying the contextual character of Christian theological views, practices, and movements through history and present-day cultures) and has just completed the first volume of *Romans: Three Exegetical Interpretations and the History of Reception* (T&T Clark, 2018) that demonstrates the contextual character of interpretations of Romans.

Camilla Raymond is a doctoral candidate and teaching assistant at the University of Denver and Iliff School of Theology since 2013. She is interested in identity and migrations within Early Christian origins, Hellenistic history, the literature and history of Second Temple Judaism, and the Dead Sea Scrolls. Having a diverse heritage produced from Afro-Caribbean and Sephardic Jewish migrations, her dissertation has deep commitments to ethnic diversity within Jewish identity. Prior to beginning her PhD, Raymond was Assistant Professor in New Testament at Southeastern University.

Angeline M. G. Song (PhD, Otago) was born and raised in Singapore but now lives in Auckland, New Zealand. The former newspaper journalist is currently a lecturer in Manukau Institute of Technology where she teaches students of predominantly Pasifika, indigenous, and Asian origins from economically unprivileged contexts or refugee backgrounds. Her monograph, *A Postcolonial Woman's Encounter with Moses and Miriam* was recently published by Palgrave Macmillan (2015).

Gerald O. West teaches Old Testament/Hebrew Bible and African Biblical Hermeneutics in the School of Religion, Philosophy, and Classics at the University of KwaZulu-Natal, South Africa. He is director of the Ujamaa Centre for Community Development and Research, a project in which socially engaged biblical scholars and ordinary African readers of the Bible from poor, working-class, and marginalized communities collaborate for social transformation. His most recent book is *The Stolen Bible: From Tool of Imperialism to African Icon* (Brill, 2016).

Ancient Sources Index

Genesis
1   111
1–2   10
1–9   11
1–15   11 n. 11
1:2   10
1:11   10
1:20   10
1:26   11
1:27–28   25
2–3   17, 111
2–4   11
2:6   11
2:10–14   11
2:18   25
2:21–22   25
3:24   17
5–9   11
12–50   150
12:1   151 n. 4
12:1–4   150–51, 161
12:1–5   150
23   152
23:4   148, 152, 153
24:4   151 n. 4
25:1   110
25:4   110
26:3   151
38   19, 144
46:11   111
50:22–26   150

Exodus
1–18   217

1:6   112
2–3   103–15, 214
2:1–10   111
2:2   111
2:7   14
2:11–15   112
2:14   113
2:16–20   126, 216
2:18   127 n. 8
2:19   110
2:21   125, 126
2:22   125, 126, 216 n. 1
3   216
3:1   127 n. 8
4   215
4:20   127
4:24   128
4:24–26   117–30, 215
4:25b   128
6:3   153
6:20   111
10:2   25
12:12   222
12:43   153
13:8   25
14   12
15   14
18   216
18:1–6   127
18:2–3   215
18:2–6   127 n. 7

Leviticus
17:3   154

Leviticus (cont.)

17:8–9	154
17:15	156
17:16	156
18:9	151
18:11	151
18:24–30	155
19:2	156
20:2	156
20:7–8	156
20:22–26	156
22:8	156
22:31–33	156
24:16	156
25	153, 155

Numbers

5:11–31	13
12	14, 216
12:1	110, 127
25:16–18	110

Deuteronomy

17:15	148
34:7	110

Joshua

3	12

Judges

4:11	126 n. 8

Ruth

1:16–18	45
2:7	190
2:15	190

1 Samuel

17:48–49	72

2 Samuel

12	76
13	95

Esther

1:9–12	209
1:12	138
2:8	135
2:9	138
2:10	137, 142
2:17	137, 138
2:20b	137
3:6	142
4:11	140
4:15	140, 142
4:16	142
4:17	142, 143
5:2	138
5:4	138
9:5–15	142
9:13	142

Psalms

22	72

Proverbs

5:3–4	64
10:1	56
13:18	57
19:20	57

Song of Songs

8:1	92, 93, 94
8:4	97
8:8	92, 96, 97
8:9	94
8:10	97

Isaiah

1:7	148
53	172 n. 5
53:4	172, 173

Lamentations

1:6	63

Jonah

1	42
1:2	40

1:3	39	8:5–13	170
1:4–16	43	8:13	171
1:12	47	8:14–15	171
1:13	46	8:16	173 n. 7, 175
1:16	45	8:16–17	171
1:16–17	45	8:17	172, 173
2	42	8:18–22	164, 168, 174, 175
2:11	37	8:19	174
3–4	15, 42, 43	8:20	174
3:2	40	9:1	174
3:3b–10	43	20:8	173
3:5–9	46	20:11	173
3:6	46	27:46	72
3:6–10	48		
3:7–8	47	Mark	
3:10	43	1:16–20	53, 63, 66
4:2	43, 49		
4:3	40, 41, 47	Luke	
4:8	41, 47	2:2	72
4:9	40	6:44	57
4:10–11	48	14:11	64
4:10–12	41	15:11–32	23–35, 206
		15:13	31, 206
Sirach		15:15	206
4:26	64	15:20–24	206
11:1	65	15:20–32	206
14:9	64	23:41	63
Jubilees		John	
1:1–5	217	3:16	74
		19:30	174
Matthew			
2:8	75	James	
3:1	173	1:8	63
3:1–4	173	1:9	64
3:4	173	1:12	63
3:11	173	2:17	64
5:1	173 n. 7	2:26	64
7:24–27	168, 169	3:10–11	63
7:24–29	168, 173	3:13	57
7:24–8:16	172	4:6	64
7:24–8:22	163–76, 205		
8:1–4	169	Revelation	
8:1–16	173	10:10	64
8:1–17	168, 169		

Modern Authors Index

Achenbach, Reinhard 216 n. 1, 219
Afutiti, Levesi Laumau viii, 5 n. 6, 6, 14, 53, 70, 195–99, 201
Ah Siu-Maliko, Mercy 164, 176
Aiono, Letagaloa F. 53–54, 59, 67
Albertz, Rainer 151–55, 155 n. 6, 156 n. 8, 159
Althusser, Louis 203, 208, 209 n.7, 210
Anae, Melani 95 n. 2, 100, 108, 115
Anum, Eric 195, 201
Arnold, Bill T. 93, 100
Ashcroft, W. D. 29, 34, 35
Aymer, Margaret 1, 18, 24, 85, 101, 133 n. 4, 134, 143–44, 163, 177
Ba, Tevita 130
Baba, Tupeni L. 119, 130
Bailey, Randall C. 1, 8, 18–19, 142, 144,
Ballantyne, Tony 139, 144
Balzac, Honoré de 136, 144
Bauks, Michaela 152, 159
Beal, Timothy K. 142, 144
Bechtel, Carol M. 142, 144
Bennett, Louise 219
Beyer, Bryan E. 93, 100
Bhabha, Homi K. 165, 176, 124
Black, Fiona C. 4, 18, 181
Bloch-Smith, Elizabeth 152, 159
Boer, Roland 3, 19
Boladuadua, Emita L. 130
Brenner, Athalya 94, 101
Brett, Mark G. 12, 19, 42, 50, 151 n. 4, 152–55, 156 n. 8, 159
Brown, George 63, 64, 67
Brueggemann, Walter 172, 176

Butler, Judith 213, 219
Capell, A. 117 n. 1, 130
Carr, David M. 61, 67
Certeau, Michel de 210
Chang, Hee Won 123, 130
Charles, Robert Henry 217, 219
Charles, Ronald 5, 129
Cohen, Jeffrey M. 141, 144
Courtés, Joseph 205 nn. 1–2, 210
Davidson, Steed Vernyl 1, 8–9, 18–19, 24, 35, 85, 101, 131, 131 n. 2, 133 n. 4, 134–35, 143–44, 163, 177, 186
Diermen, Peter van 149 n. 3, 161
Docker, John 139, 145
Douglas, Mary 88, 91, 101, 155, 156 n. 7, 159
Draper, Jonathan A. 196, 201
Dube, Musa W. 119, 123–24, 130, 136, 145, 192, 199, 202
Duran, Nicole 134–35, 145, 209–10
Duranti, Alessandro 86, 101
Efi, Tui Atua Tupua Tamasese Ta'isi 85, 97, 101
Ellis, Juniper 24, 35, 43, 50
Engler, Steven 165 n. 2, 176
Estes, Daniel J. 96, 101
Figiel, Sia 13, 37–50
Firth, Raymond 93, 101
Fisch, Harold 25, 26, 35
Fischer, Gerhard 135, 145
Fish, Stanley 90–91, 101
Foi'akau, Inise Vakabua 3 n.4, 6, 8, 12, 15, 110, 117, 192, 200, 213–15
Fontaine, Carole R. 95, 101

Fox, Michael V. 94, 96, 101
France, R. T. 173 n. 6, 176
Fredericks, Daniel C. 96, 101
Freyne, Sean 167 n. 4, 176
Fuchs, Esther 134, 141, 145
Gadamer, Hans-Georg 89, 101, 204, 210
Garrett, Duane 93, 101
Gibran, Kahlil 37, 38 n. 1, 39, 50
Gilroy, Paul 165 n. 2, 177
Gooder, Paula 205, 210
Goulder, Michael D. 94, 101
Greimas, Algirdas Julien 204, 205 nn. 1–2, 210
Guillaume, Philippe 152, 159
Hamilton, Scott 6, 19
Hanson, K. C. 66 n.11, 67
Harris, R. Laird 137, 145
Hau'ofa, Epeli 23, 35, 38, 50
Havea, Jione 1, 6, 8–9, 13, 18–19, 24, 40 n. 5, 42, 44, 50, 85–86, 101, 123, 130, 133 n. 4, 134, 143, 163, 177, 181–82, 184–85, 187, 187 n. 1, 188–90, 194–99, 207, 211, 213, 218–19
Haynes, Stephen R. 205, 211
Hengel, Martin 172 n. 5, 177
Herman, Brother 55, 58–59, 59 n. 6, 67
Hinkelammert, Franz J. 191, 201
Holladay, Carl R. 218–19
Holter, Knut 195, 201
House, Paul R. 93, 101
Hutnyk, John 165 n. 2, 177
Joosten, Jan 154–55, 156 n. 8, 159
Kennedy, Elizabeth Robertson 151, 160
Kinukawa, Hisako 3, 4, 19
Kirsch, Jonathan 126 n. 8, 130
Knohl, Israel 156 n. 8, 160
Köckert, Manfred 152, 160
Kolia, Brian Fiu ix, 2, 6, 85, 106, 129, 183–84, 190, 200, 218
Koloamatangi, Tangikefataua viii, x, 6, 11, 14, 69, 70, 181, 182, 183, 184, 190, 193, 196, 198–99, 204, 219
Kunz-Lübcke, Andreas 44, 51
Laffey, Alice L. 134, 145
Lefale, Penehuro Fatu 87, 102

Leota, Peniamina 149, 160
Liew, Tat-siong Benny 1, 8, 19
Lim, Shirley Geok-lin 140, 145
Lindsay, Rebecca 44, 51
Longman, Tremper, III 98, 102, 117, 130
Ma'ilo, Mosese 6, 8, 13–14, 19, 24, 35, 38 n. 2, 42, 43, 183, 184, 185, 187, 190, 206–8, 210
Macaskill, Grant 14, 19
Macpherson, Cluny 106, 115
Maggay, Melba Padilla 135, 145
Mariota, Martin Wilson 3 n. 4, 4, 7, 12, 103, 200, 213, 214, 215
Marshall, I. Howard 62, 67
Masenya (ngwan'a Mphahlele), Madipoane 201
Matthew, Michael 134, 145
Maude, Henry Evans 6, 20
Mbuvi, Andrew M. 193, 196, 200, 202
McKenzie, Steven L. 205, 211
Mein, Andrew 3, 4, 6, 20
Meleisea, Malama 149, 160
Middleton, J. Richard 14, 20
Mila-Schaaf, Karlo 109, 115
Milgrom, Jacob 154, 156 n. 8, 160
Mosala, Itumeleng J. 197, 198, 202
Moxnes, Halvor 167 n. 4, 177
Moyise, Steve 205, 211
Munck, Johannes 62, 67
Munro, Jill M. 98–99, 102
Nabobo-Baba, Unaisi 119, 122 n. 5, 130
Neemia, Makesi 2, 6, 10 n. 10, 15, 147, 187, 191, 194–200, 216 n. 1
Nihan, Christophe 152–56, 156 n. 8, 160
Nofoaiga, Vaitusi 2, 3, 6, 7, 163, 166 n. 3, 175, 177, 187, 200, 205–6, 210
Nolland, John 172, 177
Nzimande, Makhosazana K. 195, 202
Packer, J. W. 62, 67
Patmore, Hector 94, 102
Patte, Daniel 7, 199, 203
Penisimani 63, 64, 67
Peseta, S. Sio 56, 67
Powell, Mark Allan 62, 67
Premnath, D. N. 8, 20

Rad, Gerhard von 151, 160
Raymond, Camilla viii, 18, 213
Rees, Anthony 6, 20
Rendtorff, Rolf 152, 155, 160
Rubenstein, William B. 7, 20
Saipele, Nu'uiali'i Mulipola Ma'ilo 56, 67
Sanneh, Lamin 193, 202
Schmid, Konrad 150–53, 156, 156 n. 8, 160
Schultz, E. 55, 58–59, 59 n. 6, 67
Schüssler Fiorenza, Elisabeth 94, 102
Schwartz, Baruch J. 154, 160
Schweizer, Eduard 172, 173 n. 7, 177
Scott, James C. 138, 145, 210
Segovia, Fernando F. 1, 8, 19
Shadrake, Andrew 149 n. 3, 161
Sharrad, Paul 26–27, 29, 31, 34, 36
Ska, Jean L. 150–52, 161
Smith, Oliver 13, 20
Smith-Christopher, Daniel 61, 67
Song, Angeline M. G. viii, 3, 3 n. 4, 6, 8, 12, 133 n. 3, 134, 136, 140, 145, 185–87, 200, 208–9, 209 n. 7, 210
Sparks, Kenton L. 153, 161
Spencer Miller, Althea 14, 20, 184, 190
Sperry, Armstrong 23, 36
Stackert, Jeffrey 153, 161
Sugirtharajah, R. S. 8, 27, 36
Tamahori, Lee 23, 36
Tcherkézoff, Serge 107, 115
Thornley, Andrew 120, 130
Tiatia, Jemaima 108, 115
Ting-Toomey, Stella 92, 102
Tippett, Alan R. 122, 130
Tofighi, Fatima 208, 208 n. 6, 211
Tuwere, Ilaitia S. 120, 120 n. 4, 130
Ukpong, Justin S. 193–95, 202
Vaai, Upolu Luma 24, 36, 86, 102
Vaka'uta, Nāsili 15, 20, 44, 51
Van Houten, Christiana 153, 155–56, 156 n. 8, 157, 161
Van Seters, John 150, 161
Vatuloka, Wasevina V. 130
Wendt, Albert 13, 23–36, 43, 50, 206–7

West, Gerald O. 7, 192–93, 195–97, 199, 202
Wilson, Andrew P. 4, 9, 20
Wimbush, Vincent L. 210, 211
Winslow, Karen Strand 218–19
Wittenberg, Gunther H. 201–2
Wöhrle, Jakob 152–53, 156, 161
Young, Robert 165 n. 2, 177
Zobel, Greifswald 137–38, 145

Subject Index

allegorical, allegorize, allegory, 60 n. 7, 88, 90–92, 98–100, 129
ancestor(s), x, 6, 106, 150–53, 156, 158, 192
awkward(ness), 34, 86, 91, 99, 150, 204, 218
boundary, boundaries, 12, 34, 60, 103, 105, 108–10, 112, 114–15, 118, 123, 127, 134, 136, 167, 170–71, 215, 219
burrows, 4
church(es), viii, 18, 25–28, 31, 39, 59–61, 67, 91, 98, 100, 104–7, 114–15, 120, 122, 147 n. 1, 148, 149, 149 n. 3, 158, 163, 164 n. 1, 166 n. 3, 176, 204, 215
circumcision, 125–26, 128–29, 215, 218
climate change, 16–17, 38
climate justice, 17–18
contextual reading/biblical interpretation, viii, 1, 184, 192
corruption, 149, 195
creole, creolization, 9, 14, 61
dance, dancing, 4, 6, 14–15, 15 n. 13, 16, 58, 119, 123, 184
decolonization, decolonize, 23, 29, 122, 124
desire(s/d), 2, 30, 33, 55 n. 2, 63, 92–96, 143, 183
Deuteronomic, 153, 154
disciple(ship), 57, 66–67, 163–66, 168, 170–71, 174–76
discovery, 30, 34, 49
discriminate, discrimination, 5, 30–31, 188 n. 2
dislocation, 141

disorientation, 141
dispossession, 28, 31
dominant, 45–46, 92, 95–96, 107, 112, 114, 135, 139 n. 5, 213, 215
Egypt(ian), 13, 61, 93, 103, 105, 110–14, 125–26, 128, 214, 217–18
empower(ment), 103, 105, 109, 114–15, 133, 210, 219
erotic(ism), 88, 90–91, 95, 98–100
faith(ful/ness), 57, 64, 85, 98, 134, 151, 164 n. 1, 171, 95, 198, 201, 207
feast(s), 15–16, 32, 58, 118 n. 2, 200
fish(ing), 5 n. 6, 9, 12, 30, 37–39, 58, 58 n. 5, 63–66, 210 n.4
fisher(men), 65–66, 66 n. 11
foreplay, 93
freedom, 37, 44, 90–91, 94, 188
freshwater, vii, 9–10, 13, 64
genocide, 6, 6 n. 7, 15, 143
heal(er/ing/thy), 12, 16, 28, 34, 45, 78, 168–73
home(land), 4, 7, 9, 16 n. 14, 17, 23, 26–31, 33–35, 45–46, 56–57, 63, 64 n. 9, 70, 103–4, 126, 128, 139–40, 144, 149, 157, 164, 171, 175, 183, 185–86, 198, 204, 206–7, 215
homecoming, 34
horizon(s), 23, 34, 62, 87, 89–92, 107, 204, 213–14, 219
hospitality, 7, 70
humanistic, 85, 90, 100
humor, 16, 38 n. 2, 40 n.5
hybrid(s), hybridity, 7, 108, 139, 155, 165–66, 169, 174, 200

Subject Index

identity, 2, 3, 47, 54, 104, 106–7, 109, 111–15, 119, 127, 139–42, 152, 181, 183, 185, 187–88, 195, 213, 215, 217–18
immigrant, immigrate(d), immigration, 27, 29, 30, 31, 111, 131, 133, 135, 139–41, 144, 147, 151–53, 188 n. 2, 206, 208–9
impurity, 32
indigenous, 6, 24, 30, 31, 47, 85, 92, 97, 103, 117, 117 n. 1, 118–19, 121–22, 139, 153, 155, 158, 193–95, 201, 214–15, 219
kinship(s), 14, 129, 148
language(s), ix, x, 5, 8, 11–12, 14–15, 24, 27, 27 n. 1, 34, 40 n. 5, 42 n. 8, 53–56, 59, 60, 62, 69, 93, 96, 100, 104, 108, 129, 134, 142, 148, 156, 163, 167–68, 191, 193, 195, 199, 204–5, 214, 215–19
laugh(ter), 11, 16, 122, 127
Levite, Levitical, 111, 217
meaning(s), 5 n. 6, 7 n. 8, 14, 24–25, 34, 40 n. 5, 55, 57–59, 61–62, 76–77, 86, 88–92, 99–100, 103, 105–8, 110, 113–15, 117 n. 1, 140, 148, 148 n.2, 153, 156 n. 7, 164 n. 1, 166, 173 n. 6, 185, 191, 195, 199, 204–5, 216
metaphor(s), 7, 15, 50, 58, 69, 90, 168, 192, 204
Midian(ite), 6, 13, 103, 105, 110–13, 125, 126 nn. 7–8, 128, 214, 216–18
mimicry, 30, 215
minoritization, minoritized, 1, 7–8, 11, 11 n. 2, 43, 47, 133, 135, 140, 144, 165, 183–84, 189–90, 194, 196–97, 200
mission(ary), missionaries, 5–7, 12–13, 24, 31, 71, 85, 91, 96, 99, 120, 122, 187, 192–95, 197, 207
Nafanua, 55, 56
negotiate, negotiation, negotiating, 15–16, 49, 85, 91–92, 100, 103, 105, 109–10, 113–15, 133, 134, 140, 183, 187, 189, 213
nudity, 92, 96, 98

oral(ity), viii, ix, 2, 11, 14–15, 39, 40 n. 5, 41, 53, 70, 122–23, 129–30, 181–82, 184–85, 190, 193–94, 198, 204
poverty, 16, 57, 164, 164 n. 1
power(s), 3, 4, 8, 16 n. 14, 40 n. 5, 55, 95, 97, 113, 120, 123–24, 133, 135–37, 139, 149, 155 n.6, 169, 185, 213, 215, 219
prejudice(s), 28, 47, 133, 149, 195
protest, 8, 11, 13–17, 184, 189
pure, 3, 18, 33, 45, 165
purity, 32, 155–56, 170, 197
reception(s), 18, 204, 208
reciprocate(d), reciprocating, reciprocity, 2, 7, 15, 87, 88, 121, 124
rejection, 7, 18
relational(ity), 14, 15, 38 n. 1, 41 n. 6, 55, 92, 113, 137, 190
renegotiate. *See* negotiate, negotiation, negotiating.
resist(ed/ing), resistance, ix, 8, 11, 23, 40 n. 5, 44 n. 9, 47, 136, 141, 199
root(ed/ing/s), 3, 3 n. 4, 4–5, 30, 34, 54 n. 1, 143, 151, 165, 184–85, 200, 206, 213–14, 216, 218
saltwater, vii, 9–10, 13, 17
scripture(s), vii, 12, 50, 69, 182–83, 187 n. 1, 194, 203–5, 207–8
settler(s), 28, 107, 117 n. 1, 139, 144
sex(ism/ual), sexuality, 6, 27, 31, 85–100, 129, 134, 176, 196, 209
sinful(ness), 31, 99
subaltern(s), 8, 11, 30, 70, 182, 193–94, 213, 218–19
talanoa, x, 2, 7, 8–9, 11–12, 14–16, 23–24, 42, 49, 71–73, 76, 80, 121–22, 122 n. 5, 123, 184, 214–16, 218–19
tapu, 85–100, 183–84
tradition(al/s)
 biblical, 150–53, 156–57, 216
 Pasifika, ix, 2–4, 16, 23–24, 28, 41, 45–46, 53–54, 55 n. 2, 59–62, 70, 88, 90–92, 95–99, 104, 108, 115, 118–19, 121, 127, 136, 155, 194–96, 198

tradition(al/s) (*cont.*)
    Western, viii, 2–3, 8, 12–13, 27, 42–43, 53, 60–61, 95, 115, 120–21, 123, 136, 163–64, 174, 193–95, 197, 216, 218
trauma(tize/s), 12, 16, 46, 217
tulou, 2–3, 12, 85–100, 183–84
unfaithful, 28
unhealthy, 13, 79
wisdom, vii, 5 n. 6, 8, 14, 50, 53–67, 69–70, 77, 95, 100, 110, 117 n. 1, 123, 136–37, 193–199, 201, 216

www.ingramcontent.com/pod-product-compliance
Lightning Source LLC
Chambersburg PA
CBHW030824230426
43667CB00008B/1370